The Sociolinguistics of Narrative

Studies in Narrative

The subject of SiN is the study of narrative. Volumes published in the series draw upon a variety of approaches and methodologies in the study of narrative. Particular emphasis is placed on theoretical approaches to narrative and the analysis of narratives in human interaction.

Series Editor

Michael Bamberg
Clark University

Advisory editorial board

Volume 6

The Sociolinguistics of Narrative
Edited by Joanna Thornborrow and Jennifer Coates

University of
Hertfordshire

College Lane, Hatfield, Herts. AL10 9AB

Learning and Information Services

For renewal of Standard and One Week Loans,
please visit the web site **http://www.voyager.herts.ac.uk**

This item must be returned or the loan renewed by the due date.
The University reserves the right to recall items from loan at any time.
A fine will be charged for the late return of items.

The Sociolinguistics of Narrative

Edited by

Joanna Thornborrow
Cardiff University

Jennifer Coates
Roehampton University

John Benjamins Publishing Company
Amsterdam / Philadelphia

The paper used in this publication meets the minimum requirements of American National Standard for Information Sciences – Permanence of Paper for Printed Library Materials, ANSI z39.48-1984.

Library of Congress Cataloging-in-Publication Data

The Sociolinguistics of Narrative / edited by Joanna Thornborrow and Jennifer Coates.
      p.   cm. (Studies in Narrativity, ISSN 1568–2706 ; v. 6)
      Includes bibliographical references and indexes.
          1. Discourse analysis, Narrative. 2. Sociolinguistics. I. Thornborrow, Joanna, 1957- II. Coates, Jennifer. III. Series.

      P302.7.S65 2005
      306.44'01'4--dc22   2005043601
      ISBN 90 272 2646 6 (Eur.) / 1 58811 635 2 (US) (Hb; alk. paper)

John Benjamins Publishing Co. · P.O. Box 36224 · 1020 ME Amsterdam · The Netherlands
John Benjamins North America · P.O. Box 27519 · Philadelphia PA 19118-0519 · USA

Table of contents

CHAPTER 1

The sociolinguistics of narrative
Identity, performance, culture

Joanna Thornborrow and Jennifer Coates

Introduction

The study of narrative is no longer a literary preserve, but has emerged as
an object of enquiry in a whole range of disciplinary contexts, from sociolinguistics to social anthropology, social psychology and beyond. This is because
narrative does not exist only between the covers of books; on the contrary, stories have a pervasive role in our everyday life. From the proliferation of data
that sociolinguists and others have gathered from many different contexts, we
have ample evidence of just how central narrative discourse is to the fabric of
social interaction – whether this is in casual conversations, in legal and medical
settings, in the media, in family interactions or at school. So there is no longer
much need, at the turn of this new century, to argue the case for the increasing importance of narrative within the social sciences. However, there is, we
believe, a need to address some of the questions often left implicit whenever
stories are brought within the analytic frame of sociolinguistics. These questions are concerned with theoretical, contextual and cultural issues which need
closer attention and deeper discussion. What exactly do we mean by 'story'?
How do we use 'narrative' as a descriptive term, and what are its theoretical limits? What kind of social and contextual variations can determine the
production and shape of situated stories, and what are the core elements of narrative as a discursive unit and interactional resource? How is the relationship
between narrative discourse and social context articulated in the construction
of cultural identities?[1]

   Ever since Labov and Waletzky (1967) first turned their attention to the
structure of narratives gathered during sociolinguistic interviews, the analysis
of oral narratives has been a major concern within sociolinguistics. Analysis

has focused on how stories get told, how they are designed, and how they are received, as well as on their content, function and organisation. There is now a substantial body of work devoted to the form and function of storytelling in both conversational and institutional contexts for talk. However, there has not yet been a concerted attempt to appraise this work within sociolinguistics. Neither has there been an occasion to examine in detail the ways in which narrative constitutes a fundamental discursive resource across a range of contexts, from narrative specificity on the one hand to contextual diversity on the other. This book provides a platform for a number of these key issues to be addressed.

Many of the contributors to the book have over the years already offered valuable insights into the structural features and organisation of oral narratives in a range of contextual settings, including the analysis of stories in specific speech activities such as disputes and gossip, as well as the function of stories in talk within specific social and institutional groups, e.g. friendship talk, family interaction, the courtroom and the media. The chapters presented here bring together some of the most recent work in the theory and practice of narrative analysis from a broad sociolinguistic perspective. Our aim in presenting them is to improve our understanding of the ways in which narrative constitutes a fundamental resource in social interaction.

Theorising oral narrative

The study of narrative 'does not fit neatly within the boundaries of any scholarly field' (Riessman 1993:1): oral narrative is studied by ethnographers, by folklorists, by sociologists, by social historians, by social psychologists. This 'narrative turn' arises from a growing understanding of the importance of narrative in our lives. It has even been suggested that the ability to think in a narrative way is an innate capability of the human species and highly functional for our survival (Bruner 1987, 1991; Cronon 1992; Sarbin 1986).

However, this does not mean that analysts have arrived at a single blueprint for narrative. On the contrary, different disciplines with their different concerns have developed a variety of models. Many disciplines (for example, oral history, social psychology) focus on stories elicited in interviews, whereas sociolinguists and discourse analysts are primarily (but not uniquely) concerned with stories arising spontaneously as part of everyday interaction. Inevitably, the stories collected in these two contexts vary in predictable ways related to the constraints of these two methods of data collection.

It would be easy to take the notion of story for granted. Harvey Sacks (1995, Vol. II: 21) comments: "That it's a story, anybody knows". But *how* do we know? What is it that defines a stretch of talk as 'narrative'? These questions relate to the formal structure of narrative, while a second set of questions, including 'Why do we tell stories?', focuses more on narrative function. Questions of form and function, and the relationship between the two, are issues that are central to the research presented in the chapters of this book.

Narrative form

There have been many attempts to establish criteria which would define the well-formed story. Among the many suggested, two seem to be widely accepted. The first is that, to count as a narrative, there has to be a sequence of narrative clauses (clauses containing a verb in the simple past tense or, sometimes, the historic present tense) whose order matches the real time order of the events described in those clauses. These clauses constitute the heart of the story, or narrative 'core'. The second is that a story has to have a beginning, a middle and an end (Aristotle's definition).

The narrative sequence

At the heart of any story are, minimally, two events, represented in two narrative clauses which are linked temporally and sequentially. The story depends on the relationship between the two clauses. Sack's classic example of a child's story, "The baby cried. The mommy picked it up" (1995, Vol. I: 236) provides an illustration of this relationship. If the clauses are reversed, then the story changes. Similarly, Toolan's (2001) example: 'John fell in the river and had two whiskies', when compared to the reordering of events as 'John had two whiskies and fell in the river' is another good illustration of what happens to a story when the order of the narrative clauses is changed.

Sociolinguistic research has provided some important conceptual models of oral narrative form which have been consistently drawn upon over the past forty or so years. Of these models, Labov's (1972; see also Labov & Waletzky 1967) analysis of the structure of oral narrative has proved to be a robust formal description of both elicited and non-elicited stories. Many contributors to the present volume draw in various ways on this model (in particular, Cheshire and Ziebland, Coates, Leith, Holmes and Marra, Harris). Crucially, the model predicts that a narrative can be analysed in terms of the following components:

abstract, orientation, complicating action, evaluation, resolution, coda. Very briefly, an abstract is a brief summary that sometimes occurs at the beginning of a story; orientation refers to background information on the who, where, when of the story; complicating action and resolution refer to the narrative clauses that describe the key events of the story; evaluation is an aspect of a story that can be explicit (as when a narrator comments: 'it was so funny!') or embedded; and coda is a final comment that comes after the resolution of the story. To count as a story, it is not necessary for all components to be present: only the complicating action and resolution are essential (as the minimal, two-clause stories above illustrate).

Chafe (1980) analyses the formal structure of narrative in terms of idea units rather than narrative clauses. In his view, spontaneous speech "is produced, not in a flowing stream, but in a series of brief spurts" (Chafe 1980: 13); it is these spurts of language that he calls 'idea units'. He argues that when a narrator is telling a story, they chunk their material into units which are identifiable in terms of prosodic information (particularly intonation), pausing (idea units are typically separated by at least a brief pause) and syntax (an idea unit can consist of a word or a phrase or a clause).

Beginnings, middles and endings

Stories do not just emerge out of nowhere. They are embedded in their conversational context, often introduced by a story preface, for example, 'Did you see what happened last night?', 'Did I tell you what happened to Sue?'. Telling a story takes time; the teller needs to hold the floor over an extended series of utterances rather than just a single turn. In order to gain access to that amount of conversational space, storytellers announce that a story is coming up so that the other participants in the talk can take up the role of story recipients and suspend their next speaker rights to the floor (Sacks 1995). Prefaces are important not just because they open up the space for a story to be told, but because they often carry some indication of what the story will consist of, when it will be over, and what sort of things should happen at the end (Sacks 1995).

Elicited narratives begin differently, in the sense that the story teller does not have to negotiate space to tell the story but is invited to do so by another participant.[2] In the case of the elicited narratives presented here, it is often the researcher who acts as story elicitor, but many elicited narratives still begin with an abstract giving a brief summary of what the story will be about.

In a preface, a story teller can indicate their alignment to the story, as well as an appropriate reaction to it – setting up the way recipients should respond (for example, 'Did you see what happened last night? It was aw-ful/hilarious/disgusting'). The recipients then know what to listen for, and understand that the story will be over once an account of something aw-ful/hilarious/disgusting has been given. For a story to come to an end, the narrator needs to bring recipients back into real time, that is, into the now of the conversational present. "Tellers must smooth the way as it were from the storyworld they have created back into the embedding conversation" (Polanyi 1982:164). This is done via 'exit talk' (Jefferson 1978). Story endings may be explicitly indicated by a coda – 'it was the funniest thing I've ever seen', 'he's back in prison now' – which functions to bring the narrative sequence to a close and provides a transition from the narrative sequence back into the on-going talk. When a story falls flat, and receives a 'so what' response from its recipients, this may be because it lacks a perceivable point – in other words, the narrative in some way does not live up to the claims being made by the teller for its status as 'tellable' (Bruner 1991:12).

Narrative context

The specific form a story takes is also determined by the social context in which it is told. Shoshana Blum Kulka (1997; Chapter 8 this volume) makes the dis-tinction between 'tale', 'teller' and 'telling' to describe three different aspects of narrative activity. The 'tale' delimits the story itself, the narrative sequence of events; the 'teller' is the narrator on any given occasion; and the 'telling' specifies the context within which the story is told. Whereas the 'tale' usually re-mains constant (or it becomes a different version of the same story), the 'tellers' may of course vary. There can be more than one teller, as we see in the stories collected by Jennifer Coates (Chapter 4) and Neal Norrick (Chapter 5) which are co-narrated between couples, or groups of friends. 'Tellings' are the situ-ated narrative events, each with its unique participation framework (Goffman 1981) which includes the array of teller(s) story recipients, and sometimes story elicitors.

Stories, as Dick Leith points out in Chapter 7, need listeners. The story told by a male friend and alcoholic is received very differently on two separate occasions; the first when the teller is drunk; the second when it is elicited as part of the author's research into men's experience of illness. The 'telling', then, is very different in these two contexts, the first time the recipient does not want to hear the story and refuses the role of 'listener'; the second time he explicitly asks for the story to be told and thereby takes up the role of listener in a way he was not prepared to do the first time round. Norrick (Chapter 5) also describes how a narrative is redesigned by its tellers for a fresh context in his analysis of two consecutive tellings of the same story. The story, which is co-narrated by two women friends, is first told to one recipient, then retold shortly afterwards to another new recipient who joins the group. This locally shifting participation framework of 'listeners' affects the second telling both in terms of reshaping the 'tale' for a new audience, and the work of the narrators, i.e. who tells what.

A further aspect of context evident in the narratives collected here is the distinction between talk in public and private contexts; i.e. the forms of narrative discourse in institutional and non-institutional settings. In public contexts such as the courtroom, narrative is produced in a very different format to conversational narratives in private settings. As Sandra Harris (Chapter 11) shows, in trial discourse, narrative modes are intermeshed with non-narrative modes. Through the questioning procedures of examination and cross examination of witnesses, and judges' summing up of evidence, emerge not just factual reports, but also what she describes as 'coherent and convincing narratives'.

However, this distinction between what counts as institutional talk and what does not is not always clear cut (Thornborrow 2002). The range of narrative activity analysed here takes us through a variety of settings, from the more 'public' domains of the workplace (Holmes and Marra) and school (Blum Kulka, Sheldon and Engstrom) to the very 'private' conversations between friends (Coates, Leith, and Norrick), via the research interview (Armbruster and Meinhof, Cheshire and Ziebland, Coupland et al.). As the analyses show, narrative is a not simply a pervasive discursive form, but a resilient and versatile resource through which speakers can accomplish many different social and cultural actions.

The boundaries of narrative

Before turning to the functions of narrative in more detail, we want to consider the limits of narrative. Where do we draw the boundary between narrative and non-narrative discourse? There is a broad range of discourse which is often described as narrative in character, without necessarily corresponding to the formal description of narrative just outlined. The data presented in the chapters of this book involve many different story forms. Elicited narratives are at the heart of the first three chapters (2, 3 and 4) while collaborative narrative between friends is the subject of the Chapters 5 and 6. But there are also minimal narrative units or 'anecdotes', such as the workplace stories analysed by Janet Holmes and Meredith Marra in Chapter 10, the children's play narratives described by Amy Sheldon and Heidi Engstrom in Chapter 9; as well as the narratives produced in institutional settings such as the courtroom and news reporting (Harris, Chapter 11; Montgomery, Chapter 12). Harris argues that although trial discourse is structured according to an 'anti-narrative' mode, with constraints on the production of narrative as evidence, nevertheless narrative coherence is a central part of courtroom discourse when it comes to convincing a jury. On the other hand, Martin Montgomery challenges the established paradigm of news as 'story', questioning the narrative mode of TV news reporting which, he argues, is more akin to commentary than story telling.

Terry Threadgold's exploration of the difference between narrativity as a broad concept and narrative as a linguistic form in Chapter 13 directly addresses questions about the limits of narrative discourse. Where exactly are the limits between what we understand to be a well-formed story and a looser categorisation of narrative as a genre? Most importantly, throughout the data presented in this book we find ample empirical evidence of how stories are designed for their local, situated telling, evidence that narrative form is inevitably shaped by the social context in which it occurs, and that narrativity as a discursive mode is at the core of our social and institutional world.

Narrative function

As well as examining aspects of narrative form, many of the chapters in this book are also centrally concerned with questions of narrative function. Research has shown that narrative constitutes an important discursive resource used by speakers across a range of social contexts and settings to accomplish many different social actions. It is clearly the case that "narratives are highly portable discursive units" (Briggs 1996:29): stories can be told to entertain (jokes, folktales, anecdotes), to justify and explain (accounts, and descriptions of events), to instruct (the 'cautionary' tale, fables), and to establish social norms (gossip). But even more importantly, stories tell us who we are: they are central to our social and cultural identity.

Narrative and social identity

As the novelist Joanna Trollope puts it: "Story is how we describe ourselves to one another" (McCrum 2002), and it is now widely claimed that narrative plays a key role in the construction of the self (Brockmeier & Carbaugh 2001; De Fina 2003; Kerby 1991; Linde 1993). Through telling stories, we say who we are and who we are not. Narrative also has a key role in the location of the emergent self in a social and cultural world (Bruner 1990, 2001; Chafe 1994). The early chapters in the book explore the different selves that narrators produce and maintain in interaction.

In Chapter 2, Jenny Cheshire and Sue Ziebland explore the stability of the 'life story' in the context of illness. Through narrative, the women they interview construct a medicalised self which is coherent with their non-ill identity. In this way, their personal identity, their sense of 'the real me' is integrated with their identity as a patient through their stories of how they cope with their illness. Heidi Armbruster and Ulrike Meinhof, in Chapter 3, analyse competing versions of experience and show how three generations of people living on the German-Polish border have different ways of narrating 'what happened' to them to construct coherent socio-historical identities. Armbruster and Meinhof found that there was often more similarity between the accounts of same generation members than between members of the same family, not just in the way they represented the past and their experience of historical change, but also in the way they told their stories of 'what happened'. For these informants then, there is a generational identity which is constituted through narrative form in the telling of their 'life story' and their representation of historical experience. Nik Coupland, Peter Garrett and Angie Williams (Chapter 4) focus on stories told by teenage boys to their peers (both boys and girls). The authors show how some storytellers are successful in projecting in-group values and shared social identities that are strongly approved of by peers, while others are far less successful.

Given the role played by narrative in the construction of the self, it is not surprising that narrative also plays a key role in the construction of gender. It could be argued that one important aspect of the stories analysed by Coupland et al is their gendered nature: the boys tell stories about personal adventures, about risks to their own or other people's wellbeing, about mishaps and damage, about conflict with authority figures. While such topics are not solely the domain of male story-tellers, there is certainly evidence that such topics form the staple of male narrative (Coates 2003; Frosh et al. 2002). Many of the chapters involve narratives where the narrator's gender is a key part of the identity work going on.

The construction of professional identities in workplace settings is the focus of Holmes and Marra's chapter (Chapter 10). They analyse the function of anecdotes told by managers in two different workplace settings. They argue that narratives are central in building complex and often contradictory aspects of managerial identity; managers tell stories that display who they are to their team. Whether they construct a narrative self as the 'tough boss' or the 'ordinary, fallible person', both managers in this study use anecdotes to mitigate their position of authority. In this way, the tensions between maintaining their status as leader and showing workplace solidarity can be negotiated and reconciled.

Performance in narrative discourse

The notion of 'performance' is central to any discussion of narrative discourse. But analysts appeal to two quite distinct kinds of performance. The first, used in relation to the performance of identity and the social self, originates with Goffman's work (for example his seminal *The Performance of the Self in Everyday Life*, 1971), and has been developed in the work of Bruner (1990) and Butler (1990).

In particular, the theory of performativity has extended the idea of gender as culturally constructed. In her influential book *Gender Trouble* (1990), Judith Butler argues that gender is something that is 'done', and that it is something that has to be 'done' over and over again. 'Gender is the repeated stylisation of the body, a set of repeated acts within a rigid regulatory framework which congeal over time to produce the appearance of substance, of a 'natural' kind of being' (Butler 1990: 33). Gender is never static but is produced actively and in interaction with others every day of our lives: speakers are seen as 'performing' masculinity or femininity. In their talk, men and women can be seen to align themselves with dominant norms of masculinity and femininity as they 'do' gender with one another.

These ideas are explored and extended in the chapters by Coates, Leith and Sheldon and Engstrom (5, 7 and 9). In her analysis of stories told by heterosexual couples, Coates argues that co-narration, or 'duetting' (Falk 1980), between couples enables men to perform hegemonic masculinity; that is, it provides space to perform heterosexual connection with a female partner, whereas co-narration with other males is avoided precisely because of the performance of connection which heterosexual men tend to avoid.

The performance of masculinity and male friendship is developed in Leith's chapter, where he analyses the friendship between two men, one of whom suffers from alcoholism and the other from depression. Storytelling becomes a therapeutic activity, but only when one of the men is prepared to take up the role of story recipient. The first telling happens when the teller is drunk, 'doing familiarity' rather than 'doing friendship' and performing a version of masculinity that the story recipient deemed inappropriate to their relationship. The second telling on a later occasion is different in that the performance of friendship is at the heart of the interaction, and it becomes a mutually constructive event for both teller and recipient.

Socially performed, gendered behaviour is also evident in the data analysed by Sheldon and Engstrom in their account of the play narratives engaged in by pre-school American children. Several features of gendered language practices were identifiable among single sex groups where the children were observed to use different modes of engagement with each other. The girls tended to arrive at a co-ordinated focus for their play faster than the boys, who used a more 'side-by-side', less cohesive style which meant they took longer to achieve a mutual focus in their pretend play sequences. Sheldon and Engstrom argue that although there were clearly many similarities in the way both groups of children were interacting in their play narratives, the differences nevertheless indicate their awareness of socially differentiated ways of 'performing' gender through language and style of interaction, even at this early age.

The second use of the term 'performance' in work on narrative derives from the work of social anthropologists and ethnographers who have focused on the telling of a story as a performance (extending to narrative the everyday use of the word 'performance' in relation to plays and poems and songs being performed in public). Linguistic anthropology, particularly through the work of Richard Bauman, has developed useful accounts of factors that distinguish performance events from other sorts of communicative practice. Bauman (1992:46ff.) suggests a list of particular characteristics that all performance events share. It can be argued that performance involves a *focusing* of communicative events.

In Chapter 4, Coupland, Garrett and Williams analyse a set of teenage stories in terms of this notion of 'performance'. Why are some performances more successful than others as far as fellow teenagers are concerned? As Coupland et al show, drawing on Bauman's ideas, storytelling as a 'performance' functions as a reflexive tool for examining dominant cultural meanings, drawing attention to the culture's systems of signification and expression. Through their analysis of peer-group evaluations of a set of stories, they identify the narratives that are culturally 'resonant' for this age-group. They suggest that what makes a 'good' story is the teller's 'prat-avoidance' technique – a skill which involves a high degree of control over the tale, as well as a high level of reflexivity in the telling (e.g. the ability to stand back and laugh at oneself). Also important are intensity and incongruity, where high levels of risk-taking and exceptional events are valued over more mundane, 'boring' happenings.

From a more micro-analytic perspective, Norrick (Chapter 5) also sees story-telling in terms of a 'performance'. In the narratives he analyses, the 'editing' which goes on during the story telling is both locally and culturally informed; what makes the story funny and more streamlined as a performance the second time round is precisely the fact that it has been practised once. Thus, its 'tellability', the romantic, touching and dramatic elements of the story, have been worked on and can be better 'performed' in the second telling.

Narrative and culture

Another central theme running through many of the chapters is the relationship between narrative and culture, and more specifically, between what is *tellable* and culture. Storytelling is a powerful form of symbolic, cultural 'capital' (Bourdieu 1992) and the contributors to this book address this aspect of narrative discourse in a variety of ways. There are stories that 'work' and stories that don't; stories that are worth telling more than once, stories that play an important part in constructing life histories, group identities and practices, as well as social ideologies. They are, as Coupland et al point out in Chapter 4, full of 'rich cultural stuff'. The narratives analysed here provide many illustrations of this important articulation between narrative and culture; we examine this by looking at how the concepts of 'tellability' and 'point' relate to social and cultural issues.

Stories need to have tellability, that is, they need to have a point. The worst thing that can happen to a narrator is that their story is seen as pointless; narrators need to avoid the "So what?" challenge (Labov 1972: 362). But how a story is told for and received by particular audiences will often depend on the cultural context of the narrative event. "Stories . . . can have as their *point* [sic] only culturally salient material generally agreed upon by members of the producer's culture to be self-evidently important and true" (Polanyi 1979: 207).

While what counts as 'having a point' will differ from culture to culture, a fair generalisation seems to be that stories involve "deviations from expected norms" (Polanyi 1985: 17). Jerome Bruner explains this in terms of the concept 'the canonical script' (Bruner 1991: 11). A canonical script is the unmarked script of everyday life, the way we expect things to be. For a story to be tellable, it must involve a breach of the canonical script. In other words, Bruner argues that telling a story involves exploring the boundaries between the ordinary and the exceptional. To achieve tellability, a story needs to reach a moment where the unexpected and unusual erupts from out of the mundane and predictable.

The chapters in this book abound with examples. In Chapter 5 (Coates), the narrator of Story 3 begins with the mundane – trying to park in London's West End – and then moves on to the unexpected – a collision with a taxi. In Leith's paper (Chapter 7), the narrator tells how the mundane activity of walking down the stairs is dramatically changed when he hears voices telling him he can fly. The canonical, romantic, expectations of a 'marriage proposal' are thoroughly undermined in the 'double engagement' story analysed by Norrick (Chapter 6), where the first proposal causes the second one to fall flat.

In Chapter 4, Coupland et al argue that the peer group culture is 'performed' through narrative in so far as stories both 'entextualise' cultural values and meanings and then 'decontextualise' them, abstracting out a cultural moment as tellable in a narrative event. If this narrated moment resonates with high cultural values for the group, that story will be better received than one in which the cultural resonances are weaker. While the reception of stories told by Welsh teenagers provide insights into the cultural norms of this age group, the production of stories in preschool children's play in Chapter 8 provide another insight into the relationship between culture and narrative competence for much younger children. Blum Kulka argues that there is a strong link between what she calls the 'cultural matrix of children's lifeworlds' and their peer group narrative activity, making the point that the more grounded a story is in the children's culture, the more confident they are in telling complex tales. Furthermore, she argues that it is through this kind of narrative play that children develop their discursive competence in narrative skills.

The cultural resonance of narrative discourse is also an important theme in Harris's chapter on trial discourse (Chapter 11), where she shows how the cultural coherence of a narrative can play a crucial role in convincing the jury, and in Armbruster and Meinhof's work on the importance of cultural memory in stories of two generations with different experiences of living in pre- and post-unified Germany (Chapter 3). These chapters both explore, albeit in very different contextual modes, the relationship between narrative and culture where the point of a story, what is tellable and why, depends on culturally recognised experiences and values. Harris argues that the role of shared cultural narratives is recognised by defence lawyers, whose task is either to subvert the overarching narrative of the prosecution, or to establish a credible alternative. In the rape trial she analyses, it was the defence lawyer's construction of a coherent narrative which drew on culturally determined perceptions of a sexually abusive male, that played a key part in securing the conviction. Cultural coherence is also evident in the stories told by the different generational groups in Chapter 3, where shared 'cultural memory' within one generation produces a way of storying the past which is not found in the next. Significantly for this study, the sense of a coherent, shared historical memory seems to be absent from the middle generation of informants, whose narratives were more fragmented in their form than those of their parents.

We move closer here to the ideological function of narrative that is taken up by Threadgold in the final chapter. Describing a project involving work with asylum seekers and groups of school children, she describes how difficult it was for them to perform 'the other', in drama workshops they developed around the issue of asylum in Britain. Telling a different story means seeing and acting differently, countering dominant cultural myths which are formed through ideological bias against a social group. The reproduction of a dominant symbolic order through narrative discourse is also discussed by Sheldon and Engstrom in Chapter 9, who argue that culturally gendered ways of acting and interacting are embodied through pre-school children's play narratives.

An important function of story-telling, then, is that it allows us "to present ourselves to others (and to ourselves) as typical or characteristic or 'culture confirming' in some way" (Bruner 2001:29). As the chapters that follow demonstrate, this need to perform our selves in alignment with cultural norms, while at the same time saying something interesting, something where the normal order of things is disrupted, results in the very tension that makes stories tellable. But ultimately, it is through narrating ourselves, through constructing the self through narrative, that we construct our culture (Brockmeier & Carbaugh 2001:16).

Methodology and techniques of transcription

Reading through the chapters of this book, it will very soon become clear that there is a diversity of transcription techniques and conventions used. The issue of how to transcribe oral data is a complex one, and has been the subject of much debate within sociolinguistics (Coates & Thornborrow 1999). Transcription is inevitably always a form of interpretation, and as such, constitutes a fundamental part of the analytic process. There is no standard method of transcribing the narratives collected here; the contributors to this book present their data in relation to the focus of their approach to it, and in order to show the particular features of narrative discourse they want to highlight in their analysis. There is then a wide variety of transcription techniques which is a direct result of the range of different research designs and analytic perspectives in this book.

Thus, in transcribing television news discourse, Montgomery produces a transcript which represents not just the verbal script, but the synchronisation between verbal and visual, as well as a detailed shot analysis in some cases. Blum Kulka represents her data (collected from Israeli preschool children) in the original and in translation; while Armbruster and Meinhof use an English translation, with the original German transcript for reference in the notes. Sheldon and Engstrom choose to adopt two different methods of transcribing the play narratives produced by American preschool boys and girls to show the differences in systems of engagement in play between the two groups. The girls' talk is represented using what they call a 'verse format', whereas the boys' talk is represented in 'column format', so that the process of transcription is closely linked to the argument the authors make about gendered forms of interaction in their data. Leith captures the rhetorical aspects of an alcoholic's narrative performance by differentiating between two kinds of 'pause' in his data; the rhetorical pause used to produce dramatic effects in the story, and the non-rhetorical pause, i.e. taking breath, hesitations, and so on. Coates uses the transcription technique favoured by many researchers in conversational narrative based on Chafe's (1980) notion of 'idea units', where 'spurts of information' are represented and numbered line by line. The lines correspond to the narrator's breath-groups, or intonation units, typically a grammatical phrase or clause; Norrick too uses the intonation unit as a basis for his transcripts.

Whatever transcription technique they choose to adopt, the authors either provide a key to the notation symbols they use, or discuss their choice of transcription as part of their methodology. This diversity reflects the range of data collected here, from naturally-occurring, 'fresh' conversational narratives, to narratives elicited by a researcher, and institutionally-produced narrative discourse.

Conclusions

As we worked on this introductory chapter, we became aware that the issues that seem to us to be central to sociolinguistic work on narrative at this time are issues that are highly salient in sociolinguistics in general.

The growing confluence of social scientific ideas of social identity with social psychological ideas of the 'self' means that identity is currently centre stage in sociolinguistics.[3] Simultaneously, sociolinguistic researchers have been stimulated by Judith Butler's re-working of the notions of performance and performativity to look in new ways at narrative and at how identity is constructed through narrative performance.

Work focusing on identity and performance tends to look at the individual speaker, the individual narrator. This focus on the individual is now being challenged. The first challenge comes from psychologists and psychoanalysts who emphasize that the child's sense of self can only develop in interaction with significant others. Rare unfortunate individuals who are deprived of human interaction as infants do not develop language and therefore cannot become story-tellers (Gerhardt 2004). If we do not become story-tellers, in a very important sense we cannot become fully human.

The second challenge comes from sociologists and linguists who emphasize the importance of community for the understanding of individual behaviour. Work in this area has introduced the notion of 'Community of Practice' to sociolinguistics (a concept that originates with Etienne Wenger 1990, see also Wenger 1998). A Community of Practice can be defined as follows:

> An aggregate of people who come together around mutual engagement in an endeavour. Ways of doing things, ways of talking, beliefs, values, power relations – in short, practices – emerge in the course of this mutual endeavour.
> (Eckert & McConnell-Ginet 1992: 95)

This definition draws attention to the emphasis sociolinguists now give to the particularities of social context and to the importance of looking at language practices in the context of local groups, local Communities of Practice.

This healthy tension between individual and community-based approaches means that research focussing on narrative is hugely varied, as this collection of papers will illustrate. But narrative researchers are coming to understand that the study of narrative "involves not only examining the cultural construction of personal identity, but also the construction of one's social culture" (Brockmeier & Carbaugh 2001: 16). Narrative, after all, is central to human development, both in terms of phylogenesis and ontogenesis. Oral story-telling goes back to the beginnings of human culture: humans beings developed the ability to tell stories and thereby to define themselves and to make sense of the world. But storytelling also has a key role in the development of the human infant who drinks in the stories told by parents and other significant adults. These stories bind the child into membership of the culture. The child in turn learns to tell stories, both individually and as part of collaborative play, and thus learns to say who they are and simultaneously to demonstrate their membership of the culture.

It is unsurprising that sociolinguists have embraced the study of narrative at the beginning of the twenty-first century, given that the articulation of identity and culture and the new awareness of performance and performativity are so highly salient in sociolinguistics. The papers in this book illustrate the range of work being undertaken in the field. And, given that issues of identity, culture and performance are currently at the forefront of narrative studies, these papers demonstrate how sociolinguistics can provide a new vantage point for the analysis and understanding of story-telling in all its various manifestations.

Joanna Thornborrow, Cardiff 2004
Jennifer Coates, London 2004

Notes

1. We are using the terms 'story' and 'narrative' interchangeably here, as for us 'story' and 'narrative' are synonymous terms associated with lay and expert contexts respectively. We are however aware that some theorists – for example Eggins and Slade (1997) – make a distinction between the two terms.

2. Elicited narratives stories are of course not only found in research interview data; the role of story 'elicitor' can be taken, for example, by a mother in family discourse (Ochs & Taylor 1992) or by the host in talk show discourse (Thornborrow 2001).

3. As we were writing this introduction, a new Psychology journal, 'Self and Identity', was launched with the stated aim of providing a forum for empirical work in psychology, social psychology and other disciplines which will relate studies of the construct of 'self' to interpersonal relationships, society, and culture.

Chapter 2

Narrative as a resource in accounts of the experience of illness

Jenny Cheshire and Sue Ziebland

Queen Mary, University of London / University of Oxford

Introduction

The stories we tell about our everyday lives are an important resource for making sense of our experiences. Through narrative we structure and interpret our experiences (Labov & Fanshel 1977), create coherence in our personal life stories (Linde 1993), construct, display and reinforce our sense of self (Schiffrin 1996), and relate this sense of self to others in our social worlds (Bruner 1986). It is not surprising that narratives have been found to occur in a wide range of contexts, both public and private, from family dinner times to courts of law. In this paper we focus on the narratives that occur when people talk about their experience of illness during an interview with a researcher. Our specific concern here is not with an illness construed as a single bounded event (such as, for example, appendicitis or pneumonia) but with a chronic condition (hypertension) that becomes a permanent part of an individual's life. Hypertension is not a disease, as such, but a major risk factor for heart disease and stroke. People with hypertension need to have life-long medication to reduce this risk. We wish to examine the stories individuals tell as they talk about their experiences of the condition, to see how, through their narratives, they integrate the experience of living with hypertension into their life story and make the everyday details of coping with hypertension part of their sense of the kind of person they believe themselves to be.

DIPEx: A database of individual patients' experiences of illness

Our data come from a series of interviews carried out by Sue Ziebland for a website resource on hypertension as part of www.dipex.org (DIPEx: personal experiences of health and illness, described briefly below, and more fully in Herxheimer et al. 2000). DIPEx is the initiative of a team of medical practitioners and social scientists. Briefly, the overall aim is to provide a more patient-centred perspective on illness, which will serve as a resource for patients and their carers, and for health care professionals. Each module on the website deals with a different health problem and is developed as a stand alone qualitative study of patients' experiences. Semi-structured interviews are carried out with a maximum variation sample of 30–50 patients from different social backgrounds throughout the UK. The interviews are then used to identify issues that are important to patients. The range of conditions covered by DIPEx is increasing rapidly: in 2003 www.dipex.org included modules on hypertension, cancers of the prostate, breast, bowel, lung, testes and cervix, cervical screening and epilepsy. Work is in progress on many more.

For patients, the DIPEx website is the main resource. Each illness module has summaries of the main themes emerging from the interviews, with illustrations from video, audio and written clips. It also contains descriptions of the condition, details of its prevalence and its prevention; information about treatments; and questions and answers. There are links to other relevant websites, including support groups and voluntary organisations. The website thus acts as a reference point for patients and their carers, where they can find out about the experiences of others as well as accessing more conventional health information. For health care professionals DIPEx presents a patient-centred perspective on a range of illnesses with the aim of enabling good communication between patients and professionals. It also provides an educational resource for medical and nursing students, which can also be used for postgraduate and in-service training.

Although the website necessarily contains only short clips from the interviews, there is a wealth of information in the full transcripts about how patients have reacted to their condition and how it has affected their lives. The transcripts have been used for qualitative analysis of a range of issues (see, for example, Chapple & Ziebland 2002; Chapple et al. 2002; Rozmovits & Ziebland 2004) and further studies are in progress. This paper, however, is the first to explore the potential of the transcripts for furthering our understanding of sociolinguistic and discourse-analytic questions. Mischler (1986) points out that narratives occur frequently during interviews if those being interviewed are given room to speak. This is what we found here: many patients responded to the interviewer's questions with narratives, although some individuals, of course, related more stories than others. As we said in the introduction, we focus here on the interviews carried out with individuals diagnosed with hypertension. In particular, we will examine interviews with two women, referring to them as Rose and Josephine.[1]

Rose and Josephine

We chose these interviews for detailed analysis because there were some broad similarities in the medical histories of the two women. They had been diagnosed at about the same age – when they were in their mid-twenties – and both had been living with hypertension for many years: Rose was 72 at the time of her interview, and Josephine was 53. In addition, they each suffered from other serious illnesses that had a continuing effect on their everyday lives. Rose had a form of epilepsy that caused convulsions while she was sleeping, and throughout her life she had experienced severe migraine attacks. She had recently been hospitalised because of three "mini strokes", and she often collapsed and fell down. Josephine's medical history was more dramatic still. In her early thirties she was admitted to intensive care when her extremely high blood pressure caused heart and renal failure. Five years later she received a kidney transplant. As a result her health was under constant supervision, requiring regular attendance at hospital outpatient clinics. Both women had to take medication every day of their lives.

Despite the similarities in their medical histories, Rose and Josephine had very different reactions to the experience of living with chronic illness. They gave a first indication of this in their answers to a question put to them early in the interview: "do you have an image of the sort of person who might have high blood pressure?" Rose unhesitatingly replied "yes, someone like myself" (indicated by the arrow in extract (1) below) and went on to relate her reply to an aspect of her personality (her tendency to rush), as we see here:

Extract (1)

Sue: do you have an image of the sort of person who might have high blood
       pressure?
Rose: yes someone like myself <LAUGHS>
Sue: right and how would you =

Rose: = someone that rushed about everywhere and
        er I'm not a bit highly strung.. I wouldn't say that but I'm a real rusher…er
        I've only recently slowed down because I fractured my arm and done things
        to myself that I thought well it's because I'm rushing that I'm falling you see

Rose seems to be, then, a person who has no problem seeing her illness as a part
of her personal identity. She attributes her recent falls not to her medical condition but to her personality – to the kind of person she believes herself to be.

Josephine, by contrast, presents herself as an atypical example of a person
with high blood pressure, saying that such a person would be "not like me" (it
is relevant to note that she is slim and no longer smokes):

Extract (2)

Sue: do you have an image of the sort of person who would have high
            blood pressure?
Josephine: well er I think smokers could be… I mean as soon as you say an
            image I see a large red-faced man .. probably with a fag
            on…certainly with a big beer belly who is always going to go on
            the diet tomorrow and so on …
       →   not like me

Josephine explains later in the interview that she actively distances herself from
her experiences of illness, seeing them as not experienced by "the real me". She
describes in (3), a non-narrative passage, how her friends and family know
her as 'Jo' or 'Josie' whereas she presents herself to health care professionals as
'Josephine':

Extract (3)

er I have a way of dealing with it … I don't consider myself ill or an invalid but I
know I'm going to need treatment for the rest of my life…and in a way it's not
happening to me it's happening to someone called Josephine Smith…nobody at
the hospital knows that I'm not called Josephine by my friends and people who
know me so when I go there then it's her…it's Josephine that's being looked after
and treated and is having to waste time on this stuff… I've felt for a long time
now that the real me is a kind of observer of this and so it doesn't get to me…and
Josephine Smith takes care of all that side of it and does all that's required and
meanwhile the real me …I'm getting on with the rest of my life

Rose and Josephine, then, seem to have very different strategies for making sense of their experiences of illness, and it is for this reason that we focus on the stories they tell within their interviews. We will see that despite their different reactions to their condition each of them uses narrative to structure their experiences in such a way that they are integrated coherently into their life story and their sense of personal identity.

Defining narrative

We have worked with the classic definition of a narrative unit, taken from Labov and Waletzsky's (1967) framework. Thus a narrative, for us, contains at least two Complicating Action clauses where the verbs are in the past or historic present tense, and where we can infer that the order of the clauses matches the order in which the recounted events took place. There are also one or more Orientation clauses setting out who was involved in the events, when and where the events took place, and giving other necessary background information. In the DIPEx interviews an initial Abstract, summarising the story, is often provided by the interviewer's question. The Complicating Action section is followed by one or more clauses giving the Resolution of the story; and the narrative sometimes ends with a Coda that returns us from the story world to the present.

These sections of the narrative constitute the referential or propositional strand of meaning. They recount the facts of the story – without them there would be no story. However, narratives also have an affective strand of meaning where narrators reveal their feelings about the events they are recounting. This is equally essential to the narrative, justifying the telling and, importantly for our interests here, showing the kind of person the speaker claims to be: "narrative is a presentation of the self, and the evaluative component in particular establishes the kind of self that is presented" (Linde 1993:81). The affective strand may be expressed in separate Evaluation clauses, but evaluation may also occur through the use of intensifiers and other linguistic forms within the clauses constituting the referential strand (see further Labov & Waletzsky 1967; Labov 1972).

Rose

Classic narrative forms

Rose tells more stories than any of the other patients in the hypertension section of the database: eighteen stretches of discourse correspond to the definition of narrative outlined above, including some where the form is slightly modified, as we will see. In some of these narratives Rose's close integration of the referential and affective strands serves as a clear example of the way speakers can use narrative to integrate their experiences of illness into a coherent sense of their personal identity. We illustrate this with her account of her first experience of hypertension, in (4).

Extract (4)

	Sue:	So I wonder if I could just start by asking you to tell me how you
		originally discovered that you had high blood pressure?
1	Rose:	Yes well at the time I was 26 years old
2		I was pregnant with my daughter Gillian
3		and er I had.. I was told by the doctor that I had to go to bed
4		this was about 4 weeks before she was delivered
5		and I couldn't understand it at the time I must admit
6		and he said that he would sort it out afterwards
7		er however I did go to bed for 4 weeks before she was born
8		and er and then er I got up a couple of times whilst I was in bed
9		I was a bit naughty
	Sue:	right <LAUGHS>
10	Rose:	and I got up
11		and er when he came in to take my blood pressure
12		he found that it had gone sky high
13		and was very concerned
14		"if you don't stay there" he said
15		"well you'll have to go in hospital"
16		so I stayed there
17		and then er and then she was born within 4 weeks after that
18		er and my blood pressure still stayed high
19		so that was the first time I ever came in contact with.. with blood
20		pressure

In the referential strand of her story Rose has selected relevant factual aspects of her first experience of hypertension to produce a chronological account that answers the interviewer's question; but her story accomplishes more than this. For example, her evaluative clauses connect her subjective state in the story world she is constructing to her present attitude to her illness. Thus in line 5 the evaluation clause *I couldn't understand it at the time* is syntactically dependent on the present tense clause *I must admit*, suggesting that from her present perspective she does now understand why she had been told to go to bed. Secondly, the evaluation clause *I was a bit naughty* in line 9 displays a characteristic of her personality that she also mentions later in the interview (as we will see in the following section). In this way her account helps to construct what Rose appears to see as a stable aspect of her personal identity. Thirdly, she uses embedded external evaluation in the clauses in lines 14 and 15 to portray, through the doctor's concern, her dawning realisation that her high blood pressure was a serious condition; and she uses internal evaluation, with the choice of the adjective *sky-high* in line 12, to dramatise her blood pressure. By telling her story in this classic narrative form, then, Rose creates coherence not only through her representation of the sequence of the factual events but also through the sequencing of her subjective experience of these events. Rose's account of her first encounter with the illness that has been since been a constant part of her life makes sense of the experience both objectively and subjectively; she expresses within her account of that experience what for her is a salient aspect of her personal identity.

Habitual narratives

In classic narratives the verbs recounting the actions are in the simple past tense or historic present tense, allowing the events to be represented as a 'blow by blow' sequence. However, Rose tells several narratives where the verb phrases involve the auxiliaries *used to* or *would*. Extract (5) is an example of one such habitual narrative. As before, the interviewer's question can be analysed as the abstract. We indicate the lines where the habitual forms occur with an arrow.

Extract (5)

Sue: have you ever.. for your blood pressure have you ever used one of these self monitors these
Rose: no I've always
         my brother in law.. my brother in law had one

> but he annoyed me in a way
> → because he used to keep taking his blood pressure every…
>   it was like a toy for a bit you know
>   I mean he doesn't do it now but he did at the time
> → and er I used to think "there's no wonder he's got blood pressure
>   keep on taking it
>   it's enough to give you blood pressure.. you know"
>   and when he said "do you want me to take your blood pressure?"
> → I'd say "no thank you"
>   oh dear spoil sport really

The point of Rose's story is partly that she spoilt her brother-in-law's fun. This is consistent with the aspect of her identity that she displayed in extract (4), where she presented herself as having been 'a bit naughty'. A further point of the story, however, is that in her opinion it is more sensible not to keep thinking about your blood pressure; and that this is how she herself lives her life. This too is consistent with the kind of person she presents herself as being, as we see in (6):

Extract (6)

Sue: OK.. do you think of yourself as somebody who has high blood pressure?
Rose: no no I don't even think of it.. I just take my tablets and do as I'm told
Sue: you don't think about it normally?
Rose: I'm not a worrier in that respect…when people say they've got…they're worrying about this and to me that's so small to worry about but people do I know.. I know people do worry yes it's a natural thing to do

Habitual narratives are a less dramatic style of narration, since they cannot reproduce the blow-by-blow effect of a story about a single occasion. Instead, they tell of the general course of events over a period of time, with the verb phrases and adverbs marking repetition and routinization (Riessman 1990:1197). In Rose's narrative the habitual form allows her to bring together in a single clause a repeated series of reactions to her brother-in-law's behaviour, showing how she consistently adopts a behaviour she believes to be more sensible than his. Riessman's analysis of the narratives told during an interview with a man living with advanced multiple sclerosis also notes a large number of habitual narratives. Perhaps these are likely to occur in talk about the experience of chronic illness because that experience inevitably includes a series of repeated events and everyday small decisions about the management of the illness. In any case, here the choice of auxiliary verbs such as *used to* or *would* within the narrative form make it possible for Rose to not only display aspects of her identity that she elsewhere claims for herself (the fact that she is 'not a worrier' and that she is sometimes 'a bit naughty'), but also to show that these aspects of her self identity are constantly reinforced through the repeated events that she recounts in her narrative.

Comparison with others

The narrative in extract (5) illustrates a further characteristic of Rose's stories, many of which relate incidents where other people with the same condition as Rose behave in a less competent way than Rose herself. In (5), as we have seen, Rose contrasts her own behaviour with that of her brother-in-law. In the narrative in (7) the comparison is with her neighbour. Mention of the neighbour triggers a short narrative illustrating the sensible system Rose has adopted to ensure that she does not forget to take her medication. The beginning of the narrative is indicated by the arrow.

Extract (7)

Sue: now do you ever find that you forget to take your medication for blood pressure?

Rose: no.. no I don't… the reason being that little blue box over there on the table… underneath that top thing.. that has.. that is done every week er for 7 days

Sue: OK

Rose: so I've only got to go to that and if I found… which I never have.. if I found that they were still there I would think "oh I've forgotten today"… but I've never had that problem

Sue: right so that's your way of making sure that you're taking them?

Rose: yes, and I put them out from there into a little jar every morning so that they go from there to there and then into me so it's a sort of way that I work it because my neighbour said "I forgot the other day" well I don't think I'd get far if I did forget

→   because I only once walked out of this house going up to the bus stop and I felt my heart was beating like a drum and I felt "oh no I bet I've forgotten my tablets" and I came back

and they were still in the little jar
so yes I would know

Social identities become meaningful when we compare the behaviour of our own social group with that of other groups (Tajfel 1974, 1981). Telling stories is a way for us to locate our selves within the group to which we feel we belong, recreating the perspectives these groups have on their lives. Personal identities, similarly, are created by comparing ourselves with other people, and again we can locate ourselves as an individual through the stories we tell. This time, however, the comparison is often with people in the same social group as ourselves. It is instructive, then, to note that in her stories Rose compares her own experiences of coping with hypertension with those of other people with the same condition, and that she depicts herself as managing her condition better than they do. By locating an identity within a group of people who have the same illness as herself, Rose accepts her condition. Furthermore, by comparing her behaviour favourably with others in the group she is able to construct a positive identity for herself whilst detailing the everyday details of living with the condition. The identity she constructs in this way is in harmony with what she believes to be salient aspects of her personality, as we have seen. The story told in extract (7) provides a further illustration: here Rose portrays herself as managing her illness competently by developing a sensible system that allows her to know whether or not she has forgotten her pills. Her competence accords with what she says about herself in a non-narrative stretch of discourse, in (8):

Extract (8)

I like to be in control of myself and not being in control wouldn't go down very well with me ..I know it wouldn't ..you know what I mean?

Rose's accounts of her everyday experiences of illness, then, are presented through the lens of what to her are integral aspects of her personal identity. In this way her narratives can function in the way that Riessman (1990) has described, healing discontinuities between a person's idealised sense of who they are and the restrictions that an illness imposes on what a person can do and the kind of person they can be in reality. Rose cannot, in fact, always be in control of herself: as mentioned earlier, she has epilepsy, she has suffered three small strokes, and she falls down frequently. Some of her narratives, then, are enclaves where she creates a self that is in harmony with her ideal self (again, see Riessman 1990).

Because narratives

Interestingly, five of Rose's eighteen narratives are introduced with *because*, a story opener that has not been much commented on by other researchers. One example is shown in extract (7) above; a further, more complex example is given in (9). Again, the start of the narrative is indicated by the arrow.

Extract (9)

1	Sue:	has anybody ever mentioned er cutting down on salt?
2	Rose:	well yes but I read about Tracidrex.. it says on the packet "do not
3		cut down".. meaning "do not cut down on salt" because this
4		property.. this Tracidrex takes it out of your body...I don't think
5		many people know that
6	Sue:	right
7	Rose:	and er so therefore it says you know don't.. meaning don't cut the
8		salt out.. it doesn't say "don't cut it down" but "don't cut it out"
9	Sue:	OK
10	Rose:	because you can get low on sodium I think it's sodium..well sodium
11		is salt I think so you can become low on that... er so er no I don't
12		cut down..I don't have as much as I used to
13	Sue:	and did anyone point that out to you or do you read that in
14	Rose:	no I read everything I read all the little bits all the inner nooks and
15		crannies and I find out myself you know
16	→	because my sister said to me er er "do you cook with salt?"
17		and I said "yes I do I put a little bit in"
18		she says "well you know you've got blood pressure"
19		and I said to her "well my"
20		I says "I'll give it to you to show you"
21		and I showed it to her
22		and she said "oh I haven't read that"
23		I said "well you don't take Tracidrex
24		but you should be reading what's in yours or what you should be
25		doing may be with you you shouldn't cut it out"
26		because she's been low on sodium just lately
27		so may be it's because she cuts out you know
28		so that's a thing to think about

Here Rose again shows herself as in control, managing her illness competently; and again she creates this aspect of her personal identity by contrasting her own behaviour with that of another person with hypertension, this time her sister. *Because* clauses occur frequently in conversation, presumably because of their semantic role of explaining the speaker's thoughts, feelings or actions (Biber et al. 1999: 841). As a narrative opener Rose's *because* retains its basic meaning, indicating that the story that follows will provide a justification to explain the assertion she has just made. She claims, in line 15, that she found out for herself that she should not cut down on her salt intake, by reading the information that came with her medication. The *because* narrative then justifies this assertion by giving a specific example of an occasion when Rose showed her sister her information leaflet, demonstrating that she had indeed read it. It also, however, justifies the assertion made earlier, in line 4, where Rose claims that not many people know, despite conventional medical advice to the contrary, that some specific anti-hypertensive medication should not be combined with reduced salt intake. The *because* narrative justifies this assertion too, by providing the example of one such person who did not know this (her sister). Thus the narrative presents Rose as a person who stays in control of her health (by informing herself about the management of her illness) not only in contrast to her sister, but also in contrast to most other people who take that medication.

The narrative introduced by *because* in (7) similarly provides a justification for Rose's assertion "I don't think I'd get far if I forgot", recounting one such occasion when she did forget and when she did not get far from her home. In both these examples, then, the *because* narrative justifies the assertions Rose makes about her own attitude to her condition compared to other people's attitudes, and provides a further opportunity for her to present her own behaviour in a positive light, showing how competently she manages the everyday details of living with hypertension.

Reported speech

Like most of the patients interviewed, Rose often reports on her interactions with doctors and other health care professionals. This is not surprising, given the salience of these interactions in the experience of serious illness, for it is during such interactions that decisions are made about the management of the illness and information transmitted about the nature and the progress of the condition. Interactions between patients and health care professionals play a major role in the social construction of illness, then, and they are, therefore, highly reportable. For patients, these interactions may be highly charged: a doctor, say, may have only five or ten minutes available to spend discussing a condition with an individual patient, yet for that patient the outcome of the interaction is crucially important. Rose, like other patients interviewed, shows that she is fully aware of the time constraints:

Extract (10)

Rose: I would like to know more but you see when you go to the doctor's...
        I've got a wonderful doctor... it isn't because he wouldn't tell me ..
        he would if he had the time but he hasn't got the time and I know that

It is instructive to analyse how patients report their interactions with health care professionals, both in terms of what they choose to report, and in terms of how they report it. Who is given more speech in the reported interaction: the professionals or the patient? Do narrators give both themselves and the professionals direct speech, or do they report what they say indirectly? In extract (1), for example, Rose begins by using indirect speech to report the words of the doctor who first diagnosed her high blood pressure (*I was told by the doctor that I had to go to bed*), then uses direct speech to animate him as a character in the story and to dramatise his concern (*and when he came in to take my blood pressure he ... was very concerned "if you don't stay there" he said "well you'll have to go in hospital"*).

Research on actual interactions between doctors and patients (rather than reported interactions, as here) has found that patients behave deferentially to their doctors, tending to speak only when spoken to rather than initiating an exchange themselves. The higher status they attribute to doctors is reflected in the way that patients report their interactions: what doctors say tends to be reported in the form of direct speech whereas what the patients themselves say is more likely to be reported as indirect speech. Hamilton's (1998) study, for example, found that 60 per cent of what doctors said was reported as direct speech, but only 18 per cent of what patients said was reported in this way.

We analysed the reported speech in Rose's accounts of her interactions with health care professionals (who were mainly doctors) in both the narrative and non-narrative stretches of her interview. The results are shown in Table 1. The Table shows, firstly, that Rose reports what the doctors say more often than she reports what she herself says: of the 55 reported speech clauses, 32 are from doctors and 23 from Rose. Rose seems, then, to consider the doctors' words as more reportable and, perhaps, more important than her own. We also see, however, that she reports both what the doctors say and what she herself says almost entirely in the form of direct speech: 91 per cent of the reported

Table 1. Direct and indirect reported speech clauses in Rose's interview

	Rose speaking		Doctor speaking		Total
	N	(%)	N	(%)	N
Indirect reported speech clauses	2	(9)	3	(9)	5
Direct reported speech clauses	21	(91)	29	(91)	50
Total reported speech clauses	23	(100)	32	(100)	55

speech clauses, in both cases, are represented as direct speech. There were only 5 reported speech clauses in the form of indirect speech in the entire interview.

If giving direct speech to doctors indicates that narrators see the doctors as higher in status than themselves, we must conclude that Rose portrays her encounters with health care professionals as interactions between status equals. In this way she de-medicalises the encounters, treating the doctors almost as if they were her friends. Indeed, she explicitly comments on this, in answer to a question about the 'white coat syndrome':

Extract (11)

Sue: well there seem to be some people whose blood pressure is fairly normal most of the time …but when a doctor or a nurse or somebody with a monitor appears in front of them [their blood pressure goes up
Rose: [their blood pressure goes up…that never worries me.. I mean a doctor is a doctor.. I don't worry about it…only if they give me the wrong dose of something.. then I would worry but I never worry about doctors… I've seen too many of them in the past…I've seen so many… well I'm losing count but no that definitely wouldn't be me…
    →   I'm too friendly with them…you know I'd say "hello" I mean I do…no…but I can imagine it happening

Rose also de-medicalises her encounters with health care professionals through the content of the speech that she reports. Sometimes, for example, there is friendly banter. In addition, Rose shows her doctors as treating her with courtesy and respect, making her a partner in decisions about the management of her condition, as in (12). This is in marked contrast to the patients who took part in Hamilton's (1998) research, who reported their doctors' words using direct speech that showed the doctors as callous and unsympathetic.

Extract (12)

Sue: and do they [doctors and nurses] comment on it, do they say
      "it's not as low as the last time"?
Rose: oh yes, yesterday she [the nurse] did
      she said "your blood pressure is up"
      and I said to her "oh is it"
      "oh" she said
      I said "well I'm going in to see Dr. Clark anyway"
      so she said "well don't worry it's on the screen" or something
      so I said "well I'll tell him when I get in there"
      well when I went in I said to him "oh I've got to tell you that my blood
      pressure has gone up"
      and then he dealt with that after he dealt with the other complaint.. yes.
Sue: did he take it again or did he
Rose: he took it again..yes he did
      and that's when he said to me "well you've done so well
      and you're looking so well"
      and I said "I'm fine"
      and he said "so.. what.. we won't do anything right now..
      what I will do is I'll ask you to come back about the first of May
      and I will… we will then discuss it again..
      that's if you feel happy about that"
      because he's an excellent doctor
      "if you feel happy
      and we will go through it again
      hopefully it will have gone down by then
      if it hasn't we will discuss that"
      he's excellent in that respect
      he'll always discuss something with you
      and I said "yes that's fine"
      so yes

The representation of reported speech in Rose's narratives is a further way in which she displays and constructs a coherent sense of identity: in this extract, for example, the opening lines show Rose again presenting herself as not worrying unduly about her high blood pressure. By de-medicalising her encounters with health care professionals, Rose makes her constant visits to doctors' surgeries and hospitals part of a 'normal' everyday life in which she is able to maintain her personal identity.

Summary: Rose

As we said earlier, Rose tells more narratives than any of the other patients in the hypertension section of the database. The number is not necessarily significant; but it allows us to see some of the many ways in which narrative can be used as a resource to manage an identity as a patient and to make this identity cohere with a person's sense of self. For Rose, the experience of illness is an integral part of her life, and the narratives she tells reflect this. Through the stories she tells about her experiences of living with hypertension she displays and reinforces a positive self identity, defining herself in relation to other people with the same condition. This is one way, then, of adjusting to the necessity of living with a chronic illness.

Josephine

Josephine, as we saw earlier, has a very different approach to her condition. Far from making it an integral part of her life, she has set out to ignore it as far as it is possible to do so. Unlike Rose, she does not tell many stories during her interview: there are only five stretches of speech that fit our definition of narrative. As we have said, the number of narratives that patients tell is not necessarily significant. It is nevertheless instructive to examine Josephine's five narratives, since the events she chooses to recount in narrative form and the way in which she relates them are closely connected to the strategy she has adopted for dealing with her condition.

The first experience of illness

Josephine, like Rose, answers the question about her initial discovery of her condition by telling a narrative:

Extract (13)

	Sue:	I'd like to ask you to tell me how you originally discovered that you had high blood pressure
1	Josephine:	right er…I was living in Australia at the time
2		and er I had applied for a scholarship in Oxford
3		er and was offered one
4		and there was a medical attached

5	and er I was then about twenty-four
6	went for the medical
7	and was told I had high blood pressure
8	and they took me in as an inpatient
9	I don't think they thought it was disastrously high
10	but it was certainly
11	for a person of my age it was deemed worthy of treatment anyway
12	so they took me into hospital
13	and sorted me out in Sydney
14	and then sent me off to Oxford with my little box of pills and a
15	letter to the Radcliffe Infirmary as it was then
16	and I came under their care
17	and have been supervised one way or another ever since then
18	so that's when it was picked up

Unlike Rose, however, Josephine does not represent any of the 'blow by blow' events as a reported interaction between herself and a doctor. Instead, the events related in the Complicating Action clauses (lines 6, 7, 8, 12, 14) are represented impersonally, with indefinite *they* subjects and agentless passive clauses. The Orientation clause in 4 is an existential *there* clause (*there was a medical attached*) rather than a clause where she represents herself as the subject and the actor (she could, for example, have said *I had to have a medical*). It is important not to read too much into this, of course. It could be a general characteristic of Josephine's individual speech style: yet she does not adopt this detached speech style in her other narratives, as we will see. The internal evaluation and choice of vocabulary in the narrative clauses add to the detachment by downplaying the severity of the condition (for example, *sorted me out* in line 13 and *little* in *my little box of pills* in line 14), as does the external evaluation clause "I don't think they thought it was disastrously high" in line 9. Josephine's impersonal account of the sequence of events making up the referential strand, then, is matched by the content of the affective strand, where her emotional distancing from these events is displayed. Although Josephine's past and present reactions to her illness could hardly be more different from Rose's reactions, in both narratives the two women interweave the referential and affective strands into a coherent account of the objective and subjective aspects of their first experience. Both women have made this initial experience part of their life story, and the different linguistic choices they make in recounting the experience reflects the separate ways in which they have done so.

Comparison with others

Rose, as we saw, constructed aspects of her identity by comparing her behaviour with that of other people she knew who suffer from hypertension.
Given Josephine's desire to see the "real me" as a person unencumbered by the
details surrounding her medical condition, it is hardly surprising that when
she compares herself with others the basis of the comparison is people who are
well, rather than other people with hypertension. For example, she answers the
interviewer's question about whether she ever forgets to take her medication
by describing, in a mini hypothetical narrative, her embarrassment at the idea
that she might have to mention her medication to her friends:

Extract (14)

Josephine: I always carry two or three days dosage with me wherever I go
                 because you never know
                 say you went out for dinner
                 and someone said
                 oh you know "do stay the night
                 don't worry about driving home"
                 it would be awful …
                 I've had to do it in the past so I make sure I don't …
                 it would be awful to say
                 "well no I can't because I haven't got my tablets with me"

Two further narratives show Josephine identifying with people who are well. In
extract (15), for example, she recounts her decision to stop smoking, making
it clear that the decision was based not on her medical condition but on the
rapport she felt with the doctor, her GP. In the clauses constituting the abstract
(*I was one of the lucky ones; managed to stop easily and quickly*) she explicitly
situates herself within the general group of people who have managed to stop
smoking, with no reference to whether those people are well or ill:

Extract (15)

Josephine: I was one of the lucky ones
                 managed to stop quite easily and quickly
                 I was just having a general check up at the GP
                 and I liked the GP
                 she was a young woman about my own age

and I really liked her
and clicked with her
and she said in an extremely unpressuring sort of way
"oh I see you smoke"
she said "it's probably a good idea if you didn't really...
you know... given your history"
and it was nothing more than that
that was all she said
and because I liked her
and valued her opinion
and because she didn't come heavy on me
I just went home
and stopped
and that was that

In (16), Josephine relates her decision never to talk about her medication. Here she compares herself with her father-in-law, "still quite a healthy man" with just "a bit of hypertension", and recounts her embarrassment at having unwittingly revealed details of the amount of medication she has taken in her life.

Extract (16)

Sue: and are you aware of other people with high blood pressure... is this
            something you talk to other people about?
Josephine: I learned my lesson from my father-in-law
            who is in his eighties
            and who is now
            he's still quite a healthy man
            but he has got odd bits of angina
            and sort of a bit of hypertension
            and he's told me what he's taking
            and of course when he said to me "oh I'm on Atenolol"
            and "I'm on this and that"
            and I was saying "oh yeah I've taken those"
            "yeah I've taken those"
            not listening to how it sounded
            and then he he turned round
            and said "God she's got to do better than me
            she's always taken everything I've taken"
            and I thought "God help me from ever discussing anything like this

with anybody ever again"
<LAUGHS>
because I really actually don't talk about it that much
it seems to me it's not intrinsically interesting
how many tablets you're taking..
that stuff....
so no the answer is no I don't
and if I was ever inclined to I don't now

The only other narrative in Josephine's interview is a particularly significant one, for it relates a moment when her strategy for keeping the two parts of her life separate collapses. She rarely lets this happen, as extract (17) shows: here she mentions a single occasion when she allowed her 'ill self' to blend with her 'real self'.

Extract (17)

Josephine: I did once tell a nurse in the renal unit to call me Josie and that was a huge leap of faith on my part but I really liked her and she really liked me and we got on really well and so she was allowed into my real life ...it sounds bizarre doesn't it to talk about it like that but it's a way of keeping it where it should be I reckon

Before discussing the final narrative it is necessary to explain that Josephine developed close relationships during her stay in hospital with other patients undergoing a transplant operation:

Extract (18)

Josephine: It's like being on board ship you know...you become your own complete little world and it's wonderful ..you wouldn't get through it without ...and there's lots of jokes and stuff you know it's a tight little community...highly supportive and you never forget...you never forget the day you had it done...you never forget the people you were in with who were having it done at the same time as you...it's a very emotional experience...whether it works or whether it doesn't it's a real high point

It is also relevant to note that when Josephine attends the outpatient clinic she does not wish to be reminded of these experiences. She recounts in (19) how she identifies with like-minded patients at the clinic:

Extract (19)

Josephine: When I go to the transplant clinic for my routine visits it's actually a
             very friendly chatty place…hugely chatty…and there's always a few
             people who sort of bury their heads in a magazine and don't chat and
             ignore the overtures really because we don't need that club right now
             …when you need the club it's fantastic…it's a very supportive very
             efficient very effective unit and part of the support is that everybody is
             in there together … patients doctors nursing staff everybody … it's a
             fantastic place when you're ill…and when you're well you don't want
             the club because that would make you ill…if you responded you'd be
             ill you know … it's not everybody's view but when I look round the
             waiting room I can see the people who take the same view as me and
             they really don't want to know <LAUGHS> they don't want to catch
             anybody's eye to actually get into a chat with anybody…which you
             can easily do if you want to

We can now see that the narrative in (20) relates what must have been a traumatic occasion for Josephine, although she frames it as an amusing story by
laughing at the beginning of her story. She remembers an occasion when she
was in the outpatient transplant clinic at the same time as a woman who happened to be visually handicapped and who had received a transplant at the
same time as Josephine. This patient was, therefore, one of the people to whom
Josephine felt a great attachment, as described in (18). As a result she was forced
to bring her two selves together – the 'real me' who is well and whom she tries
to preserve in the waiting room, and the ill self of the renal unit.

Extract (20)

	Sue:	and do you ever see those people you were in with?
	Josephine:	<LAUGHS>
1		I was actually in the clinic about a year ago
2		and er one of my transplant mates was in there
3		was in clinic
4		and she is much more
5		she's quite a disabled person actually
6		she has a guide dog with her
7		and she has all kinds of ancillary problems as well as the kidney problem
8		and she was talking to someone
9		and she mentioned my name

10	and she said "oh I haven't seen Josie for ages
11	but I've seen so-and-so and so-and-so"
12	and I couldn't in all conscience sit two seats away
13	and I said "I'm here"
14	and chatted to her
15	but really broke my first rule
16	but er no when you don't need them you know
17	er it's a reminder
18	it's not what you want

Josephine does not tell many narratives, as we have said. We think it significant, therefore, that she chooses to dramatise in narrative form this traumatic encounter, where her strategy for coping with her illness broke down. It is also significant that there is a considerable amount of internal evaluation in this narrative, unlike the narrative in (13), in which she recounted her first experience of illness. For example, she describes the other patient as her 'mate' and gives details in lines 5–7 that make this patient's disability more vivid: she has a guide dog with her, she has 'all kinds' of ancillary problems, and she is 'quite a disabled person actually'. The negative clause in line 13 is also a form of internal evaluation, contrasting what Josephine tells us she did with what she might have done; there are further negative clauses in the coda, in lines 17–19. As Labov (1972) explains, negation functions as internal evaluation in narratives of personal experience. The narrative contains direct speech; this, together with the details and images, and the focus on the participants and their feelings, creates involvement (Chafe 1982).

As we mentioned earlier, in the evaluation sections of their narratives speakers can establish the kind of self they present to their interlocutor (Linde 1993: 81); they can also make the point of their story clear. Here, then, the self that Josephine presents is a good, socially proper person (as she says in line 13, *I couldn't in all conscience sit two seats away*), and the reportability of the event lies in the fact that because she is a good, socially responsible person she was forced on that occasion to break her own rule. It is significant that her narrative presents her friend as having more health problems than Josephine. She breaks off her 'she is much more' in line 4 to present details of these problems, and in this way succeeds in portraying herself as a person who is healthy compared to others. The coda to the narrative, in lines 16–18, repeats Josephine's strategy for dealing with her experiences of illness, making it clear that this occasion was a unique aberration. In this narrative, then, Josephine succeeds in displaying an identity as a relatively well person whilst repeating – and therefore reinforcing – her strategy for coping with her condition.

Reported speech

Like Rose, Josephine reports some of her interactions with doctors and other health care professionals. Unlike Rose, however, there are only three clauses where Josephine reports her own speech with, by contrast, 31 clauses where she reports the speech of the professionals. Only one of Josephine's reported speech clauses is in the form of direct speech, compared to 28 (90 per cent) of her doctors' reported speech clauses. The imbalance constructs the doctors as more powerful participants in the interactions. The content of the doctors' talk has the same effect: Josephine shows them telling her how to manage her illness and she presents herself as grateful to them for 'sorting her out' and for enabling her to live a full life. Although she mentions several doctors approvingly, such as the GP who suggested she should stop smoking, there is no attempt to construct her interactions with them as anything other than the stereotypical doctor-patient interaction, where the doctor has the upper hand. This fits with her strategy of relegating all things concerning her illness to the part of herself who is not the 'real me'. Unlike Rose, whose narratives present the doctors as her friends, Josephine uses her narratives to keep them at a distance.

Summary: Josephine

Josephine, as we have seen, copes with the experience of illness very differently from Rose, yet she appears to be equally well-adjusted to her medical condition. As in Rose's interview, this is revealed through the narratives Josephine tells, although in Josephine's case they display only rare glimpses of her personal identity. Perhaps if she were talking about something other than her experiences of illness she would be more likely to display her 'real self' in her stories. In the interview Josephine defines her identity in relation to people who are well – or, in her final narrative, in relation to a person who is far more disabled by her condition than Josephine – and she adopts a detached style when relating specific events concerning her condition. In this way she maintains and reinforces the attitude we saw earlier, in extract (3): 'the real me is a kind of observer of this and so it doesn't get to me.' Unlike Rose, Josephine has constructed a personal identity as a well person, but nevertheless she can successfully integrate her two selves – the 'ill person' and the 'real me' – when it is necessary.

Conclusion

Our analysis confirms, we believe, that narrative can be an important resource for people who have to adjust to living with a chronic condition, helping to reinforce the strategies they have developed in order to cope with the everyday demands of the condition. Although Rose and Josephine have reacted differently to the experience of living with illness, there are some similarities in the functions that their narratives fulfil in their interviews. First, narrative discourse allows them to interweave the objective and subjective aspects of knowing and understanding key events in the integration of illness into their life stories. Secondly, both women use narrative to locate themselves in their social worlds, drawing comparisons with others in ways that allow them to simultaneously display their attitude to their condition and to create a self that is in harmony with what they perceive as relevant aspects of their personal identity. Their representations of interactions with health care professionals, in the narrative and non-narrative stretches of discourse, are in harmony with the place they want to give to these interactions in their lives. For both women, narrative provides a way for them to display and construct an identity as a patient and to integrate this identity into their sense of a stable, coherent, permanent self.

Note

1. We have edited some of the non-narrative extracts to remove what we perceive as false starts, to make them easier to read. No editing of any kind has been carried out on the narrative extracts.

Transcription conventions

.	short pause (not timed)
..	longer pause (not timed)
?	question marks show the end of a stretch of talk interpreted as an question
<LAUGHTER>	angled brackets give additional information
[	extended square brackets show the beginning of an overlap
=	latching
→	an arrow indicates that the line to the right is the one where a given example occurs

CHAPTER 3

Storying East-German pasts

Memory discourses and narratives of readjustment on the German/Polish and former German/German border

Heidi Armbruster and Ulrike H. Meinhof
University of Southampton

Introduction

How do people who live through major political and historical change communicate that experience? This was one of the main questions that informed a research project on European border identities in which we are both involved. The Second World War, the redefinitions of statehood that followed in its wake, the opposition of 'East' and 'West' produced during the Cold War, the fall of the Berlin Wall and the renewed definition of a European space since, present some of the major historical events that impacted on the lives of a large number of people. Given that the events in question resulted in the drawing, redrawing and redefinition of state-borders, we assumed that they must have impinged on the lives of borderlanders in ways which remained less tangible for more centrally located citizens: through resettlement and eviction, control of daily movement, the military presence of the state, or uneasy cross-border contact, borderlanders experienced 'history' in an often dramatic way. Our project aimed at investigating the communication of these experiences along the former Iron Curtain and selected 12 border communities for study.[1]

Our analytical assumptions are based on narrative models of identity, which postulate that people can only craft a sense of who they are in narrative form. These models emphasize that crucial forms of self-experience are not constituted outside, but within narrative (e.g. Somers & Gibson 1994; Finnegan 1997; Eakin 1999: 99–102). In this discussion we are particularly interested in how a set of self-narratives categorises and 'plots' historical experience.

The two communities

This article focuses on two different sets of people who each share a border experience in Germany. The first community under research is the town of Guben on the Polish-German border. Until the end of the Second World War, Guben was a German town with the river Neisse flowing through it. Following the Allied conference of Potsdam in 1945, in which Germany's borders were redrawn, the Polish-German border was made to coincide with the rivers Oder and Neisse. This split the town of Guben into a German and a Polish half, with the Polish side being renamed as Gubin.

Our second community under research is located on the former demarcation line between East and West Germany. Our examples refer to people who live in several neighbouring villages in Thuringia (former GDR), which border on Bavaria (former FRG). Comparable to Guben these villages were Soviet occupied in 1945, later became part of the GDR and were immersed into unified Germany more than a decade ago. Thus, despite a range of local specifics and differences both sets of communities share much of the political culture and historical upheavals that affected their regions since the pre-War years.

Before 1989 the people of Guben and Gubin experienced many shifts and turns with regard to cross-border contacts. These ranged from a closed border policy until the 1970s, to open borders during that decade, a renewed closure in the 80s as a GDR response to Polish democratisation, and finally to a renewed open border policy since 1989. For Poles and Germans alike, crossing between their borders today is entirely straight-forward, usually requiring no more than an identity card.

As far as the oldest generation of people living in these towns are concerned, the majority of Germans in today's Guben had originally been evicted from the Eastern part, whereas many of those Poles living in today's Gubin had themselves been re-housed at the end of the war. They had either moved from other parts of Poland or had been evicted by the Soviets from their own home territory in eastern Poland.

In the Thuringian case people lived in close co-operation with the neighbouring Bavarians until 1949, when the two German states were founded and the Iron Curtain prohibited contact. Initially, a so-called 'kleiner Grenzübertrittsschein' ('small border-traffic pass') enabled the border population to move across to the other side for visits or work. Within a couple of years this practice was stopped. From 1952 onwards, the demarcation line between the two Germanys underwent increasing fortification and strict military control.[2] On the East German side the border zone was a restricted area (the 'Sperrgebiet'), a 5 km wide border area, which was closed to other citizens of the GDR as well as to foreigners and West Germans. Without a special permit, movement in and out of the restricted zone was impossible. Many inhabitants of the *Sperrgebiet* had to move in and out for work on a daily basis. This tight separation only ended with the fall of the Berlin wall in November 1989 and subsequent unification in October 1990.

Research methodology

Between 1999 and 2000 we conducted interviews with individual members of three-generation-families in both locations. Our aim was to elicit a type of narrative that came close to everyday speech and in which people told us about their present and past experiences. In order to activate people's own lexico-grammatical choices and language of biography we used symbolically charged photographs as communication triggers. Thus, ideally the interviewee drove the conversation and introduced lexical markers to which the interviewer then responded. These photographs represented local landmarks which would not only be easily recognisable to the interviewees but also locatable in socio-political time and space. In other words, the images indicated the interdependence between larger historical transformations and specific local realities (e.g. a bridge across the border river in its pre-war and post-war and post-unification state). (For more details and some reproduction of photographs used, see Meinhof & Galasinski 2000 and Meinhof 2004.) Assuming that identities are crafted within this interlocking dynamic of local and trans-local socio-political contexts, we were interested to see how people positioned themselves vis-à-vis these images. As the interviews showed, people's narratives were not constrained by what the photographs represented, the interviewees used them as an aide-mémoire to personal and local history, and as lead-ins into narratives about their identifications and commitments. Our extracts below will show some such responses.

Narrative and identity

Clearly, not all of our interviewees' responses can be classified as narratives that include plot-development and spatio-temporal framing. However, there were many 'storied' or narrativised layers in people's talk, particularly when it took on biographical and experiential meanings. In relation to these narratives we define identity as a sense of self, and closely relate it to its manifestation in language. Linguistically, this self-narration was accomplished by the creation of "'storied' worlds" (Schiffrin 2002: 315, 318) in which people made sense of their experiences, created links between themselves and others and between present and past. This illustrated well the relational character of identity: interviewees populated their story worlds with a number of people, creating an intersocial context, and fashioned a place for themselves within a web of others. While doing so, narrators represented themselves in relation to others who were marked as either similar or different, present or absent. In addition to the 'others' that populated the story world, there was the presence of the interviewer-other (in our case clearly identified 'West Germans') and, as will be seen in our examples, an imagined audience which narrators addressed through the interviewer. As we will show, such a highly interactive practice reveals the complexities and ambiguities of narrative self-identification.

Evidently, our interviewees also positioned themselves in relation to larger public narratives and collective memories about German history, such as the Cold War, the GDR and FRG period, and national unification. These public narratives had also undergone ideological and discursive shifts and kept reconfiguring the time and space our families have inhabited. Thus, the relationships in which people situated themselves and the stories with which they identified were crucial identity markers.

In our three-generation-approach we were interested to see whether and in which ways people's storied self-understandings changed over a period of roughly 80 years and within a communicative 'web' that was fairly intimate, i.e. the family. In this chapter we will read our data with regard to the narrative organisation of memory, and the sense of identity it underwrites. We will present several sets of key narratives that illustrate the different ways in which the middle and old generations articulate a past experience. Unlike the youngest generation, these age groups have had first hand experience of the coming and going of the border, and they were the driving forces of change in the 1980s.

The border experience meant for some a deep rupture of their lives through eviction after the war (Guben), for others it meant living for decades in highly controlled and restricted border zones (Thuringia). All had to come to terms with the sudden disappearance of their former state and the new formation of a unified Germany, which was modelled on the existing structures of the former FRG. These historical changes present potential ruptures in the experience of individuals and a concomitant sense of discontinuity between a past and a present self. Theorists of memory have shown that the experience of dissonance between present and past, as caused by a traumatic or radical life change can be a difficult challenge for individual processes of memory and for the sense of self-consistency and continuity of identity (King 2000: 2–4). We adopt those theoretical views that suggest that memory narratives are continuous re-interpretations of the past that are rooted in a particular present. Relatedly, and in contrast to what I-narratives generally suggest, personal memories are not entirely unique to the individual but closely related to cultural memories and culturally sanctioned forms of remembering (King 2000: 5; Eakin 1999: 110–116), or, as we might put it, culturally sanctioned forms of 'storying'. As will be demonstrated below, our data contained a striking overlap between memory narratives of people of a certain age. The difference between narratives thus also marked the boundaries between generations and gave shape to what might be identified as generational knowledge.

The data

We present examples of middle and older generation-narratives from two families: first from Thuringia, mother and son Tischler who used to live in the restricted GDR border zone, and secondly, mother and daughter Amsel from Guben. As indicated above, we exclude the youngest generation for the sake of this discussion, because they have had no long-term experience of the German-German border.

By focusing on two families we do not want to imply that these are 'types' or 'representatives' of a uniform group. Instead we want to show two characteristics which mark not only their narratives but also many others we collected. This is (a) the observation that the narrative configuration of the self occurs in relation to 'significant others' and larger 'storied' contexts and (b) that the narrators' linguistic behaviour reveals such contexts. Across the number of roughly 45 interviews we conducted in these regions we became aware of recurrent narrative patterns and were able to draw certain conclusions about the communication of historical change and the constitution of a 'generation'.

Our interviewees, both in Guben and Thuringia, produced specific key narratives and key periodisations of history which made comparisons according to age groups feasible. Older people in Guben related key stories about their historical experience of losing and being evicted from their home, and/or of cycles of escape-return-escape-return. Their compatriots in Thuringia often talked about suffering, fear, and victimisation. The key periodisations of personal history were pre-war, war, and post-war times, and in relation to this, the post-*Wende*[3] period appeared marginal. Most of the older people's stories implied a sense of completion. This suggests that these experiences were considered as terminated and that they no longer interfered with the present. Stories were often colourful and contained dramatised mise-en-scène elements.

This contrasts with the memory narratives of the middle generation, which included people who were born between 1945 and 1960. Their key stories dealt with life in the GDR and the subsequent demise of the state, thus establishing key periods of history relating to the GDR and post-*Wende* times. Their stories were often unfinished and contradictory, and pointed at a more continuous and not yet resolved involvement with the historical experience. Quite significantly, narrative styles in this middle generation were often argumentative: in the absence of any oppositional stance by the interviewers who adopted purely collaborative strategies, such explicit or implicit arguments presupposed an invisible 'silent opponent' as discussion partner or audience (see also Meinhof & Galasinski 2000: 344–346).

The first extract below is from an interview with Eva Tischler, a 70-year old woman, who witnessed the coming of the border and the increasingly controlled life in the GDR – *Sperrgebiet*. The extracts show how she narrativises historical experience.

Extract 1

Eva Tischler, Thuringia
THE RESTRICTED ZONE ('*Sperrgebiet*')

IR   You have just been talking about the controls at – about a big fence you have just been talking

ET   Yes it was where you enter S-village. Mmh and then you had, if visitors came they erm wrote it down in the permit, their name, how when they entered and when they leave and – and once it happened to us that my older daughter who lives in H now, she was first married down in the Thuringian forest. They came here, stayed a few days and had registered up there [i.e. at the check point]. In the meantime we had applied for a new permit which we got and they stayed a day longer – and the old permit was to expire and they hadn't registered the new one yet up there, because the old one was still valid. At HALF PAST TWELVE at night a few vehicles stop down there – they call, all of us had been to bed – they knock, we open the window, two such border guards from up there "are Mrs. Tina Schmitt and Mr. Gert Schmitt with you?" "Yes" "Their permits have expired they have to leave IMMEDIATELY!" And then we said "they have already got a new one", we took them upstairs and showed them the new permit. Well then it was ok. They took it down and made notes but they HAD ENTERED and they knew exactly how long the permit was issued for and everything and then they check in their book and well they hadn't left yet and the permit had expired. Where might they be, perhaps they left across the border or so – mmh (laughs) those who don't know who haven't experienced this – you were completely locked up here. You couldn't go over there, there was the fence and up there was another fence. With the big gate

BEING SPIED UPON
IR   Was that how you felt then really locked up?
ET   You felt locked up but as TIME went by erm we had no choice, we got used to it. What else could you do? You couldn't complain if you did, you were evicted as they did it to many people you know, if someone happened to say something wrong there were so many spies in the village and you would never have thought it of these people, they spied upon you during conversations, you thought they were nice people and then all of a sudden they informed on you, and then you were taken away. You had to really constrain yourself and had to endure it all. You had no choice. Yes and that's how the children grew up, they don't know anything else
IR   They haven't seen anything else
ET   They haven't seen ANYTHING else you know. Here our children, like my son now well he was born in 53 and – he only ever lived in this restricted zone until now when it changed
IR   Unlike you who has known the time before as well
ET   We knew it that's right. It was a hard time too, the war it wasn't easy you know. Yes - - well we left school and the war was still on, we left the church and there was an air-raid and it was well – just as terrible
IR   Really?
ET   Mmh mmh. The bombs fell up there in our village too – in the forest maybe they erm didn't drop them on purpose I don't know, on such a village they can't have seen that from the air or that there was something they had to drop bombs on but it was really it was hard hard mmh. Well yes my father was in the war, we were alone with my mother, once we came from the forest we had collected firewood there was an air-raid you lied down, my brother, he got sick, he threw up because of fear – everything because of fear you know mmh - - - well

FEAR OF THE RUSSIANS
IR   You were also in the, well, you must know the Hirschberg leather factory really well?

ET   Of course, I worked there for 30 years

IR   You worked there for such a long time?

ET   30 years in the leather factory yes. Before that, I did the obligatory year after I
     had left school in D, in the manor house that was just around 1945. I saw the
     Amis [i.e. Americans] coming over there, when the Amis left the Russians
     came, well yes it was terrible everyone was afraid

IR   Aha yes?

ET   YES YES especially if you were young

I   Of the Russians

ET   Mmh. The Russians raped a lot of women and so on, you know. I know when
     we used to sit down for evening meals in the manor house, there were many
     workers you know it was always a large table. Then all of a sudden the
     doorbell rang. A large manor house a large place "Oh" said the boss "the
     Russians are coming" and later on, they cried "Young girls", they were always
     pissed, they wanted young girls and there were two of us well then they led us
     towards the back door and locked us up in the chicken coop. We were sitting
     there sometimes for an hour together with the chicken (laughs) there were
     problems with young girls you know. They had to hide them that the Russians
     yes because they were always pissed. They came then mmh "young girls" and
     they knew that there were two of us, two young girls and while they were held
     up at the front door, she took us through the back door across the street and
     into the chicken coop (laughs) yes we have been through a lot a lot, oh dear
     one should one should have written down all these things.[4]

Features of Eva's narrative

Eva's periodisation of history shifts between war, end of war and post-war
(GDR) times. She highlights experiences of fear and victimisation but embeds
them in descriptive and colourful narratives with dramatised mise-en-scène elements (daughter called out by border police; air bombardments and brother
who vomits; hiding in the chicken-coop). These include dramatised other personas and the construction of their speech.

     These stories are narrated as completed, with an evaluative comment sum-
ming up the experience after each section. This suggests that the stories are no
longer negotiable, and are likely to have been told and rehearsed before. Eva
locates herself at a distance to her former self ("we have endured a lot"; "it was
hard"), and she tells a closed chapter of the past which no longer interferes
with her everyday life. Each episode rotates around people who relate to each
other in an oppositional 'us'-'them'-fashion: 'we vis-à-vis the border police',

'we vis-à-vis the spies in the village', and finally 'we vis-à-vis the Russians'. The varied composition of the 'we' collective is formed through the out-groups, and the link between 'us and them' is created through Eva's manifold experiences of intimidation. However, the survivor/struggler person she identifies with stands for personal continuity and integrity through time: with regard to one's victimhood there is not much difference between war, end of war and GDR period. The metaphor of "having been locked up" appears twice: when the Russians came to victimize them as sexual objects, and during the *Sperrgebiet*-time in the GDR. In both cases her experience is coloured by a mixture of self-protection to the inside and threat from the outside. She invokes very little contrast between what happened then and now, or before and after, giving the impression of continuity as well as closure. The conflictual interaction between her storied characters has not disintegrated Eva's own persona which, although victimized, always remains resourceful: all three narrated episodes contain problem resolutions and portray a stable and ultimately unscathed self.

The second extract is from an interview with Ralf, Eva's eldest son, who was born in 1953. By then, the border was a firmly established monument of the Cold War division between the two Germanys. The extract shows that Ralf's appropriation of the past is quite different from Eva's.

Extract 2

Ralf Tischler, Thuringia
THEN AND NOW

RT   No. Everything was so normal, the border installations, it was just there, well, you didn't we didn't take much notice of it definitely not it was how it was and we grew up with it

IR   And did you commute by bus to the leather factory?

RT   By bus yes. There were workers' busses which went in the morning and returned in the afternoon mmh everything was taken care of, there were no problems, things were better taken care of than now (smiles) definitely – also for the worker, he was looked after much more just, for instance, lunch or or breakfast, everything was provided, there were kitchens and refectories and and you could buy a coffee for cheap money and and and a roll with it, everything was provided. Now you have to see how you get by. Especially with food and so on like lunch

IR   Yes it's a difference mh

RT   Yes of course a big difference. Also how you get to work. Now you have to go by car that's for sure. Then there were busses, they reached Hirschberg

15 minutes before work started, and we had time to change, we had the opportunity to put on our work clothes and then we started

IR   Then you started

RT   Mmh it was much better organised definitely – but who cares, I mean you get used to things now too

THE BORDER ZONE

IR   Mmh. Did you have the feeling that there was a big difference between the border zone and other areas in the GDR?

RT   We did, we understood it, or rather we grew up knowing that this here was our home. If we applied for permits for friends and they came in here, controls up there and so on "oh my God how can you live here this is impossible, locked up and" we didn't have that feeling. It was the way it was, here was our HOUSE it belonged to us and (sighs) we never had any problems with the border guards or whatever or those who controlled or whatever you had to show the permit, so what, of course it said that you were allowed in here that you live here and so on the guards knew you, they opened the gate already from far if you approached by car. It was the border zone, it wasn't our fault, we just came to terms with it and that was how it was. How often after the Wende how often did you stop up there at the control point you took your foot off the accelerator and you wanted to stop "Oh my, there is no barrier anymore you can drive on"

IR   Really?

RT   Yes really yes. It had become your second nature, well that was just how it was. Why should you want to be rude to those up there on the border [i.e. at the check point] or whatever they were only doing their jobs doing what they had to. It wasn't their fault either. Well we I always had friendly relations with them they were only human beings, human beings exactly like us. They had to do it because the regime was that way the entire state was that way and it was just the way it was

(later)

RT   Well you were in the border zone you can't do just as you pleased like others maybe somewhere else or well there was a wall down there and you couldn't go down or rather you couldn't go behind the wall, or you can't mess with the wall that was just not possible it was the laws that was how it was and that was ok. We understood it or rather it had always been that way. Well we had absolutely no problems with it. Of course inviting friends or then when we were young your girlfriend was not allowed in and at that moment it was much harder. This is quite different now, of course, if I look at my son, his girlfriend comes here too you know.[5]

Features of Ralf's narrative

Ralf's historical periodisation is framed by GDR and post-GDR times and he highlights experiences of contrast between both periods. While the past is a source of achievement, care for the workers, and unrestrained normality, the present is full of insecurities.

Ralf's 'story world' contains no explicit in- and out-groups, his characters are all immersed in plural 'wes', 'yous', or the impersonal 'one'. Significantly his narrative is completely devoid of the personal pronoun 'I' which highlights his collective identity but leaves him unidentifiable as a person who thinks and acts individually. Instead, Ralf persistently situates himself as a member of different groups, these often unspecified 'wes' and 'yous' – which, alternately, include his family, his generation or siblings ('we grew up with it'), workers, his village community, and human beings as such. Significantly, these groups are not only internally homogenous, but relate in a harmonious fashion to each other. The only significant group of others are the border guards, with whom locals had to interact on a daily basis, and who were presented by his mother as overzealous representatives of a controlling state. For Ralf, these people are in no way adversaries, but fellow workers, ('they were only doing their jobs'), and, more poignantly, fellow 'human beings'.

In equally significant contrast to his mother, the outsiders coming in to confront locals with the limitations of the restricted zone are not family but rather more insignificantly 'irgendwelche Freunde' ('some friends'). Their direct speech of appalled reaction to the border constructs them almost emblematically as ignorant outsiders who falsely dramatise the insiders' lives, and deny them any sense of positive identification with it. This presents an interesting inversion of Eva's dramatised plot about her daughter's visit.

In clear contrast to Eva's talk, this narrative style is argumentative. Ralf engages in an argument with an unnamed but implicit opponent who challenges his experience. In response to this opponent he evaluates life in the GDR with constantly repeated phrases such as 'this is just how it was' ('das war eben so', 'das war halt so'). There is neither agency, causality nor responsibility in these expressions, nor any hint of historical reasoning and process – and yet they work as justifications. Things 'were just there' without any causes and contexts. The argumentative structure and constant mode of justification underline Ralf's portrayal of life on the border as a smooth procedure in which all people complied and where power relations were absent.

In the next section, we will again present extracts from members of two generations of the same family; this time from a mother (old generation) and her daughter (middle generation). Both have lived all their lives in what is now the German/Polish border town of Guben, surrounded by other members of their family. All three generations regularly visit each other in their homes. In the first extract, Frieda, a seventy year old grand-mother and widow talks about her dramatic westward flight from her home in Guben in the hope of escaping from the Russian troops.

Extract 3

Frieda Amsel, Guben
BREAD AND BUTTER

IR At the time, did you believe that you'd return again?

FA Yes, of course we thought that... but we wanted to get as far as the Americans, and that was Perleberg, that's in the region of Prignitz. Well with the train, when we got down, we went for ages along the road, we were attacked all the time, but when they again, when they went away, we went on and we wanted at all costs in direction west, wanted to reach Perleberg, there we had been told through the news we'd find the Americans or was it the English? I can't say that any more, but certainly not the Russians. And we finally did make it till Putlitz, that's a little village near Parchim, that is. It's all known again today, they show stuff about it on TV. In Putlitz on the day before, before the Russians caught up with us, there in that little village they cut for us huge chunks of butter, those were really big pieces that they cut for us with a knife, not pre-packaged, and they distributed those amongst the fugitives, there in that village, but not a piece of bread. Now, what were we supposed to do with that butter on its own, eh, not a piece (of bread) nothing. Well, starvation had started already on this escape, yes, we didn't have anything whilst we were on the move. And as I said, we had that butter, and then the night came and we all slept in a big barn, and all of the sudden... in the middle of the night we heard this low rumbling, those were the Russian tanks. We had wanted to leave for Perleberg, right first thing in the morning, wouldn't have been very far any more. We could have made it the next day. But, unfortunately ... walking through the entire night wasn't possible... Everyday we toddled our 50 kilometres or so, and I always had problems with my hip, my crutch is here, yes always problems with my hip (continues briefly to talk about her bad hip).

IR And so you walked all this distance? And when the Russians caught up with you, what happened then?

FA Well, they came into the barn at night, and there we thought... there we thought, now it's all over. Once its light, well in the middle of the night they won't do it, it's too dark for that, they couldn't see anything either, but when morning would dawn, then they'd put us all against the wall and kill us, we really thought that. And then one of them started, he passed something across to the other, we couldn't understand their Russian gibberish, they had this bread from the army, do you know what that is, do you know these, and in the dark they passed these to the fugitives. Whoever grabbed one, got some bread, and I fished for one, after all I was a 15 year old girl I just about made it out in the dark, and grabbed a piece of bread, and then they'd gone, the tanks had to roll on to make space for the next supply of tanks, you know. And we were over the moon, that now we could get some bread for our butter; so we cut ourselves thick slices and spread the butter, and then we really thought this is our last 'Hiob's meal' [i.e. meal that signals bad news/ last meal before the gallows]. Come the next morning and they'll definitely put us against the wall, and then it's all over for us and one didn't even get scared, I must tell you that. Those weeks when we were on the move, a with the permanent fear of the low-flying bombers, that dampens even the the feelings of a young girl. I couldn't care any more if they had stood us there and shot us point blank. One couldn't even squeeze a tear out any more. Not one, so numb one did become. Well and as I said, the morning broke and nothing happened.[6]

This passage is an extract from a continuous narrative lasting about 30 minutes, which was triggered by only one picture of the pre-war German city. This picture was quickly laid aside once the story took shape. The interviewee spoke with hardly any pause or interruption by the interviewer though she did show awareness of her interlocutor by explaining some facts which would remain obscure due to their geographical and age difference. As in Eva's narrative, Frieda also talks of fear, suffering and victimisation during the time of flight away from the encroaching Russian troops, and – with the Red Army occupying the entire eastern regions of Germany – of her subsequent return to (western) Guben. This is dramatised through colourful details of various dangerous encounters. Throughout the interview she narrates the sequence of events from the perspective of her own young self at the time. This not only permits a chronological and highly dramatic account of what happened next, but it also allows her to express the conflicting emotions and judgements of someone who in her dramatis persona of the past does not yet know that the dangers will not in fact lead to disaster. Thus within the unfolding of the story, it is the continuous expectation, that any moment might signal the end for herself and her mother which heightens the pleasure of finding food and the surprise at surviving against all the odds. In true story-teller fashion she turns this fear of the Russians and the hunger during the flight into the dramatic foil, against which the ensuing experiences provide the dramatic twist: the irony of receiving butter provisions but no bread; being surprised by Russians and expecting to get killed, but instead receiving bread from them; imagining this as their last meal before death and not really caring any longer – and finally the moment of the climactic anticlimax which closes off that section of her narrative. The morning arrived and nothing happened: 'Nischt war!'. This episode of kindness by some Russian soldiers is embedded within, and conflicts with, a larger public narrative where Russians appear foremost as potential rapists from whom one has to hide away.

In Frieda's story the emotional evaluation of events – fear of the Russians, anticipation of disaster – remains throughout the story, though the events themselves – the kindness of the soldiers – suggest an alternative reading. There are other even more notable instances in our data where the telling and dramatisation of events as remembered challenge and subvert the simple us and them divide into friends and enemies. In some cases discussed elsewhere, this alteration is even signalled by the grammar itself (see Meinhof 2004).

The coherent, assertive, highly sequential and dramatic story telling of the 70 year old Frieda could not be more different from the broken, defensive and self-contradictory accounts which her daughter Gabi gave at a separate interview (for a more detailed account of Gabi's story see Meinhof 2001), or indeed those of her articulate teenage children. Gabi was born in 1961, the same year when the erection of the wall in Berlin closed the last possibility of connection between East and West Germany. Born and raised as a GDR citizen, she and her young family saw the collapse of the only state they had ever known with German unification in 1990, but did not experience any of the less fortunate aftermath – loss of work and unemployment, decline of security in standard of living – of many of her fellow Gubenians. At the time of the interview she and her husband lived in an attractive house of their own in Guben with two children of 16 and 17 preparing for A-levels. From the outside, hers and her family's is a post-unification success story, not only materially but also ideologically. In the interview with her mother we had been told that the family had always taken a somewhat oppositional stance to the GDR since they were active church-goers who had rejected the secular politicised alternatives to church rituals and organisations which the GDR regime had put in place. I had been told by Frieda with considerable pride that all her children had received their 'Konfirmation' (confirmation into the Lutheran church) instead of the secular state ceremony – the 'Jugendweihe' (taking place at the same age but pledging allegiance to the State), and that no one had become a member of the FDJ (Free German Youth), the youth organisation of the socialist party. Gabi did not know at the stage of the interview transcribed below that her mother had made any such claims on their behalf. Nor did the interviewer know until half way into the interview, that whilst the claims were correct for her brothers and sister, she herself had in fact participated in both the church and the state rituals. The passage below is about half way through a one-hour interview when Gabi suddenly reveals that she not only wanted to join the FDJ but did in fact manage to do so against her mother's wish. The broken, hesitant, self-contradictory and defensive way in which Gabi gets to this revelation is however typical for the entire conversation: it only becomes more exaggerated at those points when she tries to narrate her conflicting emotions as a schoolgirl in the GDR.

Extract 4

Gabi Amsel, Guben
THE FDJ

GA   Yes, FDJ [Free German Youth]. Yes it.... I have to say to that, at the time I wanted to join the FDJ [laughs]

IR   That's what I wanted to know [laughter]

GA   Yes, I wanted to.... because I didn't want to be an outsider, because I felt it as a child, but er...couldn't really live it on the other hand, the faith. Because of that, er.... and everybody else in class went in this direction in any case and I wanted to join in [laughs] Although it wasn't my conviction I'd say. In fact I only wanted to be part of it, but...

IR   And did your parents not allow you....

GA   er...I have to think...I was...I even was a member of the FDJ [I laughs] Yes, yes, that's right. I did.... yes I did push it through, I'd say. Yes.

IR   And your brothers and sister, too, or where you the only one?

GA   I'd say no.

IR   No, not the others. You were the rebel [laughs]

GA   I was the.... one who...I wanted to take part in it and I think I pushed it through.

IR   Yes and er...then these.... I mean all these things that were being organized by the FDJ, I'm sure they were fun, weren't they? I'm just guessing here. For young people. I mean, I have got this picture here for example...It's a picture, no I had it with me.

GA   Well, I was.... No I didn't go to these things.

IR   You didn't go to these things?

GA   No, no.

IR   May parades or something. ...

GA Yes, apart from that there used to be meetings here in the village. Where the young people met, but…

IR But what was.…

GA I can't remember any events. I simply wanted to be part of it. That was all.

IR But I mean, that you did things together. You don't have so many memories about that. Maybe Maybe you didn't take part?

GA No, I can't think of anything. No, not really. I know that the question was raised in the eight grade and that's how it was … it even started with the pioneers. Although I was also a member of it. It was almost like a duty, that one was a member of the pioneers.[7]

The pressures which Gabi recounts are of a young woman being caught between the conflicting desires of wanting to belong to two oppositional forces: family or peer group – church or state. In an extraordinary twist to her own narrative which cannot be fully demonstrated here (but see Meinhof 2001 for more extended extracts) she moves from an initial clear division between herself, her family and the church on the one hand, and the school, the state, the teachers and her peer group on the other, to an increasingly complex set of contradictions. She finally emerges as someone who did indeed participate in both sides, whilst not really believing in either, with her family similarly divided, since her father as it later turns out supported her views against those of her mother and siblings. The wish to belong, and not to be an outsider appears as the one fundamental explanation offered time and again in her accounts, and acts as a justification for her conforming to the wishes of the state and school and peer-group pressure. But this justification is of course presented at a time when neither of these 'homes' or allegiances are much appreciated by her current outside world. This is true for her active church-going, which in an earlier passage she sees as something old-fashioned, not just then in the GDR, but also today in the modern secular unified Germany. It is even more true for her double involvement with GDR youth organisations and activities. Her discourse reflects the complex tension between her wish to recount a success at having managed to join those GDR organisations – the FDJ, the young pioneers – which now, from the point of view of the present day, are highly suspect. For instance, she twice claims not to be quite sure of whether or not she actually did join the FDJ or did take part in the *Jugendweihe* by embedding her decision into clauses such as 'I need to reflect on this' and 'actually, I might have'. Only with hedging and other modifying qualifiers does she gradually reveal her involvement. The tension not only surfaces in the choice of words, but also formally in many incomplete sentences and broken off utterances. Her narrative is thus often incoherent and disturbed at both the content and formal level, revealing a deeply uneasy relationship to her past which still affects her self-confidence in the present. Although she does claim for herself an active decision-making part in her involvement with the GDR organisations, she also retreats from time to time behind the same formulas seen in Ralf's discourse: 'That was some kind of a duty…'.

The difference between Gabi's fissured account and that of her mother's fluent colourful narrativisation of her life (including a confident though not entirely truthful account of her own children's behaviour), could not be more marked. Gabi's two confident teenage children, whom we also interviewed in a further independent session, do not exhibit any of their mother's difficulties either. In that family, as in many of the other families we interviewed in the border regions of the former GDR, it is the middle generation which exhibits major difficulties in narrating themselves as coherent agents amidst the socio-political upheavals of the outside world.

Conclusion: Narrative and memory

Both sets of narratives show that practices of self-representation are also practices of memory: the narrators reflect on their past experience and reshape it at the same time. This is where the relationship between memory, narrative and identity becomes evident. We narrate who we are by making claims about where we have come from.

While reading the stories of our informants we become aware of commonalities and differences that give hints about processes of remembering and forgetting within a single family. At the same time personal memories go beyond the individual, they are fashioned in relation to larger discursive spaces in which knowledge about the past is produced. In our case the four narratives clearly resonate with those discursive (and changing) contexts in pre-war – war – post-war – divided – and unified Germany in which historical subjects and cultural memories have been crafted. Political upheaval and change produced a fair amount of collective and personal calamity and suffering, but also periods of economic success and well-being. The older, pre-war generation appropriated historical experiences by drawing on post-war narratives that configured post-war German identities on the basis of a victim vs. perpetrator scheme. In this preoccupation with the legacy of the Second World War, east and west German old-generation narratives did not differ very markedly. The middle generation, however, emplotted themselves in different narrative contexts. Here, the most salient public narrative that informed eastern accounts was a post-unification story told by westerners, which portrayed ex-GDR citizens as misguided communists who had failed to create the economic prosperity achieved in the west (see also Armbruster & Meinhof 2002). The 'silent opponents' addressed in our extracts represented this storyline, and we, as western-identified interviewers, might have been seen as representing it too. The marked difference by which both age groups represented the past was not only visible in their presentations of people, the organisation of their relationships and the embedding of the narrator within that, but also in the wider linguistic structure, which was coherent and conclusive in the older-generation stories and more fractured and argumentative in the middle-generation accounts.

In the first family, the son Ralf's story with its absence of distinct characters, its emphasis on harmonious we-groups and its nostalgic vista of the past is also a clear rejection of the often devalued GDR identity. Contrastingly his mother Eva, who gives shape to specific characters but fractures we-groups and presents history as a continuum, appropriates a victim-status but overcomes it in the telling. Mother and son meet at the point where they portray family life in the border zone as enabled by a condition of 'getting accustomed to' unusual circumstances. This is their shared evaluation of the GDR past, echoed in many other similar extracts by the middle and older generation: Ralf: 'We just came to terms with it' ('Wir haben uns eben damit zurechtgefunne'). Eva: 'But as time went by erm we had no choice we got used to it' ('Aber mit der Zeit äh es blieb uns nichts anderes übrig wir haben uns daran gewöhnt').

However, Ralf remains entirely vague about what it was they had to get used to. Evidently, it was the 'border zone' ('Grenzgebiet'), but in his characterisation of their daily life he stresses its normality, smooth routine and humanity. Eva, on the other hand, is quite explicit. For her it was the condition of 'being locked up' ('eingesperrt') to which they had to get used, enforced by the fear of being evicted and the presence of spies in the village. Whereas she selects events to prove her point of a difficult life under exceptional and unpleasant circumstances from war to post-war, his narrative is almost event-less which proves the routine and normality he claims.

Eva tells a narrative of continuity about the past and almost omits the present. The narrative character she identifies with is that of a survivor of hardship. She clearly voiced a vision of the past which would have been sanctioned under GDR State Socialism: the suggested line of continuity between war and post-war life, the negative portrayal of the border regime, or the image of the

Russians as rapists and a source of fear. She construes a certain continuity in change.

In contrast to Eva, Ralf tells a tale of discontinuity between past and present and identifies with a narrative character we might call the ordinary dutiful citizen. He omits the past before he was born, the foundation of history starts with his birth 'we grew up with it', and undergoes a rupture with German unification. What counts is an unsatisfactory present which makes him look back at the past with a sense of nostalgia (the unique status of the worker; the state as carer, overall security). Unlike Eva, he disengages from issues of dissent, fear, or disagreement when talking about the GDR past and avoids narratives of direct encounter with the state apparatus. These issues are indirectly voiced (he couldn't bring his girlfriend in) and moved into the background.[8]

In the mother-daughter relationship of Frieda and Gabi, we find that Frieda's happy account of her children's refusal of the GDR state organisations (not extracted here) has narratively resolved what must have once been a source of great dissent in her family: of whether or not to give in to state and peer-group pressure. She has either simply forgotten or repressed it. Against her own life drama of the flight from home, these later events which so shook her daughter's life are relatively minor instances told with pride and energy. Her daughter by contrast relives in her discourse the deep division and perceived injustices felt by a young woman torn between different poles in her desire to lead a normal life. These conflicts clearly continue in the present since none of her previous choices and struggles to belong can be easily accommodated in a smooth post-GDR narrative.

When comparing narrative choices, stories and structures from all our interviewees in the former GDR, we found more overlap between generations of different families than of different generations within the same family. The middle generation exhibited far greater disturbances in the formal features of their narratives and in the contradictions between different sections – broken-off sentences, hesitations, contradictions – revealing unresolved tensions often whilst asserting the normality and ordinariness of their life. In this, the longer narratives which we analysed in our research in border communities echo the results of work with much shorter (half-page) life biographies (Meinhof 1997), where similar features pointed to the same kind of difficulty. This ongoing unease was further substantiated by the often highly defensive argumentative structure of the narratives even in the absence of any visible opponent. The older generation, by contrast, often told stories of great disturbances, of loss and fear, stories of grave danger and occasionally surprising kindness, populated by threatening and unpredictable enemies. Yet formally, their narratives were well-formed stories, through which memories of once deeply upsetting past events could be told, retold and thus laid to rest.

Notes

1. This work has been funded under the European Union's Fifth Framework Programme with a shared research project on European Border identities. For joint publications by the consortium see the collection of articles in Meinhof (Ed., 2002) and Meinhof (Ed., 2003).

2. This is generally seen as a direct consequence of the 'Deutschlandvertrag' of 1952, signed by France, Britain, the United States and West Germany. In this treaty the occupied status of West Germany was lifted and the future of a Western alliance vis-à-vis the Soviet Union took shape.

3. Lit. 'turn-over'. Established term for German unification.

4. Eva Tischler

DIE SPERRZONE
IR: Ja sie haben gerade erzählt von den Kontrollen Richtung – von nem grossen Zaun haben sie grad erzählt
ET: Ja das war wos rein nach S geht. Mhm und da musste da haben se dann wenn jetzt Besuch kam haben se ähm aufgeschrieben Passierschein Name wie wenn sie eingereist sind und wenn sie wieder rausmachen und – und einmal ist uns passiert das war die grosse Tochter die jetze in H wohnt die war erstmal verheiratet da unten im Thüringer Wald. Und die kamen waren en paar Tage da haben sich da oben angemeldet, inzwischen hatten mir aber schon wieder en neuen Paassierschein eingereicht, den hatt mir auch kriegt und dann sind die en Tag länger geblieben – und der alte Passierschein war dann abgelaufen und den neuen den hatten die noch gar nicht angemeldet da oben weil se der alte hatte noch Gültigkeit. Nachts um HALB EINS halten en paar Fahrzeuge da unten – rufen mir waren schon alles ins Bett – klopfen gucken mir naus zwei Grenzer solche Kontrolleur von da oben "sind bei ihnen die Frau Tina Schmitt und der Gerd Schmitt?" "Ja" "Denen ihr Passierschein ist abgelaufen die müssen SOFORT naus" und da ham mir gsagt "die haben doch schon wieder en neuen" haben mir sie mit rauf genommen und den neuen Passierschein dann hin. Naja dann nachher gings schon. Dann haben sie das aufgenommen und aufgeschrieben aber die sind REIN und die wussten genau wie lange der Passierschein geht und alles und die sind dann gucken die in ihr Buch, und die sind eben nicht wieder raus und der Passierschein ist abgelaufen. Wo werden die hin sein vielleicht sind sie über die Grenz oder so – mhm (laughs) wer des nit weiss gell, also nit miterlebt hat das – du warst eben richtig hier eingesperrt. Da nüber konnste nit da war der Zaun und da oben war ja nochmal en Zaun. Mit dem grossen Tor.

SPIONE IM DORF
IR: Man hat sich auch so gefühlt dann richtig eingesperrt?
ET: Man hat sich eingesperrt gefühlt aber mit der ZEIT aeh es blieb uns nichts anderes übrig mir haben uns dann dran gewöhnt. Was wollste denn anders machen? Du

konnste auch nicht rumschimpfen da biste ausgesiedelt worden, wie sies vielen gemacht haben gell wenn einer mal was Falsches gesagt hat, es gab ja so viele Spitzel im Dorf und das hast den Leuten gar nicht zugetraut. Die haben dich ausgehorcht im Gespräch, du dachtest das sind nette Leute und auf einmal haben sie dich angeschwärzt und dann kamste eben fort. Da musste eben ganz schön zurückhaltend sein und musst eben so das alles erdulden. Blieb dir nichts anders übrig. Ja und au die Kinner, die sind halt so aufgewachsen also die wissen ja überhaupt nix anders

IR: Die haben nichts anderes erlebt

ET: Die haben NICHTS anderes gekannt gell. Hier unsere Kinder eben wie mein Sohn jetze na der ist 53 geboren und – der hat nur in dere Sperrzone gelebt bis es eben jetze anders geworden ist

IR: Während Sie haben halt die andere Zeit auch noch gekannt

ET: Mir haben se noch gekannt genau. Es war ja auch ne harte Zeit der Krieg das war ja auch nit einfach gell. Ja - - tja mir sind aus der Schul kommen da war noch Krieg mir sind aus der Kirch raus da war Fliegeralarm und ach das war ja – genau so schlimm.

IR: Ja?

ET: Mhm mhm. Da sind die Bomben gefallen da oben bei uns auch – im Wald drinne die haben sie nu aus äh nicht mutwillig vielleicht runtergschmissen, ich weiss es nit auf so en Dorf, das haben sie ja nun nicht von der Luft aus irgendwie verfolgt oder dass da was war, dass sie das bombardieren mussten oder aber swar schon swar hart hart mhm. Na ja da war der Vater im Krieg da warn mir mit der Mutter alleine, dann sind wir ausm Wald Holz sammeln dann war Fliegeralarm, hingelegt mein Bruder dem ist immer schlecht worden der hat dann gebrochen vor Angst – alles vor Angst gell mhm - - - tja

ANGST VOR DEN RUSSEN

IR: Sie waren ja auch in der na da kennen sie auch die Hirschberger Lederfabrik ja auch gut

ET: Na klar ich hab 30 Jahre da drin gearbeitet.

IR: So lange haben sie drinnen gearbeitet?

ET: 30 Jahr in der Lederfabrik ja. Vorher hab ich Pflichtjahr gemacht wo ich aus der Schul kam in D im Rittergut das war eben grad so 45. Hab ich miterlebt drüben wo die Amis kommen sind nacher wo die Amis fort sind kamen die Russen na da is das war ja schlimm da hatte ja jeder Angst

IR: Ja schon?

ET: JO JO vor allem wenn de jung warst

IR: Vor den Russen

ET: Mhm. Die Russen haben viel vergewaltigt und so gell. Ich weiss wenn mir so abends zum Abendbrot dort sassen, Rittergut swar eben so viel Arbeiter eben und was halt war immer grosser Tisch. Dann auf einmal hats geklingelt draussen. Grosses Rittergut eben grosses Wohnhaus. "Ach" hat die Chefin gsagt "jetzt kommen die Russen" und nachher haben sie schon gschrien "junge Mädle!" Die waren ja immer besoffen, wollten sie junge Mädle, und mir waren so zu zweit. Dann hatten die uns da hinten naus zur Tür naus gelassen und nei in Hühnerstall gsperrt. Da standen sassen mir manchmal eine Stund mit de Hühner da drinne (laughs) da hatten sie ihre Probleme ghabt mit de junge Mädle eben gell. Mussten se verstauen, dass die Russen ja bis die waren ja immer besoffen. Na kamen sie junge Mädle mhm und die wussten, dass mir zwei da zwei junge Mädle waren und so lange die vorne die abgefertigt haben am Haupteingang, da hat die uns beim Hinterausgang naus über die Strass und dann in Hühnerstall gsperrt. (laughs) mir haben schon viel viel mitgemacht, liebe Zeit man müsste mal man hätt sich das alles mal aufschreiben solle.

5. Ralf Tischler

DAMALS UND JETZT

RT: Nee. Das war alles so selbstverständlich die Grenzanlgen, das war eben da da hast dich auch mir haben uns gar nicht da drüber gewundert auf gar keinen Fall, das war eben so und wir sind damit gross geworden –

IR: Und in die Lederfabrik sind sie mit nem Bus gefahren?

RT: Mit Bus. Da sind Arbeiterbusse gefahrn früh, nachmittag wieder zurück mhm das war alles geregelt da gabs keine Schwierigkeiten, es war besser geregelt wie jetzt auf alle Fälle (smiles) ganz klar – auch fürn Arbeiter da war eben bedeutend mehr übrig, schon allein mitn Mittagessen oder oder Frühstück das war eben alles da da gabs eben Küchen und Kantinen, und und da kannst dir en Kaffee kaufen für billiges Geld und und und en Brötchen dazu, es war eben alles da. Jetzt musst eben sehen wie de zurecht kommst ne. Grad mit Speisen oder mit irgend was mit Mittagessen

IR: Is schon en Unterschied mh

RT: Ja auf alle Fälle en grosser Unterschied. Auch wie de in die Arbeit kommst. Jetzt musst de mitm Auto fahren auf alle Fälle. Früher gabs, sind eben die Busse gefahren, die waren eben dann e Viertelstunde vor Arbeitsbeginn waren die in Hirschberg und dann konnten mir uns noch umziehen hatten die Möglichkeit gehabt die Arbeitssachen anzuziehen, und dann ging das los

IR: Dann gings los mhm

RT: Mhm. Das war schon besser geregelt auf alle Fälle – aber was solls ich mein man hat sich jetzt auch dran gewöhnt

DAS GRENZGEBIET

IR: Mhm. Hatten sie dann das Gefühl, es war ein grosser Unterschied zwischen Grenzgebiet und jetzt anderen Gegenden in der DDR?

RT: Mir sind mir haben das begriffen beziehungsweise mir sind so aufgewachsen das war unser Zuhause hier. Wenn wir Passierscheine beantragt hatten für irgendwelche Freunde und die kamen hier rein, Kontrolle oben und so "um Gottes Willen wie könnt ihr nur hier wohnen das gibts doch nicht und eingesperrt und" mir hatten das Gefühl nicht gehabt. Das war eben so, hier stand unser HAUS das war unser und (sighs) mir hatten auch nie Schwierigkeiten gehabt mit die mit die Grenzer oder was irgendwas die kontrolliert haben oder was, musst eben Ausweis vorzeigen, jawoll da stand drinne dass de rein durftest dass de hier wohnst und weiter die Grenzer haben dich gekannt, die haben schon von weitem aufgemacht wenn de mit em Auto gekommen bist. Das war halt also das Grenzgebiet war dafür konnten mir nichts, mir haben uns eben damit zurecht gfunne und das war halt so. Wie oft nach der Wende wie oft hast de da oben angehalten an der Kontrolle das Gas weggetan und wollst schon bremsen "ah ist doch gar kein Schlagbaum mehr da kannst doch weiterfahren"

IR: Wirklich?

RT: Echt wirklich ja. Das ging eben in Fleisch und Blut über das war halt hier amal so. Was
wollste die Leute jetze da oben an der Genze dumm vollpöbeln oder was, die haben ja
au bloss ihre Arbeit gemacht ihren Dienst verrichtet. Die konnten ja au nix dafür. Also
mir ich hatte immer en freundschafltiches Verhältnis gehabt zu ihnen, das warn auch
bloss Menschen genau solche Menschen wie mir. Die mussten das halt machen weil
das Regime damals so war der ganze Staat war so und das war eben so. (…)
Du warst eben im Grenzgebiet du kannst nicht tun und lassen was de wolltest wie
annere vielleicht irgendwo anderst oder da war eben unten die Mauer und da kannst
nit runtergehen beziehungsweise da kannste nicht hinter die Mauer gehen oder
kannste nit an an der Mauer rummachen das ging einfach nit das war eben einfach die
Gesetze, das war eben so und das war eben ok. Mir haben das eingesehen
beziehungsweise das war immer so. Also mir haben da keine Probleme damit gehabt
absolut nit. Freilich mit Freunden einladen oder damals wo man noch jung war mir
Freundin dann die durfte eben nicht mit rein und und in dem Moment wars schon
belastender. Das is jetze schon bedeutend andersch ganz klar, na wenn ich mein Sohn
anschau ne da ist eben die Freundin mit da ne

6. Frieda Amsel

BUTTER UND BROT

IR: Haben sie damals gemeint, dass sie wieder zurückkommen

FA: Ja, sicher haben wir gedacht…, aber wir wollten ja doch bis zum Amerikaner und das
war damals Perleberg, das is in'ner Prignitz. Also mit dem Zug, wo wir denn damals
runter sind, sind wir noch lange die Landstrasse lang, wurden ständig angegriffen,
aber wenn'se wieder mal, wenn'se denn weg waren, sind wir wieder weiter und wollten
unbedingt eben in westliche Richtung, wollten Perleberg erreichen, da hatten wir
immer noch so durch Nachrichten erfahren, dass da der Amerikaner war oder
Engländer? Das kann ich nicht mehr sagen, aber jedenfalls nicht die Russen. Und
gekommen sind wir letzendlich bis Putlitz, so'n kleines Dörfchen bei Parchim ist das.
Ist alles heut wieder bekannt, die bringen manchmal im Fernsehen davon. In Putlitz,
am Tage zuvor noch, eh uns die Russen einkriegten, haben sie da in dem Dörfchen
noch ganz grosse Butterbrocken, das waren richtig so'ne grossen Stücke, wo immer
mit Messer abgeschnitten wurde… nicht verpackte und das haben 'se noch allen
Flüchtlingen, die damals da in dem Ort allen noch verteilt, aber kein Stückchen Brot.
Was sollten wir jetzt mit der blanken Butter, ja, kein Stück gar nichts. Also, das
Hungern ging auf der Flucht denn schon los, nich, man hatte ja unterwegs nischt. Und
äh, wie gesagt, denn die Butter hatten wir nun da und denn kam die Nacht, wir hatten
alle in so'ner grossen Scheune übernachtet und mit einem Mal… mitten in der Nacht
hörten wir schon dauernd so'n dumpfes Grollen, da waren die russischen Panzer da.
Wir wollten gleich am Morgen, wollten wir zeitig weiter in Richtung Perleberg, wär
nich mehr allzu weit gewesen. Wir hätten's am nächsten Tage schaffen können. Ja,
leider… ganze Nacht durchlaufen ging ja auch nicht… Wir sind jeden Tag runde 50
Kilometer getippelt und ich hatte ja immer 'ne kranke Hüfte, meine Krücke steht
schon hier, ja mit der Hüfte immer … (continues to talk about her bad hip)

IR: Und da sind Sie diese ganze Strecke gelaufen? Und äh, wie Sie dann eingeholt wurden
von den Russen, was war da?

FA: Ja, da kamen die nachts in die Scheune rein und da haben wir schon..., da haben wir nun gedacht äh jetzt is aus. Wenn früh, also mitten in der Nacht werden 'se nicht, es war zu dunkel, die sahen ja auch nischt, aber wenn der Morgen dann graute, werden 'se uns wohl alle an die Wand stellen und umbringen, haben wir wirklich gedacht. Und mit einem fing's dann... da reichte immer einer dem anderen was hin, ... russisch quasseln konnten wir ja nicht verstehen, da haben die Komissbrote, wissen 'se die, kennen'se diese, da haben die im Dunkeln immer den den Flüchtlingen allen gereicht. Wer eben zugriff, der hatte 'n Brot und ich angelte, ich war wie gesagt 'ne 15-jährige. Ich sah das grade so im Dunkeln und griff auch nach so'm Brot, den waren die auch wieder fort, die Panzer mussten weiter, denn kommt immer der Nachschub, wissen 'se. Und da waren wir ja selig, dass wir jetzt zu unserer Butter endlich 'n Stück Brot kriegten, dann haben wir dicke Scheiben abgeschnitten und die Butter raufgeschmiert und dann haben wir wirklich alle angenommen, das ist nun unsrere Hiobsmahlzeit. Am nächsten Morgen werden 'se uns dann alle an die Wand stellen und denn is aus für uns und man hatte nicht mal Angst, muss ich ihnen sagen. Die Wochen, die wir unterwegs waren, ständig diese Angst vor den Tieffliegern, da sind sie auch als so junges Mädel so abgestumpft. Mir war ganz egal, ob die uns da hingestellt und alle abgeknallt hätten. Man konnte nich mal sich 'ne Träne rausquetschen. Gar nischt, so abgestumpt sind 'se dann. Ja, und wie gesagt, der Morgen kam denn... nischt war...

7. Gabi Amsel

DIE FDJ

GA: Ja FDJ. Ja es... Ich muss dazu sagen, ich wollte zu der Zeit auch in die FDJ [lacht]

IR: Eben, das wollt ich ja gern wissen [beide lachen]

GA: Ja, ja ich wollte... Weil ich halt nicht Außenseiter sein wollte, weil ich das halt als Kind doch eigentlich n bisschen so gespürt hab, aber äh... und andererseits das aber auch nicht so richtig leben konnte, Glauben. Dadurch äh... und alle anderen halt in der Klasse sowieso ja... diese Richtung gingen und da wollt ich halt mitmachen [lacht] Obwohl das auch nicht jetzt meine Überzeugung war, sag ich mal. Also ich wollte da eigentlich nur so mit dazu gehören, aber...

IR: Und durften sie das von zu Hause aus nich oder...

GA: Äh... Ich muss jetzt überlegen.... Ich war.... Ich war sogar inner FDJ [UM lacht] Ja, ja genau. Ich hab das... Ja ich hab das durchgedrückt, sag ich mal. Ja.

IR: Und ihre Geschwister auch oder waren sie dann die einzige?

GA: Nee. Ich möcht sagen nich.

IR: Nee, die andern nich. Sie waren die... Sie waren aufmüpfig [lacht]

GA: Ich war die... Die das... Ich wollte da gern mitmachen und hab das glaub ich durchgedrückt.

IR: Ja und äh... Das dann also... Ich mein, so die ganzen Sachen, die dann von der FDJ organisiert waren, die haben ja bestimmt auch alle viel Spaß gemacht oder? Nehm ich an mal. Also so für junge Leute. Ich mein, ich hab zum Beispiel hier jetzt... Das is ein Bild, ne das hat ich mit dabei.

GA: Also ich war da... Nee zu sowas war ich eigentlich nicht.

IR: Da waren sie dann nicht mit dabei?

GA: Nee, nee.

IR: So Maiumzug oder sowas. . . .

GA: Ja, sonst war das eigentlich nur hier so im Dorf dann immer mal so ne Versammlung halt. Wo sich auch die Jugendlichen trafen, aber…

IR: Aber was wurde denn nun…

GA: Ich hab da keine Erinnerungen groß an irgendwelche Aktionen groß. Ich wollt halt nur dazugehören. Das war alles.

IR: Aber ich mein, da sie sowas gemeinsam unternommen haben und solche Sachen. . . . Das ist weniger jetzt, dass Ihnen da was einfällt. Vielleicht durch. . . . Vielleicht sind Sie da auch gar nicht mit oder?

GA: Nee, fällt mir jetzt nischt ein. Nee, eigentlich dazu. Ich weiß, dass das die Frage damals war in der 8.Klasse oder so war das ja und… ach schon bei n Pionieren fing das ja schon an. Obwohl ich da halt auch mit drinne war. Das war wie so ne fast Pflicht, dass man da mit drin war in den Pionieren.

8. For an interesting account of middle-generation narratives in East and West-Berlin see Borneman (1992:178).

CHAPTER 4

Narrative demands, cultural performance and evaluation

Teenage boys' stories for their age-peers*

Nikolas Coupland, Peter Garrett and Angie Williams
Cardiff University

Introduction

What does it mean to view stories and their enactment as 'culturally significant'? We might point to how some stories fix and recycle cultural happenings and values that have special importance for a particular community and perhaps symbolise its distinctiveness. The cultural richness of a story may lie not so much in its documentary function as a true historical record, and more in its idealised representation of protagonists, events and outcomes. A story might have special value for a community if it represents a quest, a conflict, a stance or a resolution with particular iconic value for members. In this view, stories are repositories of rich cultural 'stuff', packaged for members to use and reuse. The telling of such stories would be a key part of the practice that constitutes the community – discourse, as Greg Urban (1996) puts it, in the service of collective social purpose.

The analyses in this chapter are an effort to establish the cultural significance of one set of stories of personal experience, designed and performed by mid-teenage boys in classroom settings in schools around Wales. The audio-records of these stories are very suggestive of the evaluative schemas and norms that are in play when these stories are told in front of the tellers' class-friends (who are boys and girls). Within predictable limits, we can infer 'cultural significance' from the referential foci of the stories – events and projected personas that tellers put into their narrative frames, motives they construct for their actions, their relationships with authority figures, and so on. Stylistic/discursive analysis of individual acts of narration provides further important evidence of what 'collective social purpose' motivates the story events. These are the usual descriptive and critical resources for a sociolinguistics of narrative. But in this case we also have a usefully direct window on recipiency, in the form of judgement data that we have collected from a substantial group of age-peers from other schools – that is, from kids of comparable ages and backgrounds who were not themselves present in the original story-telling events.

Our aim for the chapter is therefore partly methodological – to demonstrate the value of integrating researchers' commentaries on particular story texts and their telling with evaluative data from the community, centred on the same stories and their tellers. For analysing stories as cultural performances, we argue that this multi-faceted approach is in fact necessary. Evaluative response data can expose general tendencies in how a particular community engages with narrative accounts on its own terms. Such data set out the evaluative matrix within which particular stories are constructed as well as judged. We argue that stories are constructed against specifiable sets of cultural *demands* for narrative performance, and that the success or otherwise of any one act of telling will be determined by how it meets these locally operative norms of production and interpretation.

Before more comprehensively introducing the data, however, we invoke some theoretical support for, and try to clarify, our general perspective on cultural performance and the role of narrative within this process.

Narrative in cultural performance

Linguistic anthropology, particularly through Richard Bauman's work, has developed useful accounts of factors that distinguish performance events from other sorts of communicative practice. This is to argue against loose and over-inclusive senses of the term 'performance' in connection with language, where it otherwise risks becoming synonymous with 'usage' or 'talk'. Bauman (1992: 46ff.) allows us to infer a list of particular characteristics that all performance events share. He says they are *scheduled* events, typically pre-announced and planned, and therefore *programmed*. They are *temporally/spatially bounded* events, marked off from the routine flow of communicative practice. They are *co-ordinated* in the sense that they rely on specific sorts of collaborative activity, not least in that performers and audience members will establish themselves in these participant roles for the enactment of the performance. Performances are typically also *public* events, at least in that the membership of the audience will not be especially exclusive. These characteristics are material aspects of the social contextualisation of performances, but Bauman also identifies the *heightened intensity* of performance occasions. (See also Bauman 1977, 1996; Bauman & Briggs 1990.)

We can recast this list and extend it if we argue that performance involves, in several related senses, a *focusing* of communicative events. Seven dimensions seem relevant:

— *form focusing*: the poetic function of language comes to the fore and considerations of style become particularly salient
— *meaning focusing*: there is an intensity, a density and a depth to utterances or actions, or at least this is assumed to be the case by audiences
— *situation focusing*: performers and audiences are not merely co-present but are 'gathered', according to particular dispositional norms
— *performer focusing*: performers 'hold a floor' or a 'stage', rather literally or at least in participants' normative understandings of speaker rights and sequencing options
— *relational focusing*: performances are *for* audiences not just *to* audiences; although audiences are public, performers will often have designed their performances for specific groups
— *achievement focusing*: performances, as we suggested above, are enacted in relation to more or less specific *demands*; 'stakes' (gains, losses and risks) are involved, with potential for praise or censure for good or bad performance
— *repertoire focusing*: performers and audiences are generally sensitive to what is given and what is new in a performance; performances may be versions of known pieces, or at least known genres; innovative interpretation can be commended; rehearsal is relevant.

To say that an event is *framed as a performance* carries all these implications, although it is of course possible for reframings to be achieved ephemerally within communicative events, for example when a participant in a conversation (to use Dell Hymes' 1975 phrase) 'breaks through into performance'. Although Bauman's discussion of performance points primarily to institutionalised performance events, the criteria listed above can all be relevant to local communicative contingencies – shifting into 'doing performance' in the otherwise less focused here and now. Story telling will generally be frame-marked for performance, of course with some instances much more overtly marked than others. It is difficult to conceive of *any* story that is recognised to be a story by its participants not sharing at least some of the focusing features we have just introduced. All the same, it is clearly the case that stories in different contexts will range between 'full' and 'partial' performance events – they will be *focused* in the ways we have described to variable extents.

The boys' stories in our data are told in front of peers in school classrooms. These are 'gathered' events where the teller 'holds the floor' to tell a story 'for' his age-peers. We are mainly interested in the *relational* and *achievement focusing* of the boys' stories, in how they function to different degrees as successful ingroup stories for the age-peer group. They are stories 'about us' and 'for us', or 'about me as one of us', but also 'about what we and I are not'. In this vein Stephen Frosh and his colleagues write about 'canonical narratives' (a term they derive from Bruner's work) which they define as "general stories about how lives may be lived in the culture, serving to justify certain behaviours" (Frosh et al. 2002:10).[1] Our social evaluation data make it clear that some storytellers are successful in projecting ingroup values and identities that are strongly approved of by peers, while others are far less successful. Against a coherent set of normative demands for ingroup stories, particular individuals perform well and others badly. Our analysis tries to establish which narrative themes and designs correspond to these degrees of success and failure. That is, we work backwards from the evaluative data we have in hand to better appreciate what was important in the original acts of telling, in terms of cultural performance.

What precisely, then, is meant by 'cultural performance', and how should we theorise the link between performance and culture? Once again, Bauman's ideas are illuminating. Bauman stresses the role of *reflexivity* in performance, and how performance events have the particular facility of opening up cultural norms to reflexive scrutiny:

> Perhaps the principal attraction of cultural performances for the study of society lies in their nature as *reflexive* instruments of cultural expression… First of all, performance is formally reflexive – signification about signification – insofar as it calls attention to and involves self-conscious manipulation of the formal features of the communicative system… making one at least conscious of its devices. At its most encompassing, performance may be seen as broadly metacultural, a cultural means of objectifying and laying open to scrutiny culture itself, for culture is a system of systems of signification… In addition to formal reflexivity, performance is reflexive in a socio-psychological sense. Insofar as the display mode of performance constitutes the performing self as an object for itself as well as for others, performance is an especially potent and heightened means of taking the role of the other and of looking back at oneself from that perspective.   (Bauman 1996:47–48)

For Bauman, the distinction between performer and audience is one of two significant distinctions in the participation structure of performance events.

The other is between performer and audience together, and the membership of the cultural group itself. The performance frame establishes a relationship between the meanings co-articulated in the performed event and the meanings that define the wider cultural formation. This relationship and the duality of meaning is laid open to scrutiny when in some sense relevant cultural practices are performed or referred to in a particular event.

Stories clearly have potential to function 'metaculturally' in Bauman's sense. In the data we deal with in this chapter we asked the boys to tell stories that they thought their peers (males and females) would be interested to hear. A 'cultural relevance' is imposed through our elicitation strategy, although it is reasonable to suppose that all stories told to ingroups will have a metacultural aspect. The stories were generally about personal adventures, often involving movement and physicality, risks to their own or other people's wellbeing, mishaps and damage, conflict with authority figures, and so on. (See Cheshire 2000 for related issues and data. In different ways, Eckert 2000 and Hebdige 1979 discuss the iconic status of linguistic and semiotic styles for young people and their sub-cultures.) This list of topics may suggest that the cultural formation in question is not merely 'youth' but 'male youth'. On the other hand, and because at this point we have not worked with the comparable data we have from girl story-tellers, we try not to pre-judge the gendering of the data.[2] Also, to repeat, the audiences to the boys' stories which we see as generating cultural demands for performance comprise both girls and boys.

We are therefore defining 'culture' to be the cluster of practices and values that give a social group its sense of inclusion and exclusion. Relevant practices for a cultural group include what we do, how we do things, our deportment, style, our ingroup marking devices. Relevant values include what and who we like and dislike, what matters to us, what we take pleasure in and take exception to, what we take to be our ideals. A culture is therefore a set of priorities and tolerances on what we do and what we value, invoked to build a shared social identity and to distinguish it from other identities. Stories – or at least stories of the sort we have elicited in our fieldwork – are dramatisations of cultural practices which are open to evaluation. They can of course be evaluated on many dimensions, but we are mainly interested to ascertain how particular stories are evaluated for their degree of fit with cultural ideals, that is, how they match up to pre-established normative demands. We assume that the social evaluation of practice is in fact part of a cyclical process of enculturation.

To elaborate on this, drawing on Bauman and Briggs (1990), we can suggest that a story can perform and build its culture, not only in how it is 'entextualised' (put into text in the moment of telling), but also in how it is 'decontextualised'. Bauman and Briggs point out that many performances are linked through to other moments in the discursive life of a group or community (see 'repertoire' and 'versions', above). A performance in many ways abstracts away from the current situational context of telling – or at least, many performances do this. The Bakhtinian notion that "our speech... is filled with others' words, varying degrees of otherness or varying degrees of 'our-own-ness', varying degrees of awareness and detachment" (Bakhtin 1986:89; Coupland 2001), plus the presence of reflexivity in performance (Jaworski, Coupland, & Galasinski 2004), is why "performance... provides a frame that invites critical reflection on communicative processes" (Bauman & Briggs 1990:60). Performances are therefore both within and outside the culture that they characterise: "poetic patterning extracts discourse from particular speech events and explores its relationship to a diversity of social settings" (Bauman & Briggs 1990:61).

Decontextualisation is in that sense a key function of performance, and perhaps most obviously of performed narrative. As we suggested above, ingroup stories focus cultural moments and invite listeners and performers themselves to reflect on them and to work them through – perhaps to sharpen the definition of what the culture is, perhaps to draw in potential new members. Decontextualised narratives are, we might say, 'takeaway' or 'to go' cultural packages: "A text, then, from this vantage point, is discourse rendered decontextualizable. Entextualization may well incorporate aspects of context, such that the resultant text carries elements of its history of use within it" (Bauman & Briggs 1990:73).

Most obviously, because stories marshal social events, tellers can perform their own culture by selecting and representing indicative social events in which ingroup members take part. The framing, focusing and intensification work that performed narratives achieve, can lift them from being 'ordinary' to being 'salient' events. Stories can frame and project cultural rich points (see Agar 1991). In the case of a first-person narrative, the teller can represent himself or herself as a candidate for being considered an ideal or prototypical cultural member: 'this is what we are really like or should be like, as I was on this occasion'. Third persons can be constructed with attributes that define why they are *not* acceptable as ingroup members. If a story is told to a pre-designated ingroup audience, the story must work to local norms and the teller is under an obligation to assess and respond to these norms as fulsomely as s/he can. The general demand is to package up a story in ways that most members will agree is iconic of their group's preferred (actual or imagined) practices and values.

Decontextualisation through narration is a factor that encourages cultural *idealisation* and *aspiration* – working towards an idealised cultural definition, rather than representing descriptively typical or modal practices. In their character development, ingroup narratives are likely to show cultural *heroicisation*. We might even say that culture in general is an aspirational representation. Whatever attributes are most valued in a culture will be hyperbolically represented in ingroup cultural narratives – whether it is strength, daring, reticence, solidarity, vituperation, beauty, excitement, pro- or anti-establishment stances, and so on. This is because most cultural groups idealise themselves as exceptional and because performance spaces create focused opportunities to represent a group's aspirations metaculturally.

The stories and the evaluative data

We collected the narrative data and a raft of related social evaluative data for an extended series of studies on language variation and language attitudes in Wales. We have discussed the full details of these data extensively elsewhere, and here we provide just a few details that are most pertinent to the concerns of this particular chapter.[3] The audio-recorded stories were collected from schools all over Wales, in part to capture regional dialects of Welsh English that we had identified in an earlier study (see Garrett, Coupland, & Williams 2003) and from a private school in Cheltenham in England, to capture RP-like (Received Pronunciation) voices. The teenagers were told that the researcher (the third author) was interested in collecting 'stories that young people your age tell', and this general request was supplemented with the following prompt:

> All people are storytellers. You come to school every day and tell your mates about things that have happened to you. This is what I want you to do today. Think of something that has happened to you or someone you know and tell us about it. For example, a funny or embarrassing incident, a frightening story, accident or danger, or a time when you got into trouble with your parents.

There was generally no difficulty in eliciting a supply of volunteered stories from both male and female teenagers. In all, we collected 179 of them. The majority, for both sexes, are based around (actual or fictitious) events with a mildly anti-establishment character, often involving personal and physical threats or accidents, and also alcohol. Only the researcher was present with the storytellers and their classmates during these sessions; teachers were not present.

For our earlier study, we chose 14 stories – two from RP speakers, and two from each of the six dialect communities within Wales. A number of criteria were used in making the selection. For example, regionally identifying

references were avoided and the speakers had to be sociolinguistically representative of their dialect communities. We chose to limit our selected stories
to those of male speakers simply to restrict the complexity of this phase of the
study design, and also because we had more of those to choose from. The five
speakers we discuss in this chapter are a sub-sample of the 14 male voices we
used in our earlier study. As we have said, four were vernacular speakers of
different local dialects of Welsh English and one was a near-RP speaker. As a
result, the 'cultural' affiliation of each of the five speakers is unique, at least
in respect of either geographical region or social class background, although
each speaker was telling a story that was performed for an audience comprising their own immediate social network (their own school class group). The
'judges' from whom we collected evaluative data were mixed-ability groups of
teenagers from mixed-sex classes in other schools in the same regions in Wales
(though none from England). Our reason for finding different schools was to
avoid the risk that the storytellers would be recognised. Teachers helped us in
the task of finding schools that were good matches for the ones where we had
recorded the stories. In a wider sense, then, the storytellers and the groups
of young people commenting on the performed stories are all members of a
cultural group we could loosely identify as 'mid-teenage kids in Wales'. Our intention in the study is of course not to predefine cultural membership, but to
see how specific normative demands are established by the wider group, and
then to assess how individual narrative performances are deemed to match, or
fail to match, these demands.

In anonymising the speakers, it is convenient to refer to each one by the
number he was designated in the general programme of research and to refer
to the area where he lives. So we refer to the five speakers, perhaps rather incon-
gruously, as 'RP3 Cheltenham' (a near-RP speaker who was audio-recorded at
a school in Cheltenham in the west of England), 'SW4 Carmarthen' (a speaker
from Carmarthen in south-west Wales whose speech is consistent with local
norms), 'Mid6 Newtown' (a speaker from Newtown in Mid Wales), 'NW10
Blaenau Ffestiniog' (a speaker from Blaenau Ffestiniog in north-west Wales),
and 'Cardiff11' (a speaker from Cardiff, the capital city in south-east Wales).
The speaker numbers are the numbers we randomly allocated to the speakers
in the larger sample (to help with cross-referencing). Transcripts of their stories
follow in numerical order.[4]

RP3 Cheltenham   The belt sander accident

1   OK well it was er . a stupid time when . I was in a <u>play</u> er here at
2   school (.) um when I was in the . <u>third</u> year . so I us- I was I hadn't
3   <u>started</u> my GCSE course so I was still 3 doing . sort of (.) ge- or wa-
4   what<u>ever</u> <u>sub</u>ject <u>circles</u> n . <u>music</u> or . um design tech<u>nology</u> and stuff
5   like that ((er)) er . we'd been <u>up</u> it was the . <u>night</u> before I think the
6   <u>first</u> night of the <u>play</u> so we'd been <u>up</u> to about . <u>mid</u>night the last night
7   re<u>hearsing</u> the play (.) and so I was <u>really</u> <u>tired</u> . and we had er . D T
8   first lesson . design technology first lesson? . and we were . <u>finishing</u>
9   off some . <u>boxes</u> or other or something like that . and there's a <u>belt</u>
10 sander which has now been . sort of <u>stopped</u> use (.) stopped the <u>use</u> of .
11 and er I was just <u>sanding</u> something <u>down</u> . and I was <u>really</u> <u>tired</u> and
12 my fingers slipped <u>off</u> the . <u>box</u> (.) and actually <u>hit</u> (small laugh) the
13 <u>belt</u> sander (.) just the . <u>ends</u> of my <u>fingers</u> luck<u>ily</u> it didn't ((hit)) I
14 took it away in <u>time</u> (.) I I <u>didn't</u> think <u>much</u> had <u>happened</u> I thought
15 I'd just sort of <u>scraped</u> the <u>top</u> (.) and er . I I didn't feel that <u>bad</u> so I
16 just sort of <u>run</u> it under some <u>water</u> (.) some cold <u>water</u> to try and . to
17 try and stop it <u>bleeding</u> but (.) (creak) it it sort of about after about <u>two</u>
18 or three <u>minutes</u> I (.) I started feeling <u>really</u> <u>bad</u> I sort of felt <u>really</u> <u>sick</u>
19 (.) so I told . the . our teacher in <u>charge</u> of it . and he said oh well. if
20 you're feeling sick you'd better <u>go</u> . go and sit out<u>side</u> and he said it's .
21 quite <u>nasty</u> (.) so I should go up . go up and see sort of the <u>nurse</u> . in
22 <u>school</u> . so I sat out<u>side</u> for about five minutes and I I . <u>really</u> felt I was
23 going to be sick . but . I <u>wasn't</u> . and after (.) after a <u>little</u> while . I I
24 went up to . to the . <u>nurse</u> up at the . er up at the <u>junior</u> school (.) just er
25 which is our <u>house</u> matron . and so um . she sort of . she had a <u>look</u> at
26 it and cleaned it <u>up</u> (.) and just <u>ban</u>daged it <u>up</u> (.) and er (slight laugh)
27 that <u>night</u> I had to go and per<u>form</u> with sort of <u>fingers</u> about . <u>three</u>
28 inches <u>thick</u> . it was quite funny

SW4 Carmarthen   The fat rugby player

1   I got a friend called . <u>Ieuan</u> oh he's just <u>massive</u> . I just got to say he's
2   just <u>massive</u> (.) <u>um</u> . he plays <u>rugby</u> with us (.) and . he plays <u>prop</u> but
3   <u>oh</u> . <u>one</u> da- time we were playing up at Tregyb (.) and . he had to
4   come on in <u>second</u> half (.) to substitute for a . <u>small</u> . <u>chap</u> (.) he came
5   <u>on</u> the small chap . pulled his . <u>jersey</u> off (.) and then Ieuan . <u>literally</u>
6   at<u>tempted</u> . to put . the jersey <u>on</u> (.) yeah he <u>just</u> got it on his (.) his (.)
7   two hands . and he <u>tried</u> to put his head in but he just couldn't get
8   <u>through</u> (.) I was . <u>everybody</u> was <u>howling</u> (.) his e- <u>everything</u> was

9   wobbling his <u>chest</u> his <u>belly</u> his <u>back</u> his <u>legs</u> his <u>oh</u> it was disgusting
10   (.) and he's got <u>oh</u> . I I just . everybody calls him <u>Michelin</u> man it's got
11   to be . he's got <u>so</u> many rolls of <u>fat</u> (.) so disgusting (1.0) and then
12   (sighs) he came <u>on</u> (.) and he . <u>oh</u> . he can't train at <u>all</u> he's so un<u>fit</u> .
13   and it's a bit <u>sad</u> to tell the truth . but (.) it's so funny . but then .
14   playing for our local club at under fourteen <u>level</u> (.) um (.) we had
15   under <u>thir</u>teen shirts which s were <u>small</u> . <u>I</u> had quite a bit of trouble
16   getting into mine because I was . quite <u>big</u> . but um <u>Ieuan</u> <u>oh</u> it was so
17   funny (.) <u>once</u> he got <u>into</u> his shirt . it looked like it was going to <u>rip</u>
18   a<u>part</u> . at the <u>seams</u> (.) he just had to <u>tape</u> it . literally . oh he pu- he got
19   this ins<u>ul</u>ation tape ((and he was just)) <u>wrapp</u>ing it round <u>wrapp</u>ing it
20   round <u>wrapp</u>ing it round . and he had . <u>several</u> <u>lay</u>ers of it a- <u>oh</u> he
21   came on the pitch <u>oh</u> it was so <u>funny</u>

Mid6 Newtown   The tipping tractor

1   I was mucking out the <u>shed</u> I was an (1.0) on the . <u>tractor</u> (.) and I got
2   one <u>load</u> in the . front <u>fork</u> (*Researcher: mhm*) and (.) and I went <u>in</u> .
3   and I went into the . <u>mixen</u> what you do you just lift up the muck and
4   put it on the <u>top</u> (1.0) so you . dig <u>in</u> . to a bit of the mixen and get a bit
5   more in the front <u>fork</u> . and lift it up . into the <u>top</u> (.) and instead of .
6   when I put it . into the <u>mixen</u> in<u>stead</u> of the <u>front</u> <u>end</u> coming <u>up</u> with
7   the <u>muck</u> . the back w end <u>wheels</u> came up (.) cos there wasn't enough
8   <u>weight</u> on the <u>back</u> so . the back end came <u>up</u> (.) but the <u>wheels</u> still
9   going <u>round</u> (.) but the . front fork only goes <u>so</u> far <u>up</u> . so the wheels
10   <u>stopped</u> after a while (.) and the <u>back</u> wheels are . a<u>bove</u> the front ones
11   (.) and the . <u>bonnet</u> was on the <u>front</u> (.) so it was <u>sway</u>ing a<u>bout</u> a bit
12   like <u>this</u> and I . just about managed to get <u>off</u> <u>half</u> way <u>up</u> (.) so then
13   <u>dad</u> came along after and . <u>stopped</u> the tractor and . put it <u>down</u> . and I
14   just (.) there's me <u>standing</u> there getting really <u>worried</u> (laughs) what
15   am I going to <u>do</u> <u>now</u>? (small laugh) could have been <u>dangerous</u>

NW10 Blaenau Ffestiniog   The strange motorcyclist

1   er- (.) there's this <u>um</u>- (.) there's this sort of <u>pool</u> in the <u>river</u> in my
2   <u>dad's</u> <u>quarry</u> . and um- . it's really <u>deep</u> and there's this <u>about</u> . <u>twenty</u>
3   foot <u>cliff</u> a<u>bove</u> it and people <u>jump</u> <u>dive</u> and <u>jump</u> off <u>that</u> . <u>straight</u>
4   into the <u>water</u> . AB . he um (.) he went <u>up</u> there with a <u>motor</u> cycle .
5   and he wore his <u>motor</u> cycle helmet and the <u>superman</u> cape (small
6   laugh) and <u>dived</u> <u>in</u> with um <u>helmet</u> and the <u>superman</u> (laughs) <u>cape</u> .

7   cape . but um that um story's also been exaggerated and people say
8   that he was trying to kill himself and but he came up for air (1.0) um
9   (.) he's done some pretty stupid things um . with the law as well he (.)
10   stole a gate from the fire brigade place (.) and um- . cut the gate up and
11   used the bars to um . build the go-kart . with a welder (.) and stuck a
12   motorcycle engine on it and he got in some . pretty deep trouble for
13   that (1.0) um- (.) he also about three years ago . no about two years
14   ago (.) he was on . he was on a motorbike that he had built himself (.)
15   and um he he was doing a wheelie and the throttle cable . s um stuck .
16   it wouldn't go back down . so he was still going on this massive
17   wheelie . and he didn't have a clutch or anything on it (.) and um . he
18   collided with a car . and somersaulted over that car . and over a police
19   car that was um . behind that car . landed behind the police car and um
20   . well the motorcycle . you know was . just a scrambler it wasn't a road
21   bike or anything (.) and um . his um . kneecap came out of his leg (.)
22   and um he told the police officer that he'd never ride the motor cycle
23   again about . three months later he was back on the road on a motor bike

Cardiff11   The pool table

1   ah (.) ((anyway)) (.) there was one time when . you know I was in
2   Boys' Brigade an . went to adventure camp (.) you know I was the
3   only only coloured person there like an (.) you know we sort of all
4   have had a laugh they were none of them were racist or nothing (.) and
5   you know (.) few couple of days we all had a laugh on the assault
6   courses and stuff an (.) you know . they all they all took the mick out
7   of everyone you know we had this little book (.) and everyone took the
8   mick out of you (.) an (.) you know it was like everyone (.) an (.) there
9   was one time when . we were all playing pool on the pool table (.) and
10   I saw you know I saw the latch on the thing so I thought oh I know (.)
11   if I put my hand down this pool table hole you know and I can . tief a
12   few games like (.) you know keep the latch up (.) an (.) puts my hand
13   down you know . ten minutes later I realise I couldn't get it back out
14   (.) (laughing) so I thought oh no (.) I got my hand stuck down a pool
15   table (.) you know so . they had to go and find the caretaker an he was
16   he was like about three hours eventually until they found the caretaker
17   you know I had to stand in this one place w . one hand stuck in the
18   pool table you know . and one hand trying to eat my tea and my food
19   and stuff (.) an (.) you know . come across and he said oh . he said how
20   are we gonna get your hand out then? (.) an he goes oh (.) there's only

21   one thing we can do like you know (.) I said what's that he said we'll
22   have to saw the whole pool table in half (.) I said how you going to do
23   that? w he said . you know (.) go to the thing (.) goes out to the garden
24   shed like in the back and brings out this massive chainsaw (.) you
25   know he's sawing the whole pool table in half n my hand comes out
26   eventually (.) and they all take the mick out of you at the end (.) you
27   know and they all comes up to me and they goes oh (.) and we have
28   CD you know getting his hand stuck down a pool table (.) and he
29   turned round and says oh it's the first time the black's ever potted himself?

Evaluative profiles of the five speakers

In the evaluative phase of the research we collected formal, scaled quantitative responses from 169 young people from secondary schools all over Wales
who listened to a sample of the audio-recorded stories, including the five transcribed above. In our pilot work, exploratory discussion sessions with a mixed-
gender, mixed-ability sample of 35 teenagers in a Cardiff secondary school had
established a range of social dimensions on which it seemed natural to them
to evaluate the speakers they were listening to. The seven dimensions are listed
in abbreviated forms across the top of Table 1. They are: 'Overall, do you like
this speaker?', 'Do you think this speaker does well at school (e.g. gets high marks
in exams)?', 'How much like you do you think the speaker is?', 'Do you think you
could make friends easily with this speaker?', 'How Welsh do you think this speaker
sounds?', 'Do you think this speaker is a good laugh?', and 'How interesting does
this story sound?'. Fourteen speakers, including the five we are concerned with
here, were assessed along all these dimensions. The table gives the mean ratings
for each speaker on each dimension of judgement.[5]

Figure 1 then plots the mean ratings for our five storytellers along some
of the judgement criteria that are most relevant to ingroup/outgroup assess-
ments and to what the social psychology literature would define as the 'social
attractiveness' dimension of social evaluation. A very clear social attractiveness
hierarchy emerges from the figure, showing that the storyteller from Cardiff
is far and away the listeners' favourite. His story is considered the most interesting of the set, he is the person most regularly thought to be 'a good laugh',
he is liked best, he is the person thought to make friends most easily, and, interestingly, these positive judgements are supported by strong feelings overall
that he is most similar to the listeners themselves. The two storytellers from
Blaenau Ffestiniog and Carmarthen are next-best liked, with the speaker from

Table 1. Overall means for Welsh teenagers' evaluations of regional speakers (N = 169)

Speaker	Do you like	Good at school	Like you	Make friends	How Welsh	Good laugh	Interesting story
Cardiff1	2.43	2.62	1.88	2.39	2.83	2.34	1.87
Cardiff11	3.20	2.44	2.53	3.12	2.88	3.75	3.69
NE2	2.74	3.01	2.22	2.79	1.88	2.97	2.87
NE9	2.86	2.48	2.26	2.77	1.60	3.24	2.71
NW7	2.09	2.09	1.53	1.95	3.44	2.27	2.52
NW10	2.72	2.67	2.22	2.74	3.41	2.97	3.28
SW4	2.67	2.52	2.01	2.67	4.47	3.17	2.60
SW13	2.14	2.38	1.65	2.15	3.91	2.16	1.89
Valleys5	2.23	2.35	1.67	2.14	4.01	2.16	2.58
Valleys8	2.01	2.40	1.46	2.11	3.76	2.16	1.79
Mid6	2.13	3.11	1.71	2.19	2.29	1.99	1.89
Mid14	2.03	3.00	1.66	2.07	2.14	1.98	1.86
RP3	2.04	3.49	1.73	1.93	1.56	1.70	1.78
RP12	2.01	3.56	1.70	1.98	1.51	1.88	1.99

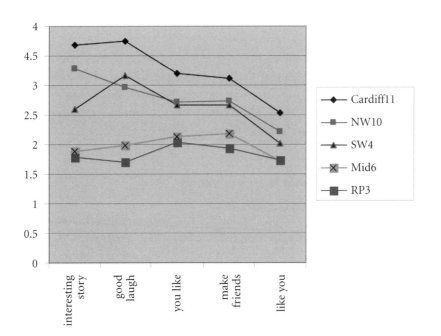

Figure 1. Summary graph of evaluative profiles

Newtown and the RP speaker being granted very meagre levels of social at-tractiveness, with little evidence of any ingroup sentiment held towards them. The RP speaker is not only 'not like the listeners', but not at all 'a good laugh'. (Table 1 shows that he is, however, held to be quite 'good at school'. The ta-ble also shows findings, unbolded, for the remaining story-tellers in the earlier study, for comparison.)

There is no simple regional or dialectal factor at work in the ordering of these particular judgements, although this is important in other aspects of the research (which we do not deal with here). Cardiff, the capital city in the south-east of Wales, Blaenau Ffestiniog in the north-west and Carmarthen in the rural south-west are widely distributed geographically, and the dialect forms associ-ated with these regions index very different cultural formations of 'Welshness' (see Garrett, Coupland, & Williams 2003). Social class and 'Englishness' are no doubt implicated to some extent in the relative outgrouping of the RP speaker (and indeed of <u>both</u> RP speakers in the larger sample – see Table 1), but these are once again not clear-cut explanatory factors. We can already infer one over-arching demand characteristic from the general negativity of peer judgements (again see Table 1, where 3.0 is a mid-scale judgement). The evaluative climate in which these stories are performed is negative, and we might say that cen-soriousness is itself part of the overall cultural climate in which the stories are operating.

To understand their highly variable degrees of 'success', we obviously need to examine the constitution of the particular narratives as discursive events performed for a peer-group. Before doing this, however, we can briefly look at another type of evaluative data which can clarify the demand conditions under which the stories were told and heard.

Performance demands for teenagers' stories

We can fill out more particular tendencies from open-ended responses made by the same 169 listeners who completed scales. They were invited to list three first-reaction comments about each of the boys they heard. What were the dominant semantic dimensions of evaluation in the 5261 'keywords' they wrote in response to a sample of 14 of the boys' stories?

It is striking that pejorative and outgrouping expressions make up the largest single category of open-ended responses, across the full range of as-sessments made. So, items like *prat, dickhead, twat, wanker, arsehole,* and *prick* make up a full 10.63% of all keywords. As summarised in Table 2, the sin-

Table 2. Keyword *boring* comments about speakers, compared to mean scores for 'interesting story' and 'good laugh' in the scales data

Speaker	'Boring' as % age of speaker's comments	Interesting story	Good laugh
Mid14	16.76	1.86	1.98
Cardiff1	15.52	1.87	2.34
Mid6	15.01	1.89	1.99
Valleys8	14.13	1.79	2.16
RP3	14.05	1.78	1.70
RP12	13.97	1.99	1.88
SW13	13.60	1.89	2.16
Valleys5	10.79	2.58	2.16
NW7	7.53	2.52	2.27
NE9	5.60	2.71	3.24
NW10	4.13	3.28	2.97
SW4	4.00	2.60	3.17
NE2	2.15	2.87	2.97
Cardiff11	1.21	3.69	3.75

gle item *boring* makes up 9.77% of all responses, although 'boringness' is very variably attributed to different storytellers. Two other major categories formed from these open-ended responses were given the headings *funny* and *boasters and bullshitters*. 6.23% of the total keywords fell into this first category and 3.52% fell into the second category.

Overall, we can infer that 'being a prat' is a highly salient if complex evaluation in this cultural context. The worst 'prats' will perhaps be ineffectual or incompetent (they were sometimes stereotyped through the expression *duh*). At the same time, based on the distributional evidence from the keywords, 'not boasting' matters, as does 'being not boring', and, more positively, 'being funny'.

We could reinterpret these facts as four rather general demands for narrative performance by (Welsh) mid-teenage boys and girls, at least when they are evaluating the boys' stories. Expressing them positively, we can say that successful and culturally resonant stories for this group need to:

a. be high or strong cultural performances (*the intensity demand*), designed to counter the generally negative and unforgiving climate of personal assessment

b. express high personal control and resilience (*the prat-avoidance demand*), for example in survivor narratives. To demonstrate high control, first-person stories might involve risks successfully negotiated. Bad stories will give us ineffectual 'prats'. In the telling of stories, successful tellers will also have to demonstrate their own control in marshalling the culture

c.   be original/extravagant/incongruous (*the boring-avoidance demand*), favouring stories that articulate exceptional happenings

Narrated events will qualify as exceptional if they transcend mundane 'boring' realities – perhaps of home, school and institutional aspects of many teenagers' existences. We can expect good stories to be about life outside the institutions, and about events that are threatening to those structures – anti-social, rebellious. The good stories may be more surreal than real, more bizarre and exotic than normal. If, as we suggested earlier, cultures are often aspirational, there will be a general appeal in transcendence and extravagance. In the telling, good stories will be immediate, graphic, unpredictable. But, working against demand (c), 'not boasting' is a predictable constraint on all this:

d.   be adequately truthful/ plausible (*the authenticity demand*)

These extrapolated demand characteristics can now be examined in turn in relation to the five stories, where they do indeed appear to have explanatory potential.

Matching and missing performance demands

The contrast between the Cardiff speaker's story and the RP speaker's is striking. The Cardiff speaker places himself at the heart of vernacular culture – pool playing is a time-out, recreational activity, trying to get free games is a mildly anti-social action – while the RP speaker's story is grounded in secondary school culture. 'Having a laugh' (Cardiff11 repeats the phrase) and 'taking the mick' (also repeated during the first seven lines) establish his community's investment in non-serious, non-literal interactional styles, universally (see emphatic 'it was like everyone', line 8). Membership in the community is referred to in the story world but is also offered to listeners in the textualising of the story: the discourse marker 'you know' is ingrouping, and it peppers the text.

Getting pool games for free is the topic, and it is iconic for this teenage culture, perhaps specifically for the boys. Cardiff11's manner of introducing it (10–12) is significant. The lexeme 'tief' ('thieve' = 'steal', probably of Caribbean origin) is familiar in Cardiff working-class usage (it is commented on by some respondents). As a restricted lexical variant it represents the act of stealing pool games as an ingroup practice. 'Like' is a multifunctional particle, but one of its functions is to downplay the need for accuracy in an account, similar to 'sort of thing'. In 12, 'like' with 'you know' familiarises the act of 'tiefing a few games'. Cardiff11 gives us access to his strategic thoughts ('so I thought oh I <u>know</u>'). He uses <u>oh</u> in conjunction with quotative 'thought', to mark transition from narrator account to protagonist strategising.

RP3's accident, unlike Cardiff11's, is told as an individual mishap. The narrative itself is definitely not *a high and strong cultural performance* (it does not meet this demand). There are many instances of 'I' subjects in the workup, and the 'we's referred to in 5–8 are fellow students doing what they should be doing in school. The only dramatic possibilities (losing fingers, being sick) don't eventuate in the story and ultimately *weaken* it as a cultural moment. RP3's belt sander and grazed fingers are real, face-value objects which refer to a degree of risk and damage caused. But Cardiff11's massive chainsaw is a far more powerful if less plausible creation, and it may earn credit in the listening group for its extravagance. Most interestingly perhaps, Cardiff11's story is *intense* through being strongly decontextualised. He makes few if any concessions to the narrating context – the presence of the researcher and the local audience being located in school. In contrast, RP3 develops his narrative from the contextual base of school in both the story and the telling frames – the belt sander is nearby at the time of telling the story and RP3 also works the school play and his 'subject circles' into the story context. He also accedes to an academic model of English usage – see his explanation of DT at 8 and his grammatical self-repair at 10 – which respects the school context of telling. Contrast this with Cardiff11's full-blown use of vernacular Cardiff grammar – double negation (4), first-person present-tense 's' morpheme in 'I puts' (12) and third-plural present 's' in 'they all comes' and 'they goes' (27). A culturally resonant story for young people is arguably one that does not defer too much to an institutional telling context. It will transcend that context (see our earlier comments about decontextualisation) – it will show high narrative control, on the culture's own terms, when institutional constraints can be bypassed.

What we called *the prat-avoidance demand* prioritises high personal control and resilience for a protagonist. Cardiff11 is certainly resilient in his first-person story. He is caught out in his attempt to 'tief'. His laughter (14) seems to be in both narrative and story telling frames – he literally laughs at his misfortune. This implies a high degree of control over unfolding events, emotionally if not materially. There is a complex reflexivity in his account: he tells his audience about himself (his strategic, 'fly', street-wise self), looking at himself (his trapped, failing self) and laughing.

All three 'good' stories (Cardiff11, NW10 and SW4) in this set are visually and perhaps filmically graphic and in that sense again *strong*: eating tea with one hand stuck in a pool table, then the prospected chainsawing; the cloaked diver who becomes the somersaulting rider; the disgusting wobbling rolls of fat. It is interesting that all three of these stories use the adjective 'massive'. They all also major on extravagance bordering on the surreal, particularly NW10. NW10's protagonist wearing a batman cape and a helmet when diving into a pool is a suitably bizarre conjunction. Building motorbikes from gate bars and doing a massive wheelie is simply *strong* action, until the kneecap freakishly comes out of his leg. NW10 is *resilient* at least to the extent that he provides this account unflinchingly, and this may be enough for him to *avoid* an accumulation of *prat* accusations.

The *authenticity demand*, which we suggested functions as a constraint on the *boring-avoidance demand*, does appear to be a second-level consideration. The patterns of judgement suggest that extravagance is the prior demand, and it seems to be on these grounds that Mid6 (from Newtown) and RP3 most evidently fail. Mid6 is not unlike RP3 in ultimately deferring to an authority figure to extricate himself from a problem with machinery. They of course avoid being 'boasters and bullshitters' because their stories and they themselves as narrators sound *authentic*, but they are also simply too dull. The audiences targeted by these tellers seem generally happy to willingly suspend their disbelief, when hyper-reality is in question. The authenticity demand appears to be more teller-focused than event-focused, and tellers are preferred if they withhold from excessive self-promotion and if they respect their audiences' interpretive norms – if they maintain personal integrity. In this way it may be that Cardiff11 navigates around the boasting and bullshitting charge more successfully than NW10 and SW4. NW10's story includes an apparently rehearsed, set-piece joke, that the protagonist was 'trying to kill himself but came up for air', which is inferably 'bullshitting'. His later account of the accident, the kneecap and its consequences positions him as an omniscient narrator, which he does not mitigate in the account. SW4 is not dissimilar in his pillorying of the fat rugby player who could not get his shirt on. His brief foray into what is clearly audible as self-deprecation – 'I had quite a bit of trouble getting into mine because I was quite big' (lines 15–16) – may not be enough to absolve him.

Discussion

It is increasingly difficult to identify a canonical sociolinguistics, and this is in many ways a state of affairs to celebrate. The diversity of perspectives and theoretical commitments that sociolinguistics entertains is broad and challenging, and it is important to remember the powerful interdisciplinarity that gave rise to sociolinguistics in the first place (Figueroa 1994). All the same, it may be useful to expose some of the contestable assumptions and perspectives that we think have surfaced in the present analysis, and which can be expected to surface in the context of a sociolinguistics of narrative.

The first relates to the terms 'culture', 'community' and 'group'. We have not addressed this range of terms explicitly in the analysis. We have paid most attention to 'culture', to engage with anthropological linguists' theories of how culture is textualised and decontextualised in discourse, not least in narrative texts. We have also referred to social groups and their boundaries (hence to intergroup relations), which adduces theory from the social psychology of language (see Giles & Coupland 1991, for an overview). What is at stake in this difference in terms? As Johnson (2000:46) says, 'group' has tended to be the default term in the study of sociolinguistic variation, where it has tended to refer to variation within a structured system of groups. The implication of social fixity in this approach is resisted in most uses of the term 'culture', stressing the admixture of evolving practices, values and norms that cultural membership entails. The distinction is therefore echoed in sociolinguistic theorising of 'communities of practice' (Holmes & Meyerhoff 1999; Wenger 1998) as a significant deviation from older sociolinguistic conceptions of the 'speech community'. (Rampton 2000 offers an illuminating critique of the history of 'speech community' in sociolinguistics and neighbouring disciplines.)

We have also held back from drawing a clear distinction between 'boys' culture' and 'girls' culture'. This is partly because (as we have mentioned) our study at this stage lacks directly contrastive findings from matched sets of male and female stories. But it is also because the wider judgement 'young people's culture' from which we have derived our account of narrative demands comprises both boys and girls, and we have noted that we found no statistically significant patterns of judgement between the gender groups. It may well be true that the male story-tellers in our data are enacting specifically male social identities, but these identities are up for evaluation and potential endorsement in a mixed-gender cultural ecosystem. If we read gender into the boys' projections, it is quite possible that similar patterns of evaluation by both boys and girls are reached on systematically different footings – different contextualisations of the performance demands we have discussed. But other sorts of analysis will be needed to confirm this.

Seeing these storytellers as taking part in a cyclical process of cultural enactment and redefinition captures the dynamic interplay between practice and evaluation that we see in the data. Intergroup theory, in Tajfel's and Giles's conceptions, has similarly been sensitive to how group members negotiate the boundaries that define them and their outgroups. It has also modelled the complex processes of social evaluation that generate group-status and group-affiliation as subjective phenomena. What mainly differentiates social psychological and anthropological/community of practice approaches in this regard is research methods. We hope to have shown in this chapter how it is useful to bring together insights from qualitative analyses of discourse with number-based analyses of social evaluation. The most positive outcome from this for us has been reassurance that what we bring forward as socially and textually meaningful in the five stories we have examined is framed in terms of young people's critical agenda rather than our own.

Our data have also, however, pointed up important differences of emphasis in sociolinguists' use of the terms 'practice' and 'performance'. We have followed linguistic anthropologists in working with a strong definition of performance, which explicitly separates 'mundane' from 'focused' communicative events and texts. Narrative of course has currency in both categories, and it is important not to overstate the boundary between them. At the same time, it seems there is much to lose by treating narrative data only as 'another form of practice'. The theoretical crux here is Bauman's idea of metaculturality, implying that performances (including at least some sorts of narrative performance) have the potential to iconise or otherwise reflexively represent cultural practice. The fact that young people readily appeal to specific demand characteristics for 'adequate' ingroup narratives (not being 'boring', not 'bullshitting', etc.) suggests to us that they are metaculturally active and adept.

Finally, there remains a tension between the neutrality inherent in the term 'practice' and issues of judgement and evaluation applied to language in use. The sociolinguistic principle of 'linguistic equality' is legendary, and this might predispose a 'descriptivist' orientation to narrative data, even when it is abundantly clear that issues of skill, individual difference and pragmatic success and failure are embedded in our experiences of storytelling. Hymes's (1996) research on 'narrative inequality' provides a crucial reminder that, as social psychologists of 'language attitudes' have demonstrated for some time, the most 'advanced' world communities are predisposed to finding incompetence rather than competence.

Competence judgements need to be visible in sociolinguistic research, but in a nuanced way that reflects what social evaluation achieves in the social world of talk. At one level, it is clearly *not* the case that 'bad storytellers' – those who know how to fashion an ingroup narrative of personal experience which conforms to general structural norms for story-telling but are not rewarded with judgement profiles as good as Cardiff11's – are excluded from a young (Welsh) person's community of practice. Narrative skill and perlocutionary 'success' are *not* straightforward inclusion criteria in that sense. It *is* appropriate to argue that 'what young people discursively do' – their 'communicative competence' in a more rounded sense, including speakership and receivership and variable degrees of individual success and acceptance – is what defines their community. But processes of social evaluation, and judgements of incompetence and failure, *do* have a key role in enculturation and a specific role in how narrative activity enacts culture. The cultural practice that we have been examining here is as much a matter of evaluative practice as it is a matter of performance practice. These two domains are linked in the concept of narrative demands. This is where we see the community establishing and negotiating its ideal forms, and performers achieving variable degrees of success in enacting them. Dialectically too, it must be where we see performers proposing and sometimes redefining cultural ideals.

Notes

* We are grateful to Jen Coates and Joanna Thornborrow for incisive comments on an earlier version. It is conventional but necessary to say that they are not at all responsible for all the unimproved bits.

1. We are grateful to the editors for helping us make this connection.

2. Jennifer Coates (2003) reports marked differences in her narratives by females and males. However, Don Kulick (2003) has pointed to the possible potency of context in this regard, commenting that, for example, the majority of the male conversations in Coates' study were recorded in pubs, while the majority of the female conversations were recorded in the home. We did not do a comprehensive content analysis of all the stories we collected to compare those by males with those by females, but no very obvious differences in the stories told by the two sexes emerged. Girls as well as boys told narratives that frequently involved conflicts with authority, acts of violence and under-age drinking, for example. British secondary schools are certainly productive sites for gender-relevant identity work. But there are few specific cues in our data (in the texts of the stories or the different sorts of evaluative data we have collected) that would have made it clear that gender was an important organising principle for these particular young people in these specific discourses.

3. An integrated account of the social evaluative findings from this research is available in Garrett, Coupland and Williams (2003). We deal only with a small subset of the young people's stories in the present chapter. A discussion of different aspects of the evaluative responses to 14 boys' stories, including the present five cases, is also available in Garrett, Coupland and Williams (1999, 2004).

4. The audio-recorded stories exist in two different versions – an original version and a version (of those stories taken for more detailed study) re-recorded under better acoustic conditions which was then edited for various phases of the evaluative work. The transcripts here are of the first versions, as originally performed to the class. Transcripts show short pauses as (.) and very minor breaks in the fluency of an utterance with a single dot. Primary syllabic stress is marked with underlining. Double brackets enclose partly audible material. Very occasionally the researcher's voice is audible in the recording, and her turns at talk are transcribed in italics. For the sake of anonymity, in the transcript of NW10, 'AB' replaces the name of a person mentioned by the storyteller, and similarly in the transcript of Cardiff11, CD replaces the name of a person.

5. In our preliminary statistical analysis of these quantitative data, we found no significant effect for gender. In other words, male and female teenagers were not evaluating the speakers differently, to a conventional level of statistical significance.

Chapter 5

Masculinity, collaborative narration and the heterosexual couple[*]

Jennifer Coates
Roehampton University

Introductory

In this paper, I shall focus on narratives produced in conversation by more than one speaker. The canonical narrative involves a single narrator, but conversational participants can choose to co-narrate stories. Collaboratively produced narratives, however, do not occur randomly throughout conversation: the evidence of my research is that male speakers in single-sex groups prefer solo narration. Collaboration in talk is typical of women's friendly conversations but is less common in all-male talk (Coates 1997a, 1997b), and this pattern seems also to be true of conversational narrative. The statistics for the narratives I've collected show a significant contrast in this aspect of story-telling: 22% of men's stories involve collaboration of some kind compared with 50% of women's stories.[1] (Where co-participants' contributions consist simply of minimal responses and laughter, stories were not counted as collaborative narratives, even though such contributions are clearly collaborative and are again more typical of women's narratives than of men's.) What these statistics show is that, in the conversations I've collected, women are as likely to tell a story in collaboration with a fellow speaker or speakers as to tell a story on their own. This is not true for male speakers, who collaborate in story-telling in less than a quarter of the stories told in all-male conversation.

By contrast, in mixed conversation involving heterosexual couples, male speakers seem happy to engage in collaborative narration. In other words, where male speakers can co-narrate with a female partner they will often choose to do so, even though the evidence is that they avoid co-narration where co-participants at talk are male. In this paper, I shall explore the phenomenon of collaborative narration involving heterosexual couples, and will attempt to answer the question: why do men choose to co-narrate in certain contexts and not in others?

The data

The narratives discussed in this paper were collected as part of a wider research project exploring gender differences in language use. The data-base resulting from this project includes all-male, all-female and mixed conversation.[2] Participants in all cases were friends (or close family in the case of some of the mixed conversations): in other words, recordings were made of groups or pairs of people who had a well-established relationship. The choice of pre-existing friendship groups as informants was determined by the need to obtain large amounts of spontaneous speech and to guarantee that such speech was relaxed and informal (Milroy 1987:35).

The methodology employed in this research is an innovative form of participant observation: after contact was made with a group, they were asked to take responsibility for recording their conversations.[3] My contact with the groups was often via an intermediary, whose relationship to the group – or to one individual in the group – might be that of friend, colleague, girlfriend, or sister. The assumption was made that any self-consciousness induced by the presence of the tape recorder would be overcome by the strong normative pressure which such groups exert over their members. Participants were simply asked to record themselves when they were with their friends.

Collaborative narration

Collaborative narration requires very careful syntactic, semantic and prosodic monitoring on the part of both speakers, and is characteristic of people who know each other well. Of course, in one sense all talk involves co-operation, and increasingly conversation is seen as an achievement which involves "the collective activity of individual social actors whose final product ... is qualitatively different from the sum of its parts" (Duranti 1986:239). But the joint telling of a story is only possible where conversational participants know each other well, have shared knowledge of the topic, and are prepared to do the work of co-narration.

Here is an example of a collaborative narrative jointly told by an older married couple, Arthur and Marian, to their daughter Kim and their grandson William. I shall follow the normal convention used by those who work on conversational narrative of presenting the story in numbered lines, each line corresponding to one of the narrator's breath-groups or intonation units, typically a grammatical phrase or clause (Chafe 1980).

(1)   THEY LOST A CHILD [BS05-15]

[*Arthur's words are in normal typeface; Marian's words are in italics; Kim's are in ITALIC CAPS*]

1   *THEY LOST A CHILD DIDN'T THEY?*
2   they lost one son
3   *they lost er- their son in his twenties*
4   *he dashed across the road to get . um-*
5   ((there's a)) big dual carriageway=
6   *=dual carriageway . um*
7   and he leapt over the=
8   *=leapt over the centre barrier=*
9   *=that's right=*
10   *=and was killed=*
11   =couldn't stop
12   cos a car came up as he- as he sort of landed from that=
13   *=yeah=*
14   *=CAR HIT HIM =*
15   *=mhm=*
16   *=yeah, he was in his twenties wasn't he*
17   she was distraught wasn't she
18   *yeah, when they came over here he was er- it w- it hadn't long happened*
19   *and they were still . very much in grief and- with it*
20   mhm
21   *MHM, SHOCK*

This is a relatively short narrative but it is a good example of the collaborative style adopted by male narrators when they co-narrate a story with a partner.

In this example, there is also collaboration with a third speaker, the daughter, whose utterance *they lost a child, didn't they?* initiates the story.

So what are the main features of collaborative narrative? Firstly, collaborative narration involves two narrators making contributions to the story which join together seamlessly (note the frequency of the latching symbol in the transcript (=) which indicates that turns follow each other without any gap).

Secondly, collaborative narration involves frequent repetition. This can involve phrases – for example, *dual carriageway,* lines 5 and 6, or whole clauses – for example, *they lost one son//they lost their son in his twenties,* lines 2–3. Speakers also rephrase each others' ideas using different words (for example, *they were very much in grief,* line 19, rephrases *she was distraught,* line 17). Another significant feature of collaborative narration is the shared construction of utterances. For example, Arthur says *and he leapt over the=* (line 7) and Marian completes the utterance: *=leapt over the centre barrier* (line 8). There is also frequent use of back channel support to signal acceptance of the other speaker's contributions (*that's right,* line 9; *yeah,* lines 13, 16, 19; *mhm,* lines 15 and 20). A collaborative narrative constitutes a powerful display of 'togetherness'. In this example, Arthur and Marian display their shared knowledge of events to their daughter and their grandson.

Storytelling as duet

The joint telling of a story is sometimes described as a 'duet'. This term was coined to describe examples like (1) above, where the two co-narrators function as a single speaker (Falk 1980). 'Duetting' is characteristic of friendly talk among women but is far less common in all-male talk. The co-construction of stories, however, is now recognised as a key way for couples to 'do' their relationship in public (Mandelbaum 1987). It seems that the very reasons that explain men's reluctance to collaborate in duetting with other men can explain their willingness to share in duetting with a female partner. The reasons are men's fear of the feminine and their need to construct themselves as heterosexual. Heterosexuality is a key component of hegemonic masculinity: co-narrating a story with another male performs connection with another male, which men try to avoid; by contrast, co-narrating a story with a female partner performs coupledom as well as heterosexuality, so is highly valued.

Let's look at two more examples of collaborative narrative where the narrators are a heterosexual couple. The first of these examples comes from a conversation involving two couples. It is an extract from a very long narrative told by Ian, a man in his 30s, about his experiences delivering parcels for a major delivery firm. The extract comes from the opening section of the narrative – Ian's partner Diane's words are in italics. (Note: lines prefixed with a vertical bracket are spoken simultaneously by Ian and Diane, as are words printed between ** and **.)

(2)   Extract from PARCEL DELIVERY [BV03B-15]

1   he said- he just said to me "Do you know the Old Kent Road?""
2   I said "Yeah",
3   he said "You'll be all right then",
4   he sent me to Rotherhithe with a hundred and two parcels,
5   *on Ian's first day <LAUGHS>*
6   my first day
7   a hundred and two drops
8   blocks of flats, shops, doctors' surgeries,
9 |there were drugs-
10 |*and you couldn't deliver half of them could you?*
11   [...]
12   I had no lunch break
13   I just went flat out
14   I did seventy drops
15   I m- I came back and |((xxx))
16 |*<LAUGHS>*
17 |((xx)) I've got thirty parcels
18 |*Ian didn't speak for twenty minutes ((xx))*
19 |I got- I got thirty parcels ((xx))
20 |*still in shock weren't you darling*
21   [...]
22   *the supervisor said "blah blah blah how many did you have?"*
23   I said "I dunno"
24   he said "Where's your sheet mate?"
25   I said "I dunno mate" [...]
26   and he went "Jesus mate what've they done to you?"
27   I was like "((xxxx))"
28 |he went "oh blimey"
29 |*((xxx)) first day ((xxx))*
30   so he- I went through it all
31   and he went and got this sheet
32   and he said "Fucking hell mate,
33   hundred and two drops" he said.
34   *"you should only have fifty"*
35 |*"you should've only have fifty to start with"*
36 |*"it was only your first day"*
37   [...]
38   and I'd done |twenty more than I should've
39 |*yeah it was just like*

40   *"oh here comes the **wanker of the week*
41   *let's see** if we can pull a fast one", yeah*
42   ***ooh I couldn't believe it***

Ian is the chief narrator of the story 'Parcel delivery'. He tells a very long story about the trials and tribulations of delivering parcels in the Rotherhithe area of London on a hot summer's day. His story fits the classic pattern observed in men's stories (Coates 2000, 2003; Johnstone 1990, 1993) where the lone protagonist engages in contest with something or someone – here, with the impossible demands of the job. Ian's super-human efforts mean he triumphs over these demands, but at enormous cost.

Ian's story makes several points: one is that delivery firms are incredibly inefficient; another is that Rotherhithe is a dangerous places; but most importantly that he was set an impossible task by the parcel delivery firm. The main theme of the story is his heroism: Ian constructs himself as a hero, but he emphasises rather than conceals the physical cost of his triumph. The final evaluative line of the full story is *it was just incredible*, a line which recapitulates *ooh I couldn't believe it* (line 42). Such statements emphasize the extraordinariness of what he experienced and make a strong claim for tellability. To claim that the events narrated were "not ordinary, plain, humdrum, everyday or run-of-the-mill" (Labov 1972: 371) is an important task for a narrator, particularly a male narrator. Male narrators, in both single-sex and mixed contexts, are concerned to communicate to story recipients that they have experienced something which deserves special attention.

So in many ways this story performs a conventional version of masculinity. But at the same time the story is a performance of coupledom. Ian is supported in his narration by his partner, Diane, and many parts of the story are told as a duet. As the example in (2) above illustrates, Diane adds significant information to the story (lines 5, 10, 18, 20, 29, 36) as well as making contributions which move the story along (for example, *the supervisor said "blah blah blah how many did you have?"*, line 22; *you should only have fifty*, line 34). There is a great deal of repetition, including whole lines such as *you should only have fifty* (lines 34 and 35); the phrase *first day* recurs throughout the narrative. Diane's contributions often overlap with Ian's (lines 10, 18, 20, 29, 36, 39, 40), a feature of the story which is highly collaborative and symbolises connection between the two speakers. Sometimes overlap results from Diane adding a comment to Ian's narrative: *still in shock weren't you darling*, line 20; *first day*, line 29. Sometimes it results from polyphonic talk, where co-narrators make parallel points simultaneously (lines 17–20, 38–42).

It is not just Diane who contributes to Ian's narrative: Jean and Martin do too (though this aspect of the narrative is not illustrated by the example given here). They comment on the inefficiency of the delivery firm (for example, Jean says *they need to organise themselves* and *that's a ridiculous waste of money*) and ask questions about what happened (for example, Martin asks *what did they say then when you said you had thirty?*). They also provide collaborative completions (for example, Ian describes putting a parcel on one side, then losing track of it, with the words *when you come to the end you think=* and Martin provides his imagined thought: *=there it is*). So Ian's narrative is multi-functional: it performs a dominant version of masculinity, which re-affirms his gender identity in front of his partner and friends, it displays coupledom in that Diane makes significant collaborative contributions which demonstrate their shared knowledge of the events recounted, and it also performs friendship in that all four conversational participants feel free to contribute to the telling. Ian's story is carefully designed to achieve all these functions.

Alternative masculinities

Sometimes the couples context allows male speakers to explore less conventional versions of masculinity. The following story is initiated by Gemma, who invites Sam to co-narrate it with her.[4] Sam takes some time to warm up but by the end of the story he is the main narrator. The story is told to their friend Adam.

(3)   INTERESTING WEEKEND (BS01-10)

[*Gemma's words are in normal typeface; Sam's in italics*]

1   you remember when we were going shopping a few weekends ago in the West End?
2   we st- we were trying to park the car in Berner Street near Middlesex Hospital about 2 o'clock in the afternoon
3   and Sam was making a second attempt to get it into the parking space
4   when the taxi just drove up behind him
5   and they have a collision
6   and um go on Sam what happened?
7   well the taxi driver says to the passengers
8   *yeah hit me from behind*
9   "Well do you believe this? can you believe this?"
10   Sam gets out of his car

11   and starts ranting and raving about who was right
12   *yes I was calling him everything under the bloody sun, yes*
13   and the taxi driver's saying you know "me, I was stationary,
14   and you- and you reversed into me,
15   I thought you were-
16   I thought you were leaving, not parking"
17   *and I said ""How on earth was I leaving if I was indicating what I was getting in- into this parking space?"*
18   [...]
19   *and then I went and lost my credit cards*
20   that wasn't that day was it?
21   *the same day, yes, yes* [...]
22   *I went to um to Oxford Street to Bookstock* [...]
23   *and I bought a few books*
24   *and I left my cards behind* [...]
25   ahh but you didn't discover until Sunday
26   you didn't realise your credit cards were missing
27   *yes I didn't realise until next Sunday*
28   *that I didn't have my- my- my wallet with me*
29   *so I lost my cheques my address my credit cards*
30   *everything in there*
31   ***my store cards***
32   **but he thought** because he'd been to Earl's Court to buy some newspapers
33   that he had dropped them **in the newsagents in Earls Court**
34   ***in the sto- in the newsagent in Earls Court***
34   [...]
35   *so that was a **beautiful weekend shopping in the West End*
36   *my car being hit from behind***
37   **so this is all- this is the outcome
38   this is all from you know because of the taxi**
39   *and I'm- I've **lost my credit cards***
40   **the taxi you know** all the incident happened from that
41   *so you know that was a very interesting weekend*

[Words printed between ** and ** are spoken simultaneously by Sam and Gemma]

This is a classic disaster story of the kind frequently found in women's friendly talk. In fact it is two disaster stories: first, Sam reverses into a taxi which mistakenly thinks he is leaving the parking space; second, Sam leaves his wallet in a bookshop because he is in such a state after the collision with the taxi. There is no way that Sam can be seen as a hero in this story: the story is told to entertain his friend Adam with its unremitting theme of things going wrong.

So this story does not construct dominant masculinity in the normal sense. What it does do, though, is construct coupledom. Through co-telling a story, Gemma and Sam "achieve the appearance of being together in interaction" (Mandelbaum 1987:147). Gemma initiates the story, a story which revolves around Sam, and she invites Sam to tell it with her (*go on Sam what happened?* line 6). Sam eventually accepts this invitation, though he allows Gemma to act as the main narrator in the first part of the story. Once the story moves on to the loss of his wallet, however, Sam narrates the story jointly with Gemma. This narrative exhibits many features of duetting: the two co-narrators say the same thing in different words (*they have a collision//yeah hit me from behind*, lines 5 and 8; *he starts ranting and raving//I was calling him everything under the bloody sun*, lines 10 and 11), they repeat each other's words (*still no sign of any police//any police* from omitted portion; *in the newsagents in Earls Court//in the newsagent in Earls Court*, lines 33–34), and they complete each other's utterances (*he thought he'd dropped them//in the sto- in the newsagents*, lines 32–34). There is also increasing use of overlapping narration as the story comes towards the end, with Sam and Gemma summing up simultaneously (lines 37–41). Sam ends the story with the (ironic) evaluative line *so that was a very interesting weekend*.

This story functions as a powerful display of 'togetherness'. Sam and Gemma display their shared knowledge of events to their friend, and their collaboration symbolises the closeness of their relationship. Note how Gemma tells us what Sam 'thought' in line 32 (*he thought … that he had dropped them in the newsagents in Earls Court*). This is a strong way of indicating how close they are: "To suggest that one has knowledge of someone else's thoughts … implicitly claims intimacy with them." (Mandelbaum 1987:163). Sam and Gemma choose to present themselves as a couple, rather than one of them telling a solo story. The topic of the story – a bad weekend – is more in the tradition of women's disaster stories than of men's more achievement-focussed narratives.

The next example again involves a man collaborating in story-telling with a woman partner in order to explore a theme untypical of classic masculine stories. This story, 'Bats', comes from a conversation involving three friends, Paul, Becky and Roger. The story is initiated by Paul but is then jointly told by Paul and his partner Becky; it follows on from talk about cockroaches.

(4)   BATS [BS01-12]

[*Becky's words are in italics; Roger's in italic capitals*]

1   but I mean you know that's nothing [..] compared to our little horror story
2   we never expected that thing remember in Italy
3   *you um do you mean Viareggio? <LAUGHS>*
4   *oh god never again*
5   *WHAT? YOU DIDN'T TELL ME ABOUT THIS*
6   *well yes in a- in a- on a holiday in Italy and um I think a few summer- a few*
     summers ago
7   *well you know when it's when it's very hot*
8   *I mean you just close **the shutters and leave the windows open you see in old*
     buildings**
9   **here when you go out you leave your windows open for the room to get
     cooler**
10   *and it was you heard all this flipping and flapping around [MHM]*
11   *and put the light on*
12   *and lo and behold the room is full of bats [LAUGHTER]*
13   *of all things [OH MY GOD]*
14   *so we're trying to get these bats out of the <LAUGHING> window with sheets*
     and goodness knows what you know
15   *and I nearly had a heart attack [OH NO]*
16   *and the next morning we went down to breakfast*
17   *and set about trying to explain to the front desk you know about this*
18   *and he says "ah si si pipistrello pipistrell- pipistrella" <MIMICS ITALIAN*
     VOICE>
19   bloody pipistrello
20   [*LAUGHTER*]
21   *I said "oh that's what it's called in Italian is it?"*
22   *I said "yeah well it's not very nice you know"*
23   you know sleeping there
24   *having those- <LAUGHING> those flying around in your room*
25   *WHAT DID THEY SAY?*
26   *they just said "well um you know-"*
27   "we'll get somebody to you know- we'll send somebody"
28   *they just shrugged their shoulders you know*
29   yeah but it's the shock isn't it you know?
30   I mean you are there, you are in- a- in a dark room
31   and then-
32   *yeah it's the shock*

33   *I mean the- the- the flapping of a- a- of wings*
34   *it sounded like it was a little bit too- too loud for just a mosquito* [MHM]
35   **I thought it was a ghost
36   I mean you know I thought a bloody ghost
37   I mean you know somebody was there you know**
38   ***first of all I thought it was birds*
39   *birds you know*
40   *a bird, birds,** a bird in the room*
41   *and switched on the light*
42   *and oh my god what a shock*
43   *can you imagine all these bats flying around you know*
44   yeah she thought they were going to come to suck her
45   and you know she thought they were bloody- you know
46   she has seen too many films of Dracula you know
47   **she thought it was Count Dracula was coming for her you know**
48   ***I was go- I was screaming***
49   screaming there
50   ***"get out!"* <LAUGHING>**
51   **you know jumping on top of the bed** with a pillow hitting them you know
52   *getting the sheets <LAUGHS> and slapping them <LAUGHS>*
53   *aw dear it was a nightmare wasn't it?*
54   *and then it's all in the morning as though oh you know pipistrello*
55   *it's like it's a- you know a regular thing you know*
56   *you have it in your hotel room in Italy*
57   *pipistrellos flying- flying around*
58   ***bats in your-* <LAUGHING>**
59   **yeah very shocking you know**
60   it was very shocking really you know
61   being woken you know by flapping you know
62   *wings ugh it's something- I'll never forget that*
63   *never never never*
64   yeah you can take it the- the- the you know the funny side of it
65   Dracula you know a real adventure but-
66   *ugh yes one of your worst nightmares come true.*

[Words printed between ** and ** are spoken simultaneously by Paul and Becky]

This is a story whose central theme is fear, a theme more typical of women's stories than of men's. Paul introduces it as *our little horror story,* a framing device which allows for the telling of frightening events. By using the pronouns *we* and *our* and by appealing to Becky's memory *we never expected that thing remem-*

ber in Italy, Paul invites her to co-narrate the story with him. This both displays their relationship, but also creates a space for him to collaborate in the expression of fear. The two co-narrators collaborate in maintaining the theme of fear throughout the story. Paul uses the word *shock* in line 29 and this is echoed by Becky in line 32 and again later in line 42. Paul repeats the phrase *very shocking* (lines 59 and 60) as part of the closing evaluation; he also confesses to having thought the bats were *a bloody ghost*. But it is Becky who presents herself, in stereotypical feminine style, as nearly having *a heart attack* (line 19) and as screaming (line 48), while Paul describes her as fantasising that *Count Dracula was coming for her* (line 47). (Paul's claim *she thought it was Count Dracula was coming for her* again involves one partner in a couple claiming to know the other's thoughts.) Becky's final line *ugh yes one of your worst nightmares come true* underlines the scariness of their experience and nicely mirrors Paul's opening (with *nightmare* balancing *horror story*).

Although each narrator gets extended turns at telling the story, there is also a great deal of overlapping talk where co-narrators make the same point in different words (for example, lines 8 and 9, where both narrators explain the Italian practice of closing the shutters in daytime in summer; lines 35–40, where both narrators recount their first response to the bats). There are also collaborative completions (for example, *screaming there//"get out"*, lines 49–50) and repetition of words and phrases (*screaming*, lines 48 and 49; *it's the shock*, lines 29 and 32).

Paul and Becky put a great deal of effort into convincing Roger that what they experienced was extremely frightening. The first half of the story concentrates on the events, the second half on their reactions. They only move on to the exploration of their reactions once Roger has shown that he is fully in sympathy with their story. His initial minimal responses develop into stronger response forms such as *oh my god* and *oh no*. He also laughs loudly when the protagonists' English horror is contrasted with Italian nonchalance (lines 18–20).

The narrative 'Bats' shows a young man reminiscing about a frightening experience and proving capable of owning feelings of vulnerability. It is significant that he manages to do this when telling a story collaboratively with a female speaker, a woman who he feels very comfortable with. Paul uses collaborative narrative to construct himself as someone in relationship with a woman and as someone who is not afraid to talk about frightening experiences.

New men?

It seems that when men are talking to other men they prefer to tell solo narratives rather than to co-construct stories (Coates 2003). But in mixed company, men will often choose to tell a story in collaboration with a female partner. In this paper I have looked at several examples which illustrate this phenomenon. The story 'They lost a child' (extract 1) is told by an elderly couple (Arthur and Marian) to their daughter and grandson. The story 'Parcel delivery' (extract 2) is told by Ian with significant collaborative support from his female partner to their friends, another couple in their 30s. The story 'Interesting weekend' (extract 3) is told by a young couple in their 20s to a male friend. The story 'Bats' (extract 4) is told by another young couple to a male friend.

As these examples show, collaboratively constructed narratives arise in a variety of settings and are told to a range of recipients. But all these examples exhibit the key features of collaborative talk: repetition, joint construction of utterances and overlapping speech. In all of them, the narrative floor is shared by two people; and in all of them, this sharing of the floor symbolises the connection between the two speakers.

Dominant discourses of masculinity assert independence and downplay connection. In all-male contexts, men have to affirm their separateness from each other in order to avoid the accusation of homosexuality (Cameron 1997; Connell 1995: 78; Frosh et al. 2001: 2; Jukes 1993: 43). But in mixed contexts, it seems that men have more latitude to explore a wider range of masculinities and to display more feminine aspects of themselves. Does this mean that the men who co-construct narratives with female partners are exemplars of the 'new man'?

To answer this question, I want to focus on two examples which occur in sequence. They come from the same conversation as 'Parcel delivery' and involve the same two couples, Diane and Ian and Jean and Martin. What is remarkable about this sequence of two stories about kittens is that both stories are collaboratively constructed, with Jean and Martin telling the first and Diane and Ian telling the second.

(5)   KITTENS 1 [BV03B-32]

  [*Jean's words are in normal typeface, Martin's in italics*]

1   we looked out of our window today
2   we saw two little kittens didn't we?
3 |I thought "what the hell is that doing out there"
4 |*dashing past the window yeah, tiny*

5   **cos I thought i- it was too young to be out
6   one of them was like that
7   just chucked in the garden**
8   ***only one of them that big and one was just a little bit bigger there*
9   *it just- they had the-* **
10   I thought |"((xxxxxxxxxxx))"
11 |*chasing each other round the garden*
12   I knocked next door,
13   I said "have you got two new kittens?",
14   and he said "yeah",
15   and I said "Have they escaped or something or what?",
16   "They're alright as long as they don't go that way",
17   like pointing to the road,
18   I thought well can't really guarantee that really can you?
19   *no the road is a- it's a busy road.*

[**** lines between double asterisks are spoken simultaneously]

This narrative is co-constructed by Jean and Martin, and recounts a shared experience. They describe an incident when their neighbour's new kittens were allowed to wander unchecked in the garden; they both express concern for the kittens and emphasise how small they were. Jean initiates the story with two narrative clauses, then Martin joins in so that the orienting details about the kittens is jointly produced in simultaneous speech (staves 2–10). This is a very good example of the way two speakers can hold the floor simultaneously for an extended period, in defiance of theoretical claims – and common-sense assumptions – that only one speaker should speak at a time.[5] Recipients have no trouble processing this kind of polyphonic talk (Chafe 1997).

Jean provides the narrative core of the story, with Martin providing a final line which extends Jean's previous line. These two last lines are essentially evaluative, expressing in different ways their anxiety over the kittens. Both the evaluative stance and the topic of the story can be seen as feminine rather than masculine, and it is only in narratives in mixed conversation that I have found men adopting such values and choosing such topics.

Jean and Martin's story is followed directly by another one, told by Ian and Diane, again on the subject of kittens. The story is initiated by Ian, who makes the topical link with the first story, but Diane provides the second line, and from then on they construct the story collaboratively, with occasional contributions from Jean and Martin. Example (6) gives an extract from this (longer) story. ('Jazz' is Ian and Diane's cat.)

(6)   KITTENS 2 [BV03B_33]

[*Ian's contributions are in normal typeface; Diane's in italics; Jean's in italic capitals*]

1   it's like that stupid bat who lived next door to me in . Allen Close
2   *she had a cat that could |never have been more than five weeks old*
3 |she- she had a . ((little)) cat that big
4   *no way maybe even four weeks old*
5   like that
6   *NOT WITH THE MOTHER? [no] OH THAT'S AWFUL*
7   ((there)) there and sh- she put it out for the day
8 |((xxxxxxxxxxxxxxxx))
9 |((*put it out there*))
10   *and Jazz used to bring it home*
11 |she just put it out
12 |*and it is so tiny*
13   *it couldn't even get through the cat flap*
14   it couldn't |reach up into the cat flap
15 |*that's how . tiny he was*
16   [...]
17   *he was completely black and just absolutely . adorable wasn't he?*
18   and on one day "bug doosh" <SOUND EFFECT>
19   through there |in the catflap ((2 words))
20 |*and one day he actually got through*
21   *and i- he was- he was hanging through the catflap with his little paws dangling*
22 |he was like <RUNNING NOISE>
23 |*but . he couldn't get the rest of his body through*
24   and he got through the cat flap
25   and that was it
26   he used to come |in and out and then out
27 |*they went up and down the stairs*
28 |they w- it didn't want to go
29 |*we used to feed him and everything*
30   and she used to put it out all day like
31   I mean this thing was like . just could not survive
32   *I used to get in from work and ((take it from)) the door and feed him and everything*

'Kittens 2' is a classic example of collaborative narration. The story is co-narrated by two speakers who share the floor to give an account of a shared experience, using repetition of words and phrases and simultaneous speech to tie their contributions together. The narrative falls into three sections. The first (lines 1–15) provides orientation (details about who, where and when) and an abstract: *it couldn't even get through the catflap*. The second section (omitted from this extract) consists of a habitual narrative, describing the relationship between the kitten and their own cat Jazz and finishing with the evaluative line *it was so funny*. The final section describes the kitten finally managing to get through the catflap. The narrative ends with evaluative lines which re-state the opening theme of the neighbour's irresponsibility, thus framing the narrative and simultaneously aligning it with the previous narrative.

This example, like the previous one, shows that male speakers can perform alternative versions of masculinity in certain contexts. Ian and Martin both choose to collaborate in narratives where the topic is kittens and where key themes are care and concern about vulnerable creatures. Such themes are not characteristic of narratives produced in all-male talk. What seems to be crucial about the circumstances of this conversation is that both men (Ian and Martin) are in stable partnerships with women, and the four speakers are also friends with each other.

So does this mean that Ian and Martin and the other men whose stories have appeared in this chapter are 'new men'? It is certainly the case that, when co-constructing stories with female partners, men engage with topics which are rare in (or absent from) all-male talk, topics such as death ('They lost a child'), fear ('Bats'), concern for small animals ('Kittens 1' and 'Kittens 2'). Moreover, in co-constructing a narrative with another speaker, male narrators display human connection, something they tend to avoid in all-male contexts. So in some ways it is true to say that collaborative narration involving a man and a female partner performs a different kind of masculinity and displays more feminine aspects of manhood.

But if we examine Ian and Diane's contributions to 'Kittens 2' carefully, we can see that as co-narrators they still take up conventional gender positions relative to each other.[6] Diane's contributions draw on a nurturing or maternal discourse; examples are *Jazz used to bring it home* (line 10), *we used to feed him and everything* (line 29), *I used to get in from work and ((take it from)) the door and feed him and everything* (line 32). They also pay attention to the kitten's adorability and smallness: *he was [..] just absolutely adorable wasn't he?* (line 17), *that's how tiny he was* (line 15), *with his little paws dangling* (line 20). Ian contributes more narrative clauses than Diane (compare lines 11 and 12 where Ian's narrative clause *she just put it out* is said at the same time as Diane's evaluative line *and it is so tiny*). Ian's contributions focus more on the kitten achieving its goals: *and within the week he learned how to get there* (from the omitted central section); *and he got through the cat flap and that was it* (lines 24–25). So Ian and Diane simultaneously perform coupledom through collaborating in story-telling and also maintain gender distinctions through subtle differences in the perspectives they adopt as co-narrators.

Another question which needs asking is: why is it that men *only* co-construct stories in mixed talk with female speakers? The mixed conversations are full of collaborative narration, involving heterosexual couples, male and female friends, fathers and daughters, mothers and male family members, as well as mothers and daughters, sisters, female friends. But there are no examples in the mixed conversations of men collaborating with other men to tell a narrative. Why should men avoid collaborative talk in the company of male peers and in mixed company? Is it the case that, given the homophobia which informs hegemonic masculinity, men avoid ways of talking which display closeness with men for fear of being accused of being gay? And in mixed talk do men choose to co-construct talk with a female partner to display their non-gayness? Heterosexuality is at the heart of dominant versions of masculinity, so when male speakers perform the heterosexual couple through co-narration with a female partner, they are by definition also performing hegemonic masculinity.

In other words, far from being 'new men', the male speakers who collaborate in story-telling with female partners are very much 'old men'. They may exploit the potential of co-narration with a woman to tell stories on less macho topics, but through displaying their connection to a woman they are performing heterosexuality and therefore (hegemonic) masculinity.

Conclusions

As the examples in this chapter demonstrate, the collaborative construction of talk, specifically of narrative, is not confined to female speakers. But male speakers, in the conversations I've collected, are more likely to construct talk collaboratively in mixed company rather than in all-male company. Perhaps the most significant finding to come out of my analysis of mixed talk is that male speakers only share the construction of narrative with female speakers: there are no examples in the mixed conversations of collaboratively constructed narratives involving two male speakers. This suggests that collaborative modes of talk may be avoided by male speakers in contexts where the closeness symbolised by co-construction threatens hegemonic masculinity, and, by contrast, may be chosen in contexts where the closeness symbolised by co-construction functions as a display of heterosexuality.

Notes

* This paper is a revised version of the one I gave at the Cardiff University Round Table held at Grygynog in July 2001 (a slightly different version appears as Chapter 7 of my book, *Men Talk*). I am grateful to all participants at the Round Table, whose comments have helped me in the revision process.

1. The statistics for collaboration are given in Table 1 below:

Table 1. Collaboration in male and female narrative

	Men's stories [N = 203]	Women's stories [N = 257]
Collaborative narration	45 [22.2%]	128 [49.8%]

2. I am extremely grateful to all those who agreed to allow their conversations to be used in this project, particularly those whose mixed conversations are included here. Some of the recordings were made initially by other researchers, including students taking my Conversational Narrative course at Roehampton University. I would like to put on record my gratitude to the following for giving me access to these recordings: Robert Clark, Joanne Fieldhouse, Elinor Green, Sarah Pascall, Sarah Prince, Julia Stevens, Karl Stuart, Jonathan Waldron.

3. I started using this methodology in 1985. Other sociolinguists who have collected conversational data using a similar approach are John Wilson *On the Boundaries of Conversation* and Ben Rampton *Crossing*.

4. This story has been edited for reasons of space. Omissions are marked by the symbol [...].

5. The classic exposition of the one-at-a-time theory of conversational turn-taking is found in Sacks, Schegloff and Jefferson's article 'A simplest systematics for the organisation of turn-taking in conversation' (1974). Sacks, however, was well aware that overlapping speech is a regular feature of relaxed conversation among equals (see his *Lectures on Conversation*). For further discussion of this issue, see Coates (1994, 1997a, 1997b).

6. I am indebted to Julia Stevens for this insight.

Chapter 6

Contextualizing and recontextualizing interlaced stories in conversation

Neal R. Norrick
Saarland University

Introduction

This chapter explores how two tellers contextualize and recontextualize their interlaced stories in collaboration with one another and the other participants in a natural conversational situation. In what I call *interlaced* stories, two tellers team up to perform related personal narratives as sequential stories with common characters and events, where the second presents a continuation of the first. Interlaced stories represent a resource for conversational narrative performance, ranging between first story-second story organization and collaborative narration of a shared story. The recording described also contains retellings of the stories, related for a new arrival to the conversation, and in the retelling the tellers coordinate their performances and interlace their stories more closely. These retellings afford an unusual opportunity to investigate how tellers accommodate their stories to each other after they have already 'practised' once. The primary tellers accomplish the recontextualization of their stories the second time through with plenty of input from the other participants, giving us a window through which we can observe the ongoing re-interpretation of life stories and the events they describe.

Interlaced stories, response stories, and co-narration

The stories to be considered here constitute a special case of narrative sequencing and co-narration. They differ from first story-second story sequences, in which the second teller constructs a narrative matching the foregoing one in topic or point. They also differ in organization from collaborative narrative performances involving two or more participants telling a shared story. Response stories are produced in reply to previous stories by another participant. They may be second stories, responding thematically to the immediately foregoing story, in the sense of Sacks (1995), or responses to various preceding stories, perhaps in a longer series of related stories, as described in Norrick (2000). Response stories either seek to establish common experience, saying 'the same thing happened to me, . . .' or they competitively seek to 'top' previous stories in some way, saying, for instance, 'an even funnier/scarier thing happened to me.' Either way, response stories ratify foregoing stories and provide participants with a resource for saying 'me too.'

In collaborative co-narration, all co-tellers have had access to some common previous (at least vicarious) event, so that there is no need to establish common experience and no competitive 'story topping', though participants may still vie for the right to tell. Instead, participants routinely subordinate their personal perspectives to the effort of performing their co-narration as a 'team', in the sense of Goffman (1959). Co-narration of this kind provides participants with a resource for saying 'we two' to each other or portraying it for an audience (see also Coates this volume).

In performing interlaced stories, the participants again have no need to establish common experience, since the personal events they are recounting are dovetailed; and they have no basis for competition, since they must both subordinate their personal narratives to the common performance in order to get the story told. Their narratives are not topically the same, but rather concerned with interdependent events. Furthermore, since the boundary between the two interlaced narratives is clear, there should be no vying for the turn. Indeed, in the example below, the transfer of the floor is accomplished so explicitly that even a first-time listener recognizes when the telling responsibilities have shifted. Interlaced stories provide participants with a resource for organizing interrelated experiences into an ordered sequence.

In interlaced stories, the first story leads into the second, while the second story continues and complements the first. The two stories share characters and even events, in addition to sharing a theme and perspective, as we expect from an initial and a response story. In the present example, the man who proposes marriage in the first story was staying with the couple whose proposal event is reported in the second story, and the proposal described in the first has a real effect on the reception of the proposal in the second.

Moreover, since the recording contains a retelling of the two stories melded together into another 'double proposal story', it reveals special processes of recontextualization as the tellers adjust their respective contributions to interlace their stories more closely the second time around for a newly arrived recipient. Practice and subsequent discussion of the interlaced stories apparently results in identification of a central narrative point and streamlining the rest to lead up to it. The tellers in effect 'edit' their performance with the help of co-participants. We will see in particular (1) how the tellers clearly demarcate their respective roles within the unified story; (2) how they subordinate their personal stories and telling goals to the team performance; (3) how they shorten their parts to highlight the humor; and (4) how they focus on a single punchline identified during the first telling and subsequent talk.

In a recent article based on these same stories (Norrick 2005), I concentrated on how the tellers co-construct conflicting cultural models of marriage proposals for humor. Except for that article, the literature on narrative contains no references to what I call interlaced stories, though collaborative telling of shared past experience has received attention from such authors as Watson (1975), Tannen (1978), Falk (1980), Quasthoff (1980), Goodwin (1986), Schegloff (1992), Boggs (1985) and Norrick (1997, 2000). Watson, Boggs and Goodwin especially have documented the influence of co-tellers on the trajectory of a narrative through differential interest and competence in the details of talk. Tannen brings out the importance of differing expectations about what counts as a story and how this can lead to dissonance between co-narrators, while Quasthoff identifies various strategies by which listeners become co-tellers. Falk describes 'conversational duets' between two co-narrators presenting a story for a third party; she shows how collaborative telling affects turn-taking and related matters such as simultaneous speech. Chafe (1998) analyzed two spontaneously produced tellings of the same story, drawing out "things we can learn from repeated tellings of the same experience" as he puts it in the title of the article (see Norrick 1998 for comment). My own work has explored both co-narration and retelling of a wide range of story types. In particular, I have investigated when and how stories are retold, including cases of retelling by multiple co-narrators, and co-narration as a team performance (Norrick 2004).

Although I shall focus on the contextualization and subsequent recontextualization in the telling and retelling of these stories, interlaced stories are quite interesting for their own sake; in particular, interlaced stories raise questions of how tellers decide where their respective parts begin and end, and how they effect the transition from one story to the next. They shed special light on the question of 'storytelling rights' in the sense of Shuman (1986) and Blum-Kulka (1993): when stories are so closely related, the sequential tellers may more easily participate in each others' stories, even becoming full-fledged co-tellers. The fact that we have retellings here gives us a special purchase on these issues, but my focus on recontextualization means I will be most interested to explore how the tellers alter their stories the second time through and the role other participants play in re-contextualizing the stories.

Both the interlaced stories I examine here tell how two women recently received proposals of marriage. Proposal stories belong to the more general class of 'life stories' in the sense of Linde (1993). In particular, they count as stories about 'landmark events', in describing a salient juncture in a person's life. The proposal stories in my data again represent a special class of landmark event stories, because they are told as funny personal anecdotes, obviously as much for their entertainment value as to inform hearers about the events leading to a new personal status. Unlike typically funny landmark events such as 'my first job' or 'learning to drive', proposals might be expected to yield serious and romantic stories rather than funny ones, so that this is a significant feature for the classification of the stories here as well. The contextualization of a story as humorous affects the performance in various ways, as we shall see.

The data and context

Cordelia, Lois and Emma are young German university academics and good friends. They are visiting acquaintances in Birmingham. The three women all speak English quite fluently, though they occasionally produce somewhat unidiomatic constructions and suffer from different word-finding difficulties than native speakers. Neither of these problems seems significantly to affect their ability to present their interlaced stories quite effectively, then to re-present them, even more closely interlaced. Cordelia and Lois had already related their proposal stories to Emma and each other before the evening's recording, as comes out in the passage of conversation following the first tellings.

James and Lucy are their hosts, and George comes to visit shortly after the proposal stories were told for the first time. These three participants are all monolingual British English speakers. James alone is the recipient of the first version of the stories, while Lucy and he both act as recipients of the retelling. During the retelling, Emma and George are engaged in a parallel conversation on a separate topic. Their two-party talk is clearly audible on the tape, and both conversations were, in principle, accessible to the other group, though neither conversation was being attended to by the participants of the other.

The conversation was recorded on a mini-disc player, and everyone but Lucy knew they were being recorded. In any case, all the participants are accustomed to Emma recording whenever she comes to visit, so that there are no obvious taping effects of the kinds one sometimes finds, such as speakers addressing the recorder directly or shying away from speaking (see Norrick 2000). All participants' permission to use the tape was, of course, secured later, and all the personal and place names have been changed to preserve the anonymity of the participants. Since the taping, I have conducted sociolinguistic interviews with some of the participants to gain insights about their relationships and their impressions of the taped conversation.

A summary of my transcription conventions appears in an appendix. The first tellings run to line 137 of the transcription. They are followed immediately by some discussion about the prehistory of the stories and their primary tellers (lines 138–168). Although about nineteen minutes intervene before the retellings commence, I have numbered the second excerpt consecutively from 169–238 to avoid confusion.

The two proposal stories

Let's begin at the beginning and set the scene for the initial telling of the first proposal story. It has developed that Cordelia is pregnant and that the date of conception was the day she was proposed to. Lois speculates (line 1–2) and Cordelia immediately confirms: 'it was exactly that night'. James' response, 'That's great' at line 4 prompts Emma to state, 'You should hear the story of the proposal'. This sort of story elicitation shows that Emma already knows the story herself and that she finds it tellable (see Labov 1972 and Sacks 1992 on 'reportability' and 'tellability' of stories). She goes on to explain why, starting in line 7: 'this is so funny, 'cause the two of them were proposed to' within such a brief period. At first it sounds as if Emma intends only to elicit Cordelia's story in relation to the discussion of her pregnancy, but she justifies its tellability with the humor of the close connection between the two proposals. Thus, Emma initially contextualizes the two stories as funny due to their interrelation, though not necessarily taken separately.

THE PROPOSAL STORIES

1	Lois:	… I said to Hank,
2		I bet it was exactly that night.

3	Cordelia:	it was exactly that night.
4	James:	that's great. {clapping his hands}
5	Emma:	and you should, you should hear the story of the ehm proposal
6	Cordelia:	{laughing} yeah that,
7	Emma:	I mean this is so funny,
8		'cause the two of them were proposed to
9		within I don't know, [three]
10	Lois:	[twenty-four hours]
11	Emma:	two days, yeah
12	James:	oh really?
13	Emma:	it was so funny.
14	Lois:	it was so funny.
15	James:	fantastic.
16	Cordelia:	yeah, (1 sec.) we had the dramatic version,
17		they had the- what is it?
18	Lois:	the romantic, [slash funny]
19	Cordelia:	[the romantic]
20		{general laughter}
21	James:	let's have it then
22	Cordelia:	well, I don't know,
23		for some reason Ernie had to move out first
24		and then two days,
25		we were both kind of
26		you know
27		on the the verge of a nervous breakdown,
28		to realize that maybe it wasn't a good idea, {chuckles}
29		I went to him and I wanted to talk
30		eh with him about some problems,
31		we were having
32		and he kind of thought
33		I wanted to break up or something,
34		I don't know
35		anyway, he moved out,
36		and then (3 sec.)
37		well, he realized it was the wrong idea
38		{laughing} to move out
39	James:	yeah, yeah
40	Cordelia:	yeah, and then,
41		he proposed in a park in Stuttgart,

42		it was really cute,
43		in a little hut,
44		on a ehm children's
45		what is it?
46	Emma:	[playground]
47	Lois:	[playground]
48	Cordelia:	yeah, on a playground,
49		we sat like this in one of these little huts
50		and we had a little ehm,
51		well, candles and everything
52		and we were just,
53		I just went there to have a talk with him
54		you know, to know,
55		what he was going to do,
56		if he was going to come back
57		or you know
58		something like that
59		and then he just-
60	Emma:	and it [rained]
61	Cordelia:	[proposed] and [it was raining like hell]
62	James:	[o:hh]
63	Cordelia:	[yeah, it was raining]
64	James:	[o:hh], oh God, it's like a film.
65	Emma:	[yeah.]
66	Cordelia:	[yeah,] and our poor dog,
67		I always had to look at Spot, you know,
68		because the hut was so small,
69		so the dog had to stand outside in the rain.
70	Emma and James:	{laughing}
71	Cordelia:	and the ears like that
72	Emma:	{laughing} (6 sec.)
73	Lois:	and Hank and me, we we're sitting ehm at home,
74		waiting f- you know, eh, uh,
75		and when Ernie did didn't come home,
76		I thought: "okay, he made it."
77		or "they made it."
78	James:	uehh {laughing}
79	Emma:	Ernie had moved to them
80	Lois:	yeah, exactly
81	James:	Oh, really?

82	Emma:	and they were there waiting for him.
83	James:	oh God, that's a great [story.]
84	Cordelia:	[mmh,] well, it was (2 sec.)
85	Lois:	yeah, in the end,
86		it turned out to be
87		really romantic, didn't it?
88	James:	{laughs}
89	Emma:	and then it really spoiled [Hank's plan to propose to Lois]
90	Lois:	[Hank's (1 sec.) yeah]
91	Cordelia:	yeah.
92		{general laughter}
93	James:	oh no, he'd, he had already planned it?
94	Lois:	he had planned it for ages, you know.
95	James:	[oh no:]
96	Lois:	[he'd told his friends and stuff,]
97		and the, the moment he asked me,
98		I just didn't get it, you know, so,
99		because it was our ehm anniversary,
100		you know, when- the day we met.
101	James:	mmh
102	Lois:	and I gave him a ring, you know,
103		and he opened the little box
104		and he looked at me and said:
105		{door bell ringing} "you know, but now,
106		now you've you've got to marry me"
107		and I said: "yeah, sure, yeah, yeah."
108		and he was like: "no,
109		do you want to marry me?" {squeaking door}
110	James and Cordelia:	{laughing}
111	Lois:	yea:h.
112		and he was like:
113		"you got it all wrong, you know,
114		that's because of Ernie."
115		because I was so preoccupied with Ernie and Cordelia's
116		thing that I didn't really,
117		I didn't think that there would be
118		something s- serious going on in my relationship.
119	James:	that's neat.
120		oh that is terrible.
121	Lois:	so it took him a third time to to to

122		make me ehm realize that this is a serious proposal
123		[oh my God]
124	James:	[so you eventually] got it?
125	Lois:	yeah, I got it.
126	Cordelia:	yeah and then you'd
127		you didn't say that you said:
128		"you don't have to do this just because [of Ernie"]
129	James:	[oh no:]
130	Lois:	and he was like: "uahh"
131		and he, {laughing and slapping her thighs}
132	James:	oh no, that's terrible!
133	Lois:	yeah
134	James:	that's terrible. {squeaking door} how funny.
135	Emma:	yeah, that's funny.{laughing}
136	James:	that's a ga-
137		that's a great combination of [stories that is.]
138	Emma:	[yeah, isn't it?]
139		and we met like a few days later at a friend's house,
140		the three of us,
141		and this friend,
142		and they were both telling their stories
143		and then I
144	Lois:	yeah
145	Emma:	knew already that Lois had been asked too,
146		and I kind of
147	Lois:	yah {laughing}
148	Emma:	pushed her and said:,
149		"now, come on."
150	Lois:	{slapping her thighs}
151	Emma:	and then Lois started to tell this long story
152		of how they went
153		and had dinner on their anniversary.
154		and ehm we thought, you know,
155		we thought the punchline was somewhere else.
156	James:	yeah
157	Emma:	because he surprised her with a certain restaurant
158		and we thought:
159		"ah that was it, that was the story."
160	Cordelia:	{laughing}
161	Emma:	that was, you know {laughing}

162		but then, it went on and on
163		and finally it was the proposal
164		and we were all {gasping}
165		{general laughter}
166	Lois:	Steven couldn't believe it, you know.
167	Emma:	he was so envious. {laughing}
168	James:	that's classic.

Cordelia comprehends the proposals and stories as separate, at least initially. As well she might, inasmuch as her story is tellable and humorous independent of Lois's. Moreover, the original impetus for the storytelling is Cordelia's pregnancy; and the proposal scene she describes is 'like a film', according to James. She characterizes her own story as 'the dramatic version' in line 16, and is not sure how to characterize Lois's, saying 'they had the- what is it?' When Lois offers 'the romantic, slash funny', Cordelia accepts at least the term 'romantic' at line 19. And when, following the general laughter, James requests 'let's have it then' in line 21, it sounds as if he were asking Cordelia for her story alone. Though Emma seems to want to contextualize the two stories as a funny interrelated event from the start, Cordelia and James are focussed on Cordelia's story alone. As the telling progresses, we shall see Cordelia come around to Emma's perspective on the two proposal events as constituting an overarching narrative with a single major humorous crux.

Still, this first time through, Cordelia tells her story as if it were an independent composition. Her initial statement at line 22, 'well, I don't know, for some reason Ernie had to move out first', sets up the story as a progression of events with the proposal as its goal. The initial discourse marker *well* signals an introductory passage with background information (see Norrick 2001 on specifically narrative discourse markers). Cordelia describes the proposal scene itself as 'really cute' (line 42), and the following details about the little playground hut, sitting 'like this' (with appropriate body language), the candles, the rain and the unfortunate dog present a touching vignette, definitely tellable for its own sake. As noted above, James even comments, 'Oh God, it's like a film' at line 64. Thus, Cordelia's story meets the description, 'romantic slash funny', which Lois seems to intend for her own story in line 18. The locale and characters shared by the two narratives will appear only once Lois begins her story. And even Lois seems to take the relationships between the stories for granted, leaving it up to Emma to explain: 'Ernie had moved to them' at line 79 and 'they were waiting for him' at line 82.

By contrast with Cordelia's self-contained story, Lois' story develops only as a result of the foregoing narrative. We have observed that Lois and Hank were at home waiting to see what happened with Ernie and Cordelia. Emma really initiates Lois' story with her summary preface (line 89) that Ernie's proposal to Cordelia 'spoiled Hank's plan to propose to Lois'. Hank's proposal seems to be triggered by Ernie's: indeed, Lois hears it that way, because she 'was so preoccupied with Ernie and Cordelia's thing' (line 115). Lois reports at lines 113–114 that Hank said, 'you got it wrong, you know, that was because of Ernie'. Ironically, Cordelia even delivers the punchline of Lois' story this first time through. In saying at lines 127–128, 'you didn't say that you said, "You don't have to do this just because of Ernie"'. Cordelia reminds Lois of the salient speech she presumably recalls from a pre-England version of the story. This speech serves as more than the humorous punchline of Lois' story; it locates the decisive connection between the two proposal stories. After all, Ernie's proposal is both facilitative and inimical to Hank's, it both leads to and spoils Hank's proposal. Cordelia's formulation of the punchline for Lois here marks her growing acceptance of Emma's perspective that the two stories ultimately constitute parts of a more comprehensive narrative. The punchline speech parallels the one attributed to Hank in lines 113–114: both speeches end in 'because of Ernie', and Lois may be telling a different version here. In any case, Lois immediately latches onto this speech, adding, 'and he was like "uahh" and he', {laughing and slapping her thighs}. This elicits a flurry of evaluations and laughter, thus effectively ending her story. We shall see below that Lois recalls this formulation and cites these words almost verbatim in her retelling.

Let's return for a moment to the differentiation of the original stories as 'dramatic' versus 'romantic slash funny', starting in line 16. The tellers had referred to their respective stories with these terms before the trip to England. While Cordelia calls her own story 'dramatic', and Lois apparently calls her own story 'romantic slash funny' in line 18, she can be heard as modifying or replacing the word 'dramatic' from Cordelia's previous phrase. Cordelia herself repeats 'the romantic' overlapping with the end of Lois' turn, again presumably referring to Lois' story, though the extraneous noise and laughter surrounding her comment, as well as the reaction to it, make it difficult to determine just how the recipient, James, receives the identifications. When James says, 'let's have it then', as the laughter dies down, it sounds as if he was requesting the 'romantic slash funny' story just mentioned, and Cordelia naturally begins. After all, Emma prefaced the whole event by saying 'this is so funny, because the two of them were proposed to so close together': if the humor lies in the temporal proximity of the proposals, either one or both might be romantic in and of itself.

Furthermore, Cordelia calls her own proposal scene 'really cute' at line 42; and Lois says of Cordelia's story in lines 86–87 'it turned out to be really romantic, didn't it?' Now, this is just the sort of comment someone makes who has seen her initial assessment realized. (Compare James' comment 'it's great, isn't it?' at the end of the second telling – a comment which confirms his remarks introducing the story for Lucy.) In any case, Lois' evaluation of Cordelia's story stands as the final assessment, leading directly into Emma's clear initiation of the second story with 'and then it really spoiled Hank's plan to propose to Lois' at line 89. And indeed, Lois' story is both more dramatic than Cordelia's and less romantic. Except for the brief scene where Lois presents a gift to Hank, he opens it and broaches the subject of marriage for the first time, the story thrives mostly on the dramatic irony that Lois repeatedly fails to understand the serious nature of Hank's proposal. From an outsider's perspective, then, Cordelia's story is romantic slash funny, Lois' story is dramatic slash funny, and the two stories together as 'the double engagement story' develop a special humor through the interlacing of the two proposals and the characters involved. The women reflect this vision in their initial contextualization for James, whom they entrust with more personal details, since the stories grow out of Cordelia's pregnancy story, and in their recontextualization for the new hearer, Lucy, for whom they reorient the stories toward the dramatic humor of the interlaced proposals rather than their personal landmark events.

There is some confusion about time in the stories. In her initial justification for telling the stories, Emma begins by saying the two women 'were proposed to within I don't know, three ... ' Now, this could mean three hours or three days. As the only person present who should know the time frame exactly, Lois interrupts Emma to say 'twenty four hours', which Emma immediately changes to 'two days', with no further correction from Lois. In Lois' actual story, it sounds as if Hank proposed the very same evening as Ernie. That is, the listener gets the impression that Lois and Hank waited to see what happened with Ernie and Cordelia, and when Ernie did not return, they celebrated their anniversary and Hank proposed. A little reflection after the fact makes it clear that their proposal episode must have taken place the following day, once they knew for sure about Cordelia and Ernie, and on the proper day of their anniversary. In fact, in her retelling, Lois clearly states, 'and the next day, Hank and me, had our anniversary' (lines 208–210). The problem of the time frame of the story is attended to in the recontextualistion of the story, as we will see.

As the only uninitiated listener, and thus the primary recipient of the story, James has considerable influence on the trajectory of the first tellings. His appeal, 'let's have it then', at line 21 effectively ends the evaluatory prefacing and segues into the story proper. When James responds to Cordelia's scene of the proposal in the park in the rain with 'oh, oh God it's like a film', he ratifies this initial performance as a story tellable for its own sake and marks a potential end for the story. Cordelia, however, tacks the short description of the poor dog, rounding out the image she characterized as 'really cute' at the outset in line 42. Here again, Cordelia validates her own story as independently tellable.

Even when Lois seems to have begun her story, James is still fixed on the initial proposal. He apparently hears Lois' initial information about Hank and her waiting simply as part of Cordelia's story, and reacts to it with 'oh God, that's a great story' at line 83. His evaluation actually causes Lois to backtrack and produce her own final comment on Cordelia's story: 'yeah, in the end, it turned out to be really romantic, didn't it?' (lines 86–87). Emma gets Lois' story rolling again with her summary preface, 'and then it really spoiled Hank's plan to propose to Lois'. James reacts to this preface with appropriate surprise and a question, 'oh no, he'd he had already planned it?' (line 93). James prepares a potential end to this story as well with a double, somewhat paradoxical evaluation in lines 119–120: 'that's neat. Oh that is terrible'. When Lois continues with an apparent coda, James again responds with a potential pre-closing, 'so you eventually got it?' at line 124. This time, Cordelia extends the story, because she feels Lois has forgotten the punchline, as noted above. Lois then describes Hank's reaction, and James once again offers closure with 'oh no, that's terrible' at line 132 and again 'that's terrible. how funny' at line 134. He then concludes and summarizes the dual telling in line 137 with 'that's a great combination of stories that is'. We shall see how James continues to influence the telling and trajectory of the stories through their retelling below.

Emma plays a significant role in the organization of the telling performance. As we have seen, Emma first mentions the proposal stories in the context of discussion about Cordelia's pregnancy: 'You should hear the story of the proposal' (line 4). She justifies the telling of Cordelia's story with its relationship to Lois' story from the very beginning: 'because the two of them were proposed to', thereby linking the stories and setting the stage for the dual telling. It is Emma who first supplies the missing word 'playground' at line 46, and it's Emma who inserts the detail that it rained at line 60. The fact that it was raining elicits James' remark that 'it's like a film' at line 64, and prompts Cordelia's digression about the dog. Emma is also responsible for getting Lois' story back on track by saying that Ernie's proposal 'spoiled Hank's plan to propose to

Lois' at line 89. Following the first set of stories, from line 138 onwards, Emma gives some background on events preceding the trip from Germany to England. In that passage, Emma describes Lois' pre-trip report of the proposal as 'this long story' (line 151) that 'went on and on' (line 162), saying 'we thought the punchline was somewhere else' (line 155). At the time, Lois was drawing out the story to build up to the actual proposal, which was new information at the time. For an audience already aware that the two women have become engaged, the stories must be recontextualized, and Lois must identify a new 'punchline'. Emma's evaluation of Lois' pre-England story is not lost on Lois herself, who has apparently streamlined her telling here in Birmingham, leaving out 'how they went and had dinner' (lines 152–153) and the 'certain restaurant' (line 157). Clearly, Emma's influence on the stories started even before the evening of the recording.

There is another brief recontextualization accomplished by Lois and Emma apparently just for one another, and perhaps for Cordelia, right at the end of the passage following the first telling. After Emma's assessment that 'it was the proposal, and we were all {gasping}' in lines 163–164, Lois evokes a different response to the stories, namely that of another friend Steven, who heard that very first presentation of the two stories back in Germany. Since James does not know Steven, this comment can only be addressed to Emma and Cordelia. Emma then laughingly recalls Steven's reaction to the proposal stories: 'he was so envious' at line 167. For a recipient who wishes he might experience a romantic engagement of his own, the stories clearly bear a different significance.

Retelling: The double engagement story

Turning now to the retellings, this time it is James who elicits the stories. He asks Lucy, who has been in the adjacent kitchen, if she has 'heard the eh story, the engagement story' in lines 169–170, insisting that there is but one story, namely 'the double engagement story' (line 173). This leads Lucy to make the explicit request, 'well, tell me' at line 178.

THE DOUBLE ENGAGEMENT STORY

169 James: have you heard the eh (2 sec.) story?
170   the engagement story.
171 Lucy: what do you mean?
172   no, I don't know.

173	James:	the double engagement story.
174	Lucy:	no. no.
175	James:	it's a peach.
176	Lucy:	oh no
177	James:	it is total quality.
178	Lucy:	well, tell me,
179		I didn't know.
180	Cordelia:	it's really strange,
181		you know, Ernie and I quarreled,
182		oh we didn't really quarrel.
183		I wanted a serious talk,
184		and he moved out.
185		right.
186		and then two days or three days,
187		I don't remember, later,
188		we decided to have a talk,
189		and we met in a little park,
190	Lucy:	o:h
191	Cordelia:	and then, when I got there,
192		he asked me to- if I wanted to be his wife.
193		you know, so he had really decided it wasn't a good idea.
194		yes, and then mea- meanwhile,
195		he was staying at Hank's and Lois' place,
196		you know, and ehm yeah
197	Lois:	yeah
198	Cordelia:	you- your turn.
199	Lucy:	your part, your part
200	Lois:	{clearing her throat}
201		uah, and and the thing was we actually
202		at that, you know, at that night
203		we were sitting there waiting
204		whether Ernie would come back or not.
205		and he didn't.
206		so, we knew.
207	Lucy:	it was good news, yeah
208	Lois:	and the next day,
209		Hank and me,
210		we had our anniversary,
211	Lucy:	yeah.
212	Lois:	and Hank asked me whether I

213		I'd wanted to become his wife, you know.
214	Lucy:	no?
215	Lois:	and at first I just didn't get it, you know.
216	Lucy:	yeah
217	Lois:	so he opened his present
218		he said:
219		"you know, but now you have to marry me."
220	Lucy:	{gasps} [o:h] {very high pitch}
221	Lois:	["yeah sure, sure"]
222		"no, no, no, no.
223		do you want to marry me?"
224		and "yeah, of course,
225		I mean, you must know that, yeah, sure"
226		and then he, he ha- had a third try
227		and then I realized
228		and then I said:
229		"you don't have to do that,
230		just because Ernie asked Cordelia"
231	Lucy:	{gasps}
232	Lois:	"oh uahh, I've planned that for ages,
233		all my friends know it,
234		how can you say that?"
235	Lucy:	oh no:,
236		o:h fantastic,
237	James:	it's great isn't it?
238	Lucy:	that's- tha- I can't believe it.

James not only recontextualizes the two interlaced stories as a unitary 'double engagement' story, he also insists on his perception of their cohesion in a single unit, referring to 'it' twice: 'it's a peach' in line 175 and 'it is total quality' in line 177. Given Emma's determination that the 'punchline was somewhere else' during the discussion following the first tellings (line 155) and Cordelia's own identification of the punchline in the remark Lois forgot to report, namely: 'you didn't say that you said, "You don't have to do this just because of Ernie"' at line 128, it is hardly surprising that Cordelia keeps her own part of the story to a minimum. She really just sets up the background for the now central portion by Lois. After all, the first telling grew out of interest in Cordelia's pregnancy, but this time around the context has been reduced to this humorous double story with Hank's misunderstood proposal at its center. James and the story-tellers seem to judge that the new recipient Lucy will be more interested in

the humorous 'double engagement story' than in the personal life stories of
Cordelia and Lois.

While Cordelia's story was slightly longer than Lois' in the first tellings, in
the retelling Lois' part comes out significantly longer than Cordelia's. Thus, in
the first tellings, Cordelia's story is the central topic for about 63 lines (from
around line 7 to line 69), compared to about 59 lines (line 73 to line 131) for
Lois, whereas in the second telling, Lois' part runs for about 35 lines (from 200–
234), compared to only about 15 lines (from 180–194) for Cordelia. Cordelia
leaves out all the 'romantic slash funny' details about the little children's hut,
the candles, the rain and the dog. Somewhat curiously, although she reduces
her story in all other respects, Cordelia expands her account of the span of
time intervening between Ernie's leaving and their meeting. In the first telling,
she says simply 'and then two days' (line 24), while in the second, she records
her uncertainty about the chronology, saying 'and then two days or three days,
I don't remember, later' (lines 186–187). Except for this digression about the
elapsed time, Cordelia gives the impression of rushing to the point where she
can report that Ernie had been 'staying at Hank's and Lois' place' (line 195),
so that she can hand the telling over to Lois with the words 'you- your turn' at
line 198. In pointedly saying 'your turn' to Lois, Cordelia explicitly recognizes
the intimate connectedness of the two stories, and the team character of the
performance. In doing so, she further contributes to the impression that her
story serves as the build-up to Lois' punchline.

Nevertheless, Lois has also streamlined her story, reconceptualizing it as
the logical consequence of Cordelia's story. After the transitional passage about
her waiting at home with Hank, Lois clarifies the somewhat confusing time
relationship from the first telling, saying: 'and the next day, Hank and me, we
had our anniversary' (lines 208–210). Lois reorganizes her story to focus on the
salient piece of dialogue which makes it a humorous personal anecdote rather
than a serious narrative describing a landmark event of personal achievement
or self-recognition, namely her response to Hank's proposal: 'you don't have
to do that, just because Ernie asked Cordelia' in lines 229–230. This statement
not only marks the climax of Lois' story, but also displays the bond between
the two stories, since Ernie's proposal prepares for but also frustrates Hank's
proposal. Emma's comment that 'the punchline was somewhere else' at line
155 in the passage following the first telling, and Cordelia's identification and
insertion of the so-called punchline into the first telling at line 128 impel Lois
to incorporate the speech in her retelling practically verbatim from Cordelia,
as we have seen. At the same time, Lois leaves out the whole section containing
the parallel speech attributed to Hank ('you got it all wrong, you know, that's

because of Ernie' in lines 113–114 of the first telling) in this second telling. She also includes the information, prompted by James' question in the first telling, that Hank had been planning his proposal for a long time already. She even dramatizes it in this second version as dialogue by Hank himself: 'oh uahh, I've planned that for ages, all my friends know it' in lines 232–233.

At this point we should note what a supportive audience Lucy makes, as her immediate response 'your part, your part' at line 199 demonstrates. She, too, hears the sequenced performances as 'parts' of a larger narrative. Following the transitional passage, Lucy immediately affirms: 'it was good news, yeah' (line 207). Her other back-channels are frequent and carefully placed. Her gasp and ingressive 'oh' (at line 220) and the gasp (at line 231) surrounding the central passage are especially effective, and her pre-final comment in lines 235–236 have some of the paradoxical quality we noted in James' comment above: 'oh, no:, o:h fantastic'. James also continues to register his interest. Since he elicited the story, and praised it highly in advance, his final contribution is more a request for confirmation of his original assessment than a new evaluation as such: 'it's great, isn't it?'

In their retellings, both Cordelia and Lois have reoriented their stories toward the crucial punchline in the second (part of the) story. This reorientation stresses the humorous interlacing between the subdivisions of the shared story. From the outset, the women have negotiated two incongruent views of proposals. On the one hand, they evoke the traditional model with such 'romantic' trappings as candles, dinner and rings, but on the other hand they display a more 'modern' attitude, according to which women play a more active role and men may be inept without losing face and risking failure. This incongruency between the romantic and modern models creates distance and humor. When James and his wife Lucy co-narrate their own proposal story later on, they, too, draw out the incongruencies between the romantic model and their own proposal 'lost in a peat bog'. The co-construction of conflicting cultural models in a series of narratives also creates a window through which we can observe the ongoing negotiation of attitudes in and through stories. This aspect of the tellings and retellings is treated in depth in Norrick (2005); important here is the way the women recontextualize their stories toward humor for a new recipient and as a result of having recently 'practised' telling their shared story with considerable input from the other participants.

Conclusions

First, to summarize the observations, we have seen how two women tell in-terlaced stories, then recontextualize them as a unitary, humorous narrative during a second telling. The news that Cordelia is pregnant prompts Emma to announce 'the story of the proposal'. Emma bases the tellability of the story on the humor of the paired proposals received by Cordelia and Lois, but Cordelia tells her story as independent the first time through, and James re-sponds as if to a story tellable in its own right. Emma initiates Lois' story by stating the relationship between the stories, saying Ernie's proposal to Cordelia 'spoiled Hank's plan to propose to Lois'. Lois must construct her story around Cordelia's, but she fails to identify the crucial punchline linking the proposals. Cordelia reminds her to report her statement: 'You don't have to do this just because of Ernie.' Cordelia's formulation of the punchline for Lois here serves to more closely lace the two stories together into a single comprehensive nar-rative for both tellers. Talk following the initial telling further underlines the perception of the separate performances as an indivisible narrative whole.

When Lucy arrives, James announces 'the double engagement story', rec-ognizing the two stories as parts of a single whole, in the sense of Emma's initial announcement, and the tellers launch into a coordinated retelling. This second time, Cordelia revises her story as the set-up for Lucy's part, and even marks the transition by saying 'your turn' to Lois. Lois takes over, and cites the punch-line Cordelia identified almost verbatim. This close accord in the content and presentation of the two related strands produces a unified performance of a hu-morous narrative, and demonstrates a special case of recontextualization and team performance by two primary tellers, with the aid of their co-participants.

Finally, to expand the conclusions reached, through these data I have in-vestigated a case of co-ordinated telling which lies between response stories (about similar but separate experiences) and collaborative narration (about shared past experience), namely telling related events in relatively separate parts, with a tendency toward team performance, reinforced through practice and retelling. We have seen how a first telling, the co-narration with intrusions and recipient comments, functions as a resource for tellers to find the point of story and identify their parts for a second telling of interlaced stories. We have observed the role co-participants can play as co-editors in identifying the crux or punchline of a narrative and helping streamline the performance toward this crux in a subsequent performance. This process of telling, co-editing and retelling is a resource for group members to get their story straight, figure out the point of events, and to redesign their story for new recipients in the group.

Further, the investigation of interlaced stories through tellings and retellings yields special insights into the contextualization and recontextualization of narratives in conversation. We have seen the effects of 'practising' with input from co-participants as a resource for revising stories for future tellings. We have noted particularly the significant role played by the other participants in eliciting stories, shaping them in various ways, guiding the teller along a particular path, inserting details and dialogue. Co-participants aid tellers' memories, help them see connections, and may even help them locate the punchlines in their stories. Telling and retelling stories reveals new perspectives on the events they relate and new ways of organizing them.

Practising stories changes them. Personal stories do not simply rehearse a remembered series of events; they reconceptualize the events of the tellers' lives. In particular, we have seen how: (1) co-editing can occur during and after performance; (2) retelling with co-editing by co-participants can streamline and focus stories; (3) in the case of interlaced stories, co-editing can lead to teamwork, where the co-tellers subordinate their personal perspectives to the overall effect of the narrative performance. We recognized important differences between stories which indicate 'me too' and those which indicate 'we two' in areas of (1) establishing common experience, (2) competition through story topping, (3) the organization of conarration, and (4) the potential for team performance. The interlacing of interdependent stories thus offers conversational storytellers a special resource for narrative performance, ranging between first story-second story organization and full-blown collaborative narration of a shared story.

Appendix

The transcription was produced from a mini-disc recording by my students and me according to the conventions summarized below.

Transcription conventions

Each line of transcription contains a single intonation unit.

she's out.	Period shows falling tone in the preceding element.
oh yeah?	Question mark shows rising tone in the preceding element.
well, okay	Comma indicates a continuing intonation, drawling out the preceding element.
bu- but	A single dash indicates a cutoff with a glottal stop.

says "oh"	Double quotes mark speech set off by a shift in the speaker's voice.
[**and so**-]	Square brackets on successive lines mark
[**why**] **her?**	beginning and end of overlapping talk.
da:mn	colon marks unusual length in preceding vowel
(**2 sec.**)	Numbers in parentheses indicate timed pauses.
{**sigh**}	Curly braces enclose editorial comments and untranscribable elements.

CHAPTER 7

Hearing voices

Evasion and self-disclosure in a man's narratives of alcohol addiction

Dick Leith

Introduction

The American anthropologist Dennis Tedlock was once asked by a Native American informant, "When I tell you these stories, do you picture it, or do you just write it down?" (1983:55). The question implies a challenge to any researcher collecting data 'in the field', particularly, perhaps, to the student of narratives. Stories need listeners, and a narrative needs to be listened to as a story, not merely as a sequence of narrative clauses interspersed with asides and bounded by a frame. Listening to a story means acting not just as a scholar but also as a human being, with a heart as well as a head.

So implied within the question is the assumption that the fieldworker has more than one self; and this is also something we can say about the people we collect stories from. Much has been made of the claim that we tell stories to establish an 'identity', or, more precisely, identities. When the story is likely to be one of personal experience, the acts of telling and listening may become highly charged. In narrating incidents of great personal weight we sometimes put our identities on the line, so to speak; and as listeners we are sometimes made to feel conscious of a trust that is being invested in us. At least as far as the teller is concerned, such stories often have great therapeutic value.

A great deal of narrative research, both within sociolinguistics and beyond, seems to have been undertaken on the (tacit) assumption that storytelling is a positive, enriching experience for listeners as well as narrators. One thing I would like to do at the outset of this dicussion, however, is to question this assumption. Sometimes, hearing a story may feel like an imposition. Instead of feeling grateful, or touched, we may feel dumped on. This is most likely to occur, perhaps, when the narrator has simply taken the listener's interest for granted, without first preparing the ground.[1]

The material on which this chapter is based was not conceived as sociolinguistic research; indeed, it did not originate as research in any way. Its origins lie in a story told by one friend to another, at a time when the listener was actually reluctant to listen. The listener was myself; the teller, who I shall call Mac, tells narratives of personal experience referred to in the title of this chapter. At the heart of our relationship is friendship, and this raises ethical issues which I, as the listener, feel I need to take seriously. I have a responsibility to honour that relationship, and I have sought my friend's collaboration throughout the writing of this account. So before discussing the stories in question I need to talk about friendship: first in general terms, and then this one in particular.

Friendship, gender and storytelling

Friendship is the subject of a recent study by the sociologist Ray Pahl. "Every generation", he suggests, "has to rethink friendship in its own terms". By the end of the twentieth century social, economic, democratic and cultural changes "emphasised choice, individualism and individuality". But we still need the support of, and commitment from, others. "Friendship", he concludes, "can cope with these tensions better than the fixed and formal ties associated with family and organisations. Friendship has to be egalitarian and democratic: it has no place in hierarchies or authoritarian structures" (2000: 166). Friendship can be a vital way of negotiating, or re-negotiating, our sense of identity, and it is perhaps most valuable when we are undergoing a profound change in our life-course.

Friendship can be realised, or performed, through shared activities and shared talk, and there is a general feeling that friends ought to help you in times of crisis (summed up by such utterances as 'you find out who your real friends are'). So friends can function as quasi-therapists, and one way they do this is by attentive listening.[2] But there is also a widely-held view that men differ from women in the ways they 'do' friendship. Jennifer Coates refers to a number of such differences. "...(M)en have a history of friendships which stress sociability rather than intimacy, which could be described as 'side-by-side' rather than 'face-to-face'" (Coates 2003: 104). Sociability is often expressed by 'having a laugh', taboo-breaking speech such as swearing, making sexist and homophobic remarks, competitive banter, and the exchange of ritual insults. In behaving like this, men attempt to demonstrate a dominant form of 'masculinity', which means keeping women and gays in their place, and refusing to reveal vulnerability or doubt (although the last-mentioned characteristics can be disclosed to a female confidante).[3]

According to Coates, however, men do have ways of achieving greater intimacy with each other through the exchange of stories. While men are generally keen to display through their stories a 'heroic' identity, and therefore compete with each other, they sometimes share stories in less competitive ways. One of these is to tell a story collaboratively. Another involves the careful sequencing of stories, such that a listener 'replies' to a story he has just heard by himself telling one that reinforces a point made in the earlier story. In this way the second storyteller shows that he has listened to and understood the first one – as if to say 'my mind is with you' (Coates 2003: Chapters 3 and 4).

Coates's corpus of men's stories also includes examples in which men do 'open up' to another male, and display the kind of emotional intimacy more commonly associated with women. Significantly, this is most likely to occur when only two friends are present (op. cit.: 198–199). It is this kind of interaction which characterises my friendship with Mac. In fact, the relationship was based on it from the beginning. It is now time to examine in more detail the nature of our friendship.

A male friendship, and an alcoholic's narratives

I met Mac at a time of 'profound change' (to use my earlier phrase) in my own life. Recently retired from lecturing on the grounds of ill-health, I struggled with questions of identity throughout the 1990s. During what might be called a mid-life crisis (I was in my forties) I became a 'house-husband', spending a great deal of my time helping my wife care for our two young daughters while she worked. Ties with my family of origin were also changing, my mother dying in 1992. I became immersed in Gestalt therapy as a patient, trying to find some meaning in the chronic asthma and depression I have suffered from since the age of two.

As an academic, my friendships had often been with other academics; many of these were conducted at great physical distance. Mac, however, was a building labourer, and lived only a street away. I first got to know him as a father whose daughter attended the same primary school as my own. Walking our daughters to school one morning, Mac and I struck up a conversation in which he enthused about a book he was reading. We gradually found we had a lot in common: a love of mimicry, larking about and play-acting, of digging and other manual jobs, of exploring the local countryside, of visiting ancient churches, of Westerns and, above all, of singing. Mac has a rich, powerful voice of great range and, like myself, loves Country and Western. We formed a duo with myself accompanying him on the guitar and singing in harmony, Everley Brothers style.[4]

But our friendship was based on much more than shared interests. I realise now that Mac reminds me of my mother, who died around the time I first got to know him. One thing they had in common was a manic personality. Like him, she was prone to depression, anxiety and despair, but had too the same exuberant streak of irreverence and mischief. Our relationship reminded me also of the one I enjoy with my older brother. The latter, like Mac, is a practical man who has worked in the building and construction industries. Our relationship has its laddish side, but is based primarily on mutual self-disclosure. We share experiences of growing up in a dysfunctional family and the problems this presents to us in day-to-day living. Like me, Mac is the youngest child of a father who could be bullying and physically abusive. Some of our childhood experiences were similar. Perhaps inevitably, I came to see Mac as a kind of younger brother, whom I could support as my own brother has supported me. And I also had the support of a therapist. I came to realise that I had been helped, and that I, perhaps, could in turn be a help to Mac.

Mutual help and support is one thing many people seek in friendship. Mac helped me re-connect with aspects of myself that, as an academic, I had repressed. He also mirrored the manic side of my own temperament. Mac, on the other hand, has always explicitly valued the fact that I am prepared to listen to him. I am a male to whom he can reveal his feminine side.[5]

There is, however, another aspect of our relationship which has always been problematic. For much of his life Mac has struggled with alcohol. Like many of his family, friends and neighbours in the local Irish community, Mac was brought up to drink. In the ten or so years since I have known him, Mac has seen his older brother and father die from alcohol-related illness; his only sister died from the same cause many years ago, and Mac has been haunted by the possibility that he may soon meet the same fate.

Although I do not misuse alcohol (or other substances) I have felt a powerful sense of kinship with Mac's problem. First, I too have an addictive personality. I am easily 'carried away', for instance, by academic work, and on more than one occasion Mac has recognised in me its depressive after-effects. As the poet Gwyneth Lewis writes in a book about depression, "(a)lcoholism dovetails disastrously well with depression because both are symptoms of a refusal to face reality" (2002: 159). Secondly, alcohol misuse was apparently endemic in the lives of my maternal grandmother and paternal grandfather, both of whom had died before I was born.

The problem for our friendship was that once Mac had had one of his drinking bouts the relationship between us could no longer be one of equality. I was reduced to the role of listener, but it was impossible to know what purpose, if any, was served by my listening. An individual can use drunkenness as a way of signalling neediness, but puts themselves beyond help while drunk. One day Mac turned up for a singing session blind drunk, and I showed him the door. Shortly after, while in the process of detoxification, he told me the first story discussed here. He claimed to have heard voices the night before, directing him to do absurd things which, when he carried them out, landed him in hospital. What I found intolerable was his assumption that I would be as interested in the details of his story as he was. I wasn't, partly because there was no equality nor mutuality in the relationship at that point. I was just a shoulder to cry on. I felt used, and gave his story a frosty reception.

Another reason why I did not want to listen to his story was my feeling that in narrating it Mac was performing a version of masculinity which, ultimately, we both knew was inappropriate for our friendship. His was a story of epic suffering, of the kind identified by Coates (2003) as quintessentially 'male'. I was confused about what reaction he wanted to elicit. Was I to be impressed by his capacity for endurance? Was I to feel, and express, sympathy? Or was I to pity him, and forgive any of his shortcomings on the grounds that his lot in life was insufferable?

Another way of responding to Mac's story would have been to focus on its narrative impact rather than its status as a recent and very painful experience. I could, therefore, have told him a story from my own experience of suffering, as if to say 'my mind is with you', in the sense referred to above. But Mac was in no condition to listen to any story of mine. Since an alcoholic 'bender' precludes intimacy, it felt instead as though Mac were addressing me with a rather mechanical kind of 'blokish' familiarity.

To put this in sociolinguistic terms, Mac had not designed his story with me, as recipient, in mind. And to use Labov's terminology, his story had been largely unevaluated (Labov 1972: 366ff.). The main function of evaluation is to build a bridge between speaker and listener, so that some sort of point to the narrative emerges. Instead, I got a string of narrative clauses detailing a sequence of actions and their physical consequences.

Re-telling and recording the story, and its sequel

The experience of hearing voices – voices which deceived, then threatened to torture and kill him – was a turning-point for Mac. He went into rehabilitation and kept off alcohol for four whole years. When he eventually relapsed, I felt able to encourage him to press on. I could do this partly because I had become increasingly aware of my own cycles of depression. A turning-point for me occurred during those four years, when, for the first time, I was prescribed Prozac. Like many Prozac users, I hated the thought of dependency on a drug. I kept coming off it only to find that I would eventually need to take it again. This cycle of dependence reminded me of Mac's relationship with alcohol.[6]

Increasingly, my concern with my own health widened to an interest in men's health in general. I attended Health Promotion courses and became actively involved in a local regeneration project, which included setting up a Healthy Living Network. I began tape-recording local men on the topic of health. I mentioned this to Mac, who had become increasingly reflective and self-aware over the last few years. He was keen to participate. We went for a walk and talked through his perceptions about alcoholism. He referred to the story I had been reluctant to listen to. As he re-told it, it became clear how important it still was for him, and, moreover, how firmly many of its details had lodged in my own memory. I now wanted not only to hear it but also to record it for my project. Mac re-told it, but also added other stories on the same theme. We arranged to meet the next day, and Mac talked long after my 90 minute cassette had run out.

The taping session began with the story I had been so reluctant to hear. He then recounted several other experiences. It needs to be said that Mac is an extremely fluent and vivid storyteller. But during the taping session he was able to set each narrative in a wider frame, in pursuit of answers to questions he himself had begun to pose. What is it about him, for instance, that he has had these experiences? How far, if at all, have other people had them? It turned out that Mac himself had attempted his own research, by questioning other alcoholics. Above all, he wanted to know more about the meanings of addiction and how addiction varies from person to person. It was the sharedness of his suffering, rather than the dramatic experience of individual pain, that now exercised him.[7]

One reason why Mac agreed to our taped conversation is that when he was in rehab. no-one was available to listen to his experiences. He felt a lack in the provision of care. Our friendship helped to fill it, but at the crucial time Mac needed more than that. On the other hand, it was our friendship that made the tape possible. As he says on the tape, he is only telling me these stories because I am a 'mate'. The material on the tape became our joint possession which, once transcribed, could form the basis for further discussion between us.

The transcript

There are three general points to be made about the transcript below. First, it represents a sequence of two narratives, interspersed with conversation, on the theme of 'hearing voices'. The first deals with the damage Mac did to himself by listening to 'the voices', the second with Mac's fear of what the owners of the voices are threatening to do with him.

Secondly, the narratives have been transcribed in a form that may be unfamiliar to readers acquainted with the conventions of sociolinguistics. It may be more familiar, however, to those used to the work of some anthropological linguists and folklorists who are keen to try to capture the artistic aspects of oral storytelling. One such aspect is pausing. Especially at the beginnings of their stories, many narrators can be said to pause rhetorically (as is also the case in political oratory).[8] They thus segment their utterances into what Tedlock calls *lines* (Tedlock 1983). Each line tends to have a characteristic intonation pattern consisting of a somewhat exaggerated rise near the beginning of a line and a fall (or fall/rise) near the end; and part of the storyteller's art lies in their ability to prolong the ensuing pause to maximum dramatic effect. Accordingly the transcription leaves a line space after each rhetorical pause. Where the storyteller pauses non-rhetorically (for breath, while hesitating, etc.) a simple gap of four spaces is indicated in the transcript.[9]

The advantage of this style of transcription is that by distinguishing between these types of pauses it signals the importance of rhetorical pausing in oral storytelling (as in music, where a pause is not simply the absence of sound, but part of the overall aesthetic pattern). It helps us to feel the story as a story, and it can help to suggest how storytelling performance (in this case Mac's) can be both vivid and highly accomplished.[10]

Mac's storytelling in general can be described as "fully performed", in the sense outlined by Wolfson (1982:25). Although his use of gesture has not been represented in the transcript, I have tried to indicate words or syllables given extra prominence (heightened pitch, greater volume) by an 'expressive' use of the voice: these are indicated by bold style. Another performance device, the aside, is used by Mac to both frequent and powerful effect. Asides can be seen as a kind of comment on the material in the story, addressed to the listener: they therefore have an evaluative function. I have marked these asides with square brackets.

The final point concerns the way in which the narratives emerge from an ongoing conversation. I have included the utterances of the listener (D) as well as those of the narrator (M). Not only do they 'frame' the narratives, they are a reminder that the material in them is, at the time of recording, shared knowledge between two friends. There is therefore a 'collaborative' aspect to the storytelling (Coates 2003). The listener helps to guide the narrator, especially in his use of questions. These often have a quasi-therapeutic flavour, since they were designed to provide for Mac the kind of listening experience he felt he'd been denied. They show how the performance of friendship often includes an informal 'therapeutic' dimension. And at the same time, it needs to be remembered that the recording session was part of a wider project on men's narratives of ill-health – a point that Mac was well aware of.

Voices in the wind

```
1    D  You were telling me the other day on that walk about the –
2       what happened when you heard the voices.
3    M  Oh, when I was when I was bad with the drink?
4       Er      well      it was about      one o'clock in the morning
5       I suppose      I got down to go to the loo

6       And there's some steps leading down from my room left
7       to the toilet and er three steps down three steps up and then
8       you got the toilet

9       And I came out of the toilet

10      And as I turned to face- to go back up to my room
11      [You can see the hallway at the bottom      and stairs leading
12      down]

13      As I was looking down towards the hallway
14      The voices in my head
15      [Now these voices      are not loud voices at all they're more
16      or less a whisper      so all you're getting is

17      It's like hearing voices on the wind you were just hearing

18   D  Voices that you knew? They weren't people that you knew they
19      weren't the voices of people you knew?
```

20 M Sometimes yes
21   And sometimes no you- you- you get a mixture

22   Now I suppose you know everybody's on the verge of madness
23   it only takes just a little bit- it's a thin line you know]

24   Well I was-I was standing there and I was looking towards
25   the front door and

26   [Now you've got to realise this time I 'm- I'm DTing   I've been
27   like this for a couple of days 'cause that's what drink does to
28   you   I mean you don't- nobody]

29   Anyway

30   [I mean if you're a drinker   and this happens and you know it's
31   not happened before   I mean it's enough to frighten you

32   I mean really frighten you

33   But even though it happened to me two or three times it's still
34   you still don't know what 's going on inside your head you're
35   thinking 'well am I?' 'cause   you know when you hear
36   these voices I mean there' s nobody there no-one can hear- if
37   there's anyone around you they're not hearing anything

38   They're just watching your actions you know]

39   So anyway these- these voices turned round to me and says
40   'Mac you don't have to walk down there you can fly'

41   Well I did I just spread my arms

42   I just leapt and went for it as if I was diving into a swimming
43   pool and as I- as I- as I approached the bottom (*laughs*)
44   the wooden ball at the end of the bannister that was the
45   first thing my head hit

46 D oh gosh
47 M so I bounced off that and   as I bounced off that my body
48   was turning and I   the radiator I hit the radiator on the
49   wall   which gave me a hole in my side   which has healed
50   now   and then I land- I landed sort of   on my feet but not

51   on my feet but on my tip-toes   and my toes bent under and I got-
52   all my toes were bruised and   then   as I managed to bend my
53   toes I was in- I was in motion anyway and I banged into the wall
54   and I damaged my sternum and while the ambulance came 'cause
55   my brother was there at the time   and my dad   and er they
56   bandaged me up took me to hospital and stitched me up
57   I had eight stitches I think on my head left-hand side of my head
58   and er I came back I think it was after half an hour or an hour and
59   er the voices started again and   so I done it   again so they had to
60   take me to hospital

61   D   You did exactly the same thing again?

62   M   I done exactly the same thing again

63   D   You flew down

64   M   I flew I did fly yeah   I was even better than (*laughs*)
65   and er I opened it all up again so they had to take me back
66   to hospital and stitch me again [but some of these some of
67   these   I mean some of these   some of these voices 'cause it's
68   so realistic

69   D   Weren't there some- weren't you also- didn't you also feel
70   there were people who were going to come and kill you?

71   M   Oh yeah yeah I mean

72   D   What was that about?

73   M   This- it's er]

74   I was lying   [I knew   you see- when you're hearing these voices
75   you- you can't take   too much in   because it's happening these
76   what I- I mean if you haven't experienced it   it's very very hard
77   to explain   but I'll try I'll try my best bit anyway seeing as
78   you're a mate]

79   but er I'm sitting there like it's like I'm sitting
80   there one night and   er   I'm on my own   and er   I'm
81   lying on the bed I've just had this drink [I mean I'm drinking
82   continuously for   more or less for twenty-four hours   because I

83   mean if   if you haven't got a drink   I mean if you're an
84   alcoholic and you haven't- I mean it's the worst thing
85   possible to be without a drink   I mean because that's all you live
86   for really   I mean that's all I lived for]   but er as I'm
87   saying I was laying there in bed   and these voices came- came to
88   me I mean this is about one o' clock in the morning   and er they
89   told me they'd be back at three

90   now   I'm hearing these voices from outside the window

91   now the window's quite close to my bed

93   now I jumps up and I- I'm trying to I'm trying to find out if
      (****************)
94   I was I – something happened I was afraid to go back to bed
95   so what I done was got a blanket and slept by the door   the main
96   door to my room the only door to my room 'cos I said 'if I bar that
97   they can't get in'
98   [but I mean nothing was happening but I wasn't to know that
99   you know?

100 D And did you know who these people were?

101 M I- the voices- I did then the voices they were friends two mates
102   of mine   who I used to play in the band with   and they came
103   back I mean I haven't seen
      (*******************)
104   'cause when the band split they   they moved
      (******************)
105   but I had (their) voices in my head   and I mean they was as
106   clear as day it was like me talking to you   now   when they are
107   talking   other times   when it starts off you see when these
108   voices start off   it's like something on the wind   you're
109   hearing it from a distance   and then it'll get   very   very
110   close   it'll get closer   and then you can make the words out
111   yeah?]

112   so

113   I lay down by the door   [and what they told me was   they'll be
114   back at three   so there was no way I could have gone to sleep] so
115   what I done was drank another bottle of cider   [which was

116   making yourself worse all the time anyway   'cause I think the
117   more alcohol that you drink   the keener or wha- I don't know if
118   it's the keener the senses or whatever but you pick up- you pick up
119   a lot- a lot more d'you know what I mean?   I'm not quite sure
120   Dick I'm just- this is the way I'm   sort of trying to   figure it
121   out

122   anyway what they were going to do]   er I lay- I lay down
123   anyway by the pillow- with the pillow and the blanket by the door
124   yeah [and they said I'd see a bright light   first of all yeah?]

125   so

126   [I mean there was no light outside- usually if the light's on on
127   the landing outside you can see it under the door whichev-)
128   I opened the door but there was no light on so I closed it
129   but when I lie down and open my eyes and looked under the (door)
130   there was a bright light as if I-

131   [you- you ever see these sci-fi films these spaceship films and
132   you see the light coming shining? Well that's the way- that's
133   the way it was

134 D And they said you'd see this light?

135 M They said I'd see this light and then they'd come in and
136   they'd- they'd put   hot knives in my eyes first and then-
137   they'd start with my eyes   and then they'd work down the body
138   like]

139   well I was lying I was lying there [you see?] and
140   [I- I don't really know what happened] but

141   morning came

142   and all I can remember was seeing these two people dressed
143   in white

144   floating under the door

145   and when I seen them [you see I- I just   I don't know what
146   happened] but I woke up the next morning   [but what went on in
147   between times I haven't- I haven't- I didn't- I didn't get

148 round to that er- if I had a video camera or anything I
149 wouldn't have caught nothing because it was all in my own
150 head]

Analysing the transcript

The first thing many readers may notice from the transcript is the sheer number of asides. As stated above, they tend to have an evaluative function. Mac's
re-telling of his experiences keeps the details of the first telling, for example
the injuries he suffered (a hole in his side, toes bruised, damaged sternum
and gashed head) and the effects of hearing the voices, but the asides effectively delay the development of the complicating action (beginning at 14, '*the
voices in my head…*). The asides, of course, are partly in response to my own
questions about the nature of the voices. In this respect they are partly co-
created. The storytelling event has some of the characteristics of what Polanyi
calls the "diffuse story", in that "the evaluation of crucial material is accomplished largely through the turn-taking system of the conversation", providing
"a strategy for telling a … story with significant emotional impact but few
events" (1989: 85).[11]

  The asides therefore are a reminder of the 'collaborative' aspect of the narration. Similarly collaborative is the joint establishment of an abstract for the
first narrative (lines 1–3). Mac then goes on to supply orientating information
(4–8), and his focus is firmly on the spatial relationships important to the story;
the whereabouts of the toilet in relation to the stairs, etc. Orientating information is also given in asides (11–12). But more typical is the long evaluative aside
as in lines 15–28, incorporating a question from the listener, which deals with
the volume level of the voices and whether or not they are known to the narrator. At 30–38 it is their frightening, and subsequently disorienting quality, that
is referred to. From 39, Mac returns to the role of the voices in the complicating
action, narrated in the past tense (with some interesting dramatic inversions:
both the wooden ball on the bannister and the radiator are mentioned before
the damage done to a part of the body, as though Mac is re-experiencing seeing
these objects appear to hurtle towards him). The hospital section (lines 55–
60) constitutes the resolution of the action, while 67–68 acts as a coda: it was
because the voices were so 'realistic' that these singular events occurred.[12]

  The second narrative is inspired by D's question at 69–70. The narrative
starts at 74 with the orientating statement "I was lying" but once again, the
complication is delayed by Mac's attempts to explain the process of detoxification and its effects. The first aside stresses the sheer difficulty of explaining

what it feels like to hear the voices (lines 74–78); the second (81–86) what it feels like for an alcoholic to be without a drink. At 105–111 Mac returns to what the voices sound like; at 115–122 he returns to the effects of alcohol on perception. At 131–138 he deals with the nature of the lights he sees and, in response to a question, their relationship with the voices; and at the end of the narrative, acting as a coda, he questions whether or not anything actually happened in the first place (145–150).

So preoccupied is Mac with the provenance of the voices that I have felt it necessary to cut sections of the second narrative. Between lines 93 and 94 he explains how he has mistakenly heard voices in the telephone box across the road from his house; between 103 and 104, and between 104 and 105, he explains who the two mates in his former band are. It could be argued that the overall emphasis on asides is necessary because, strictly speaking, very little in this second narrative actually happens. So little happens, in fact, that what does happen tends to get repeated, and the storyteller finds ways of eking out any dramatic interest he can find.

Thus, Mac's initial orientation clause 'I was lying' (line 74), is repeated (with lexical variation) at 79–80, but this time he shifts the tense to the present (*'I'm sitting there'*, *'I'm lying on the bed'*) at 80–81. (There is another repetition of the orientation at 86–88, this time with past tense verbs.) The onset of the complication at 90 is, interestingly, marked by a shift back to present tense 'I'm hearing these voices', followed at 93 by 'now I jumps up'. The rest of the complicating action is in past tense: 'so what I done was got a blanket and slept by the door' at 94–95, (repeated, with lexical variation, at 113 and 122–124); 'what I done was drank another bottle of cider' at 115. The tense-shifts themselves can be described as evaluative, since certain actions (e.g. jumping up) are foregrounded by virtue of the shift to the so-called historic present.[13]

The narrative moves to a kind of anti-resolution. After the orientating 'morning came' at 141, all that clearly happens is that Mac wakes up (line 146). His 'seeing these two people dressed in white floating under the door' was ultimately, all in his own head (149–150).

Victimhood, identity, gender and narrative

For many, a sense of personal identity is very largely built up out of the narratives we tell of our own experiences. In telling these stories we 're-present' to others periods in our lives. But our perception of the meaning of those stories can change. In this process the role of the audience is crucial. As Hollway writes:

> I know from paying close attention to myself giving accounts in a variety of different settings, that I have a stock of ready narratives to draw on which fit particular situations and which tell me nothing new unless the person I am talking to helps me to produce something new.   (1989: 39)

In Mac's case, it was myself, as the person he was talking to, who could help him 'produce something new'. This was because I, too, had changed since hearing his story for the first time. So it is important to re-affirm the view mentioned at the beginning of this chapter that listeners, as well as narrators, have biographies, and that the issue of identity for both is a fluid and multi-layered one.

The complexities of constructing, and re-constructing, personal identity through 'self-narration' are explored by Mary Jane Kehily (1995). She describes how she wrote autobiographical pieces to present to a gender and sexuality group at the University of Birmingham. Her audience were accordingly focussed on the issue of how personal experience is represented and interpreted in the light of gender identity. Kehily found that in her stories she presented herself as a 'victim', in this case of patriarchal power. But she also found that through adopting certain narrative conventions she could "reclaim some control by refusing to dwell on the pain and infusing the narratives with a sense of humour and irony" (op.cit.: 27).

It was also as a victim that Mac presented himself in his original narration. A victim is someone unable, for one reason or another, to *choose*. So they have little or no control over their lives. The first time he told me his story Mac presented himself as entirely at the mercy of alcoholic addiction. He was therefore the passive recipient of the voices. In the version discussed here, however, he has moved beyond that presentation – not so much by the use of 'humour and irony' (although these are by no means absent) but by acknowledging the possibility of including the experience of fellow-sufferers in his account. In this respect Mac's self-development can be said to parallel that described by Kehily.

As I know from my own personal experience, a sense of victimhood often arises in the context of chronic illness. Alcoholism, like depression and asthma, poses the sufferer powerful, sometimes overwhelming questions about the meaning of suffering and its relationship with personal identity.[14] It is an understandable response to identify oneself as a victim. In the end, however, victimhood is a way of evading the issue of taking personal responsibility for one's life. By portraying himself as at the mercy of alcohol and threatening voices, Mac was ultimately evading the issue of his addiction and what it represented in his life (hence the use of the word in the title of this chapter).

One problem with the term *victim* is its frequent association with judgemental attitudes. But the role of victim could be the one of last resort for those individuals or groups whose voices are systematically overlooked or ignored in society. Perhaps these feel that 'playing the victim' is the only way they can attract attention. It could be argued, then, that we live in a culture which in some respects actually encourages a sense of victimhood. A recent manifestation of this is the growing popularity of 'sickness narratives', in which people narrate, often at great length, what it feels like to suffer from a particular ailment, which are then read "out of aimless inquistiveness, out of schadenfreude, out of boredom" (Bennett 1999). Ill-health, especially mental illness, is often isolating; it also inspires feelings of inadequacy and guilt, precisely because our culture finds it hard to accept.[15]

On this view, sickness may be said to have become a contemporary 'master narrative', giving people the opportunity to present a self-image of assertive victimhood. For Kehily, much the same function is served, for women at least, by gender. On this view, women are 'victims' of patriarchy, and we should expect many of their narratives to show this. Men, on the other hand, we might expect to assert dominance through their stories, and given the high incidence of narratives of physical prowess, sexual conquest, laddish risk-taking, and stoical endurance among all-male groups, this is what we find. In stories such as these crucial issues are, in fact, evaded: self-reflection, responsibility, outcome, danger to others, and the emotional and social 'hinterland' of the action.

On the face of it Mac's first story, while narrated when he was still deeply involved in de-toxification, was typical of this male pattern. He presented a picture of 'laddish risk-taking' (trying to fly) and a state of stoical suffering in which, crucially, the hero *suffers alone*. Responsibility for what happened to him was laid firmly at the door of 'the voices'. There is a curious paradox in this performance of masculinity. The hero is presented as the *doer* of actions, but what is often celebrated is the sense of being *out of control*. The male hero in his most 'macho' guise has no control over his aggression (so he lashes out in anger and hurts someone else), his sexuality (so he fornicates whenever and wherever the opportunity arises) or, as here, his neediness (so he drinks himself silly). So fundamental parts of the self remain unintegrated; they even seem to make a 'victim' of the other parts.

Modes of masculinity are ultimately learned; but they are learned in different ways in different places at different times. Gender is always historically and geographically contingent. Mac's performance of masculinity has been shaped by his working-class Irishness, and how that identity has been accommodated within the English midlands. Interestingly enough, there is much in that background that contributes to a sense of victimhood. For instance, there is long tradition of the Irish seeing themselves as victims of English oppression (a response to an even longer tradition of English disparagement of the Irish). Emigration, especially from the west, has been a central fact of Irish life since the famine of the 1840s, and has had profound effects on the lives of Irish men, especially labourers. Isolated from their womenfolk, relegated to the hardest forms of manual work, Irishmen came to depend on the pub as the sole source of consolation (it was also the only place where you could be hired for work; see Cowley 2001). Furthermore, their reception within English society was less than whole-hearted. Mac's family came to England at a time when 'No Irish' signs were commonplace outside boarding-houses. In short, a sense of victimhood for Mac has a cultural as well as a personal source.

Catholicism is a further aspect of Mac's cultural background that reinforces, for him, a sense of victimhood. As the child of a bullying father Mac learned early to feel shame, a condition exacerbated by the priestly emphasis on sin. Angered by what he feels is its hypocrisy, he has since rejected the Church; but like many people in this situation, Mac feels a powerful mixture of loss and guilt about this rejection, and is constantly seeking a home for his strongly spiritual nature.

There is one final point to make about victimhood in relation to Mac's Irish background. To feel a victim to one's situation can be frightening; and Mac makes it clear that hearing the voices was a harrowing experience. In *Telling the American Story* Livia Polanyi (1989:115) asks "why is something frightening narratable?"

> Fear in general is an interesting topic for a story, because it is painful and confusing. People are supposed to be happy and unafraid, yet fear is often justified. Knowing when to be afraid is one mark of an adult. Tension can be created in stories which involve fear because there is always a question of whether that fear will be shown to be justified; fearing unnecessarily makes us children; not fearing when there are grounds for fear is a sign of madmen and fools.
>
> (op. cit.: 116)

These cultural presuppositions are also widely accepted in contemporary English culture. But it is arguable that part of Mac's difficulty with the voices may arise from the possibility that in the Ireland he left behind, there was less expectation that '(p)eople are supposed to be happy and unafraid', and that hearing 'voices in the wind' would not be such an 'unexpected' occurrence (Wooffitt 1992). As Mac struggles to find a newer, less egocentric view of his experience through his re-tellings, he has to negotiate not only different masculinities but cultural identities as well.[16]

Conclusion

One theme of this chapter is paradox. Its beginnings lie in a story which the listener did not want to hear, because the teller was in the grip of alcohol; yet the teller needed to be heard, and it is alcoholism that makes the story possible in the first place. Another story is then told in which nothing seems to happen. Both stories are narrated masterfully by a man who, at the time the events occurred, was not in control, and whose 'masculine' attributes seemed precarious. The chapter is also about male friendship, and how it can support someone struggling heroically to re-invent himself. It amplifies Polanyi's point about the sheer complexity of conversational storytelling by highlighting the complexities of gender and identity. And I hope it also reinforces the validity of her contention that "one is always, inescapably, part of one's work" (Polanyi 1989: 201). I make no apology for the autobiographical matter here.

Notes

1. Another example, also from personal experience, is the relaying of a traumatic early experience by a mother to a young son, who, by definition, is too young to respond with the compassion the story deserves (see Leith 1999 and 2002).

2. Polanyi (1989: 132ff.) stresses the importance of honesty and volition to friendship, and adds that neediness undermines true friendship. In my experience, however, a dependence on friends is a response to inadequate support from my family of origin.

3. Coates uses the term hegemonic masculinity (2002: 13 and passim).

4. It should be said that my friendship with Mac was able to flourish because we both had plenty of time on our hands: I was retired, he was often out of work or on sickness benefit. The lack of regular employment (and therefore structure) in Mac's life felt threatening for him, but it also presented him with an opportunity to examine himself.

5. Mac still makes jokes about my need to wear a plastic mac while he 'cries' on my shoulder (see further Note 16). For both of us, fatherhood was a 'feminising' influence, and we both had close relationships with our mothers and sisters in early life.

6. I had a similar problem accepting the need for a steroid inhaler to control asthma. My attitude is summed up by Kay Redfield Jamison's account of her 'warrings with lithium': "underneath it all, I was actually terrified that lithium might not work: What if I took it, and I still got sick?" (1996: 163).

7. As revealed in the following exchanges which took place after Mac narrated his second story (see pp. 138–141ff.):

```
150   D   Horrible experience
151   M   And this-and this it is frightening        I mean I can laugh at it
152       now   but at the time man it is
153   D   Well I remember when you actually told me at the time
154       I mean quite soon after
155   M                                              yeah
156   D                                                    you were really afraid of
157       those (   ) fellows coming to your place
158   M                                   yeah I was- I was- I was frightened
(…)
159   D   And- I mean talking about it like this have you you- you say
160       you've talked to other      kind of alcoholics
161   M   Not in a group
162   D   Not in a group               well just individually
163   M   Not even       not even
164       Er- I see some of the- I see some of the lads sometimes now that
165       are still going around now that- I mean they're still heavy
166       drinkers
167       And I-I've just- I've asked some of them er I've said 'Have you
168       have you ever heard- have you ever heard the voices?' I called
169       them the voices      without to say more or less they're
170       mine     and I'm saying to them 'Have you heard my voices? Have
171       you heard the voices?' yeah? Whether or not it's- whether or not
172       it's the same I don't know well I don't know
173   D   Were they able to talk about their own experiences?
174   M                                              No       no
175   D   like you have yours?
176   M                                 No they don't bo- they don't
177       bother I think maybe they're still too much involved with the
178       drink
179       It's only since I've been off the drink that I could I mean OK
180       I used to see * remember I used to see * once a- once a
181       month
182       but she's in * now but I haven't spoken I haven't spoken like
183       this for a – only to you now
184   D   'Cause you did say the other day that you- you felt that- there
185       wasn't really anybody       interested
186   M                                              no
187   D                                                    in listening
188   M   I don't- I don't- I don't think
189       I wish I could write a book on it
190       I wish I could write a book on well maybe not just- maybe a book
```

191   but er I wish I could put it if I could put it down to paper I think
192   I'd have a great story

8. See Leith and Myerson (1989: Chapter 1). See Leith (1995) for an application of these transcription principles to a Scottish folktale. A recent American example is McCarthy (Ed., 1994).

9. As the narrative progresses the 'lines' often get increasingly longer and the tempo of narration faster.

10. My approach is also inspired by the American ethno-poeticist Richard Bauman, whose "representation of spoken language is, frankly, intended to have more expressive than linguistic accuracy in a strictly technical sense. I am more interested here in the narratives as oral literature than as dialectological data" (1986: x). For this reason I have tried to keep the transcript as uncluttered as possible.

11. In Labov's terms, this is 'external evaluation', which, interestingly enough, he says "is common in therapeutic interviews, where it may form the main substance of an hour's discussion" (1972: 371). There is an example of internal evaluation at 96: "cos I said if I bar that they can't get in".

12. It could be argued that by mentioning 'going to the toilet' in his orientation Mac is emphasising the 'everydayness' of his situation before hearing the voices: see Wooffitt (1992) Chapter 6, 'I was just doing X when Y': a device for describing recollections of extraordinary events'. The problem with this notion of the 'extraordinary' is that it presupposes a category of 'the normal' recognised by all 'rational' people: this in itself can be a source of anxiety for someone in Mac's position, since hearing voices can be taken as a sign of schizophrenic or psychotic disorder (see [p. 137], and Note 16).

13. See Leith (1995) for a discussion of the use of the historic present.

14. Gwyneth Lewis documents this in relation to depression (2002).

15. According to Bennett, "ailments are becoming a vehicle for self-expression, a life-style choice", and our interest in these stories is made possible because of the advances of medical science: "The healthier we get, the brighter the future for illness as entertainment" (1999: ??).

16. There is an obvious danger of stereotyping Ireland and Irishness in terms of some dreamy 'Celtic Otherworld' of supernatural encounters, religious miracles and artistic sensitivity. This stereotype was very useful in Victorian English thought since it could help 'define' Englishness as down-to-earth and practical. On the other hand, it was exploited by one strand of 19th-century Irish nationalism and could therefore be self-fulfilling: some of Mac's characteristics, such as his musicality, lively sense of humour and highly emotional nature could be described as stereotypically Irish (and it is also possible that the images of torture in his narrative derive from accounts of Hell given by Irish priests in his childhood).

Chapter 8

Modes of meaning making in young children's conversational storytelling

Shoshana Blum-Kulka
Hebrew University Jerusalem

Introduction

Conversational stories provide dynamic, open-ended, often collaborative ways of sense making. Conversational stories are often reshaped in the telling, are co-constructed rather than autonomous, may relate to past as well as to future events, and can entertain, point to a moral or be part of an explanation without necessarily abiding by structural constraints of well-formedness (Blum-Kulka 2004; Eggins & Slade 1997; Martin & Plum 1997; Ochs & Capps 2001). To understand how they unfold and achieve their social goals, we need to decipher the secret of their tellability. What is exceptional and worth telling might be locally determined, vary with gender or age, and be highly culture bound (Blum-Kulka 1997; Heath 1982; Shuman 1986). Children's conversational storytelling is especially sensitive to the riches and constraints of childhood culture. Arguably, stories that emerge in peer interaction among young children are deeply embedded in the cultural matrix of children's lifeworlds, deriving their tellability and emergent meanings from the resources and norms of childhood culture.

Consider the following conversation. It took place in the yard of a Jerusalemite preschool, among a group of children playing inside a wooden construction. This construction changes function as the play develops – first it serves as 'a jail', and later as 'the babies' cage'. In the extract presented, the children negotiate play-entry, drawing up rules for inclusion and exclusion.

Extract 1. Tarzan-part 1[1]

Dafna (f; 6;1) Racheli (f; 4;5); Daniela (f; 5;8) Rafael (m; 5;11); Guy (m; 5;11) Michal (f; 4;1); and four unidentified children.
Date: 3.1.00; filename: Dafna; original transcript turns: 258–270 (simplified and abbreviated).

1   Rachel: Can I join?
2   Child: <u>No.</u> [ya]
3   Dafna: Anyone who likes Tarzan can't join in, only those who don't like him.
4   Daniela: I <u>hate</u> Tar(zan)
5   Dafna: ALON you don't play because you like Ta/ra/zan
6   Child: >anyone who likes Tarzan< (...) doesn't even know the code.
7   Guy: #I will <u>never</u>↑ tell# ((in a mysterious tone))
8   Child: <u>They</u> don't know the code either, <u>just</u> me
9   Child: What what is the code for the babies' cage?
10 Child: "I don't like Tarazan" ((quoting))

For any stretch of peer talk between children, the culture of childhood may be a given, or, as here, be constructed collaboratively 'on line'. In our example one child makes up a rule, the others accept it, and hence a new social contract for exclusion and inclusion is drawn up, and all collaborate in its upholding. The rule is announced by Dafna (turn 3): '*Anyone who likes Tarzan can't join in, only those who do not like him*'. In the next turn (4) Daniela immediately responds to the implicit invitation to declare alliance and be included by announcing '*I hate Tarzan*'. Exclusion is just as important: now that a rule has been established, a child can be excluded on the grounds of liking Tarzan (turn 5). A further development occurs when Dafna's rule is elevated to the status of a code – and a new division is constructed, between those who know '*the code for the babies' cage*' (and will never tell – see turns 8 and 9) and those who do not. We can see here how a coherent imaginary world of childhood culture is being constructed by the merging of language and imagination – it has a location (the 'babies cage'), a community (of Tarzan haters) a secret language (the code) and even an epistemology (knowing or not knowing the code).

Arguably, to understand peer talk in general and narratives in particular we need to look at peer talk as a *double opportunity space*, as talk functioning simultaneously in two discursive planes or spaces. The first space is created within childhood culture; it is the social space within which children negotiate meanings and relationships unique to their local age culture. It is this space which is the focus of social anthropology of childhood. As noted by James, Jenks and Prout (1998), anthropologists are interested in the 'tribal child' – ethnographies of childhood, carried out from a social constructivist perspective, are geared to understanding the processes of cultural reproduction in childhood from an emic point of view. Language becomes important for understanding this process for the complementary perspective provided by sociologists of childhood like William Corsaro. For Corsaro (1985) children are active social agents, busy constructing their peer culture through interactional displays, creating a web of multiple realities unique to childhood.

Viewing talk as an arena for development creates the second space; it is peer talk considered as an opportunity for the development of discursive skills, as stepping stones for adult-like uses of language and for gaining membership of adult cultures. This space is the focus of developmental psycholinguistics (e.g. Berman & Slobin 1994) and language socialization studies (e.g. Blum-Kulka 1997; Aukrust & Snow 1998), both with an etic, top-down stance towards children's discourse. Thus psycholinguistic studies ask questions about stages in the development of specific genres, like narratives, and language socialization studies examine the discursive practices provided by adults in different cultures for easing children's way into gaining membership rights to 'Culture' with a capital C.

Observing children telling stories in the natural setting of the preschool sheds a different light on language socialization. It reveals the way peer talk, storytelling included, functions for children themselves as a double opportunity space; it functions simultaneously on the plane of meaning making within childhood culture, while at the same time providing opportunities for discursive learning of narrative conventions. It follows that we need to adopt such a double perspective in trying to understand the processes of meaning making through storytelling. Specifically, I propose to consider children's conversational stories:

1. as a socio-cultural arena for the negotiation of issues like the division between the real and the imaginary, notions of time and space, social norms and gender identities; and
2. as a discursive arena for the negotiation and learning of performative and structural aspects of narrative construction.

Conversational storytelling can be conceptualized as encompassing three dimensions of narrativity: *telling*, i.e. performance, *tale*, i.e. the story-text and *teller(s)*, i.e. the actual animators of the story (Blum-Kulka 1997). In peer talk narrative events, issues related to telling, tales and tellers are negotiated on both the sociocultural and the discursive plane.

The discussion in this chapter is guided by the following questions:

1. *Issues pertaining to telling*:

How do narrative genres emerge in peer interaction? More specifically, (a) what are the conversational skills used by the children to introduce, frame for a particular audience, sustain and close stories within the framework of an ongoing conversation or play? And (b) what is the role of story audiences? How do the stories enfold in real time? What types of conversational collaboration and/or support do children receive from their peers in constructing coherent story lines and evaluating their stories?

2. *Issues pertaining to the tale*:

What are the criteria of tellability for peer interaction? What makes events (real and imaginary) worth telling? What types of tales (in terms of genre variation) emerge in young children's peer talk?

3. *Issues pertaining to tellers*:

What compels children to tell stories to each other? What types of social functions are served by story telling?

The stories analyzed in this chapter were all audio-taped in two Israeli preschools during periods of free play.[2] The narrative events observed range tremendously in terms of topics, length, number of participants and most notably, mix and transitions between the real and the imaginary. The following examples are meant to show how, despite this variation, conversational stories function simultaneously as resources for meaning making in the world of childhood culture, as well as arenas for practising and learning modes of performance and the structural conventions of narrative genres. Issues related to telling are considered first, then issues related to the point and structure of tales, and finally the positioning of tellers in relation to their tales and audiences. In each case the discussion focuses on the discursive practices the children are presumably learning from the narrative experience, and on how they are using the experience to make sense of their cultural world.

Telling: Negotiating story entry and supporting fellow-tellers

Prospective storytellers need to negotiate the right for an extended narrative turn, to justify their bid for temporary conversational dominance. Story entry has been noted to proceed normally in two turns or stages, being projected in the first and ratified in the second (Jefferson 1978; Polanyi 1989; Polss 1990).

Polss has conceptualized such negotiation as geared towards two types of conversational work. First, negotiation related to justifying the topical relevance of the projected story, achieved through its *textual embedding,* by the use of devices like discourse markers, cohesion, evaluation of preceding talk or just assumed topical relevance. Second, negotiation related to introducing the necessary *change in participation structure.* Such changes are achieved by signaling intent to tell by devices like story alerts, turn allocation, meta-linguistic comment and orientation information, and by aligning participants with devices like address summons, teller question, and rising intonation.

In adult-child conversations, like family dinners, children can rely on adults to scaffold their story entry in different ways. Adults elicit stories by direct questioning ('*What did you do in school today?*'), allocate narrative turns in response to turns spotted as potential story alerts ('*Mommy you know what happened – Yes dear*'), and both support and challenge the validity of children's tales and their modes of telling. All members of the family, children included, share familial assumptions of relevance and sometimes skip the participant aligning story-entry phase altogether ('*today we went to a school for teachers or something*' (Child (11)), (Blum-Kulka 1997).

In the multi-party, potentially egalitarian, participation structure of peer interaction, story-entry seems to require more conversational work, and offers different types of audience support and challenge.

Extract 2. The Swimming Contest

Dafna (f; 6;1); Raxeli (f; 4;8). The children are playing in the backyard outside.
Date: 3.1.01; filename: Dafna; original transcript turns: 58–66.

1	Raxeli:	°at yoda'at, (0.7) shhhh. at roca lavo elay ayom?°	°You know, (0.7) shhhh. Do you want to come to my ((house)) today?°
2	Dafna:	ani lo yexola.	I can't.
3	Raxeli:	°lama?°	°Why?°
4	Dafna:	ki (0.5) ki ayom yesh li xug ad a-erev.	Because (0) because today I have a class until the evening.
5	Raxeli:	(1.7) be↑-eze yom at yexola?	(1.7) On ↑ which day you can?
6	Dafna:	ulay e, maxar.	Maybe e, tomorrow.
7	Raxeli:	maxar (nira) lax? (0.8) tishali et a-orim shelax eze yom [at yexola.]	Tomorrow (is good) for you? (0.8) ask your parents which day [you can.]
8	*Dafna:	[ve-ulay] be-yom revi'i. (1.2) ve-ulay shavua a-ba be-yom rishon. (0.7)	[and maybe] on Wednesday. (1.2) and maybe next week on Sunday. (0.7) On Sunday I can as well, only

be-yom rishon ani gam yexola, rak etmol lo ayiti yexola, (0.8) ki aya li:: kaze: taxarut.(0.8) sxiya. (0.5) zaxiti makom sheni. (2.9) makom sheni ze axi↑ (0.4) tov↓. (0) (xavlim), mekaplim ((mekablim)) maxzik maftexot meod meod yafe.

yesterday I would not have been able to, (0.8) because I ha::d thi:s contest. (0.5) Swimming. I won second place. (2.9) second place is the↑ best ↓(0.4) (ropes) , you gep ((get)) a very very pretty key chain.

In Extract 2, the children are playing in the backyard and two girls are making plans about visiting. The conversation is firmly situated in the future until turn 8, when in the middle of the turn Dafna introduces a surprising shift in the time frame (*only yesterday I would not have been able to*), pauses, and then goes on to offer a story as a justification (*because I ha::d thi:s contest..*). First Dafna takes care to embed the story textually through the use of lexical cohesion devices, reiterating the lexeme *day* (from turn 4) in naming the days she can or she can't meet with her friend, and referring to another word from the same semantic field (*next week*).[3] Taken together, these devices create a cohesive relation of co-classification across turns (Halliday & Hasan 1989). Next, she introduces *only* as a discourse marker to mark the transition in both time frame (from future to past), topic (from visit to swimming-contest) and genre (from chat to narrative). Even if the transition strikes us as somewhat abrupt, it is noteworthy that though no ratification for story telling is asked for or granted, the child still makes a considerable verbal effort to ease the conversational shift needed for her to tell (Avni, Habib, & Hacohen 2002).

Extract 3. Pokémon in the Laundry

Gadi (m; 6;5); Oded (m; 5; 4); Amir (m; 6;5). The children are standing next to the drawing table and looking at a Pokémon sticker booklet. Ditto is a Pokémon. Amir talks extremely slowly.
Date: 11.5.00; filename: Gadi; original transcript turns: 1–10.

1	Gadi:	derex agav samta lev she- (0.6) she::ani'lo yodea efo ditto? ((scratches his palm))	By the way have you noticed that (0.6) that::I'don't know where's Ditto? ((scratches his palm))
2	Amir:	<ditto.> (1.3) ditto? (0.8) bo, rega ani <axapes lexa.> ((takes the booklet))	<Ditto.> (1.3) Ditto? (0.8) come, wait I'll <search for you.> ((takes the booklet))
3	Gadi:	LO, >DITTO KVAR LO BA-MAXBERET.< (0.8) a::ata yodea, pa'am u nidbak la-regel	NO, >DITTO IS NO LONGER IN THE BOOKLET.< (0.8) y::you know, once he got stuck to my mother's leg

		shel ima sheli (1.0) ((sits down)) ve-a::z [samti oto al] ha-xulca,	(1.0) ((sits down)) and the::n [I put him on] the shirt,
4	Amir:	[SHEL MI?]	[WHOSE?]
5	Gadi:	shel ima sheli ve-a:z samti oto al ha-xulca ((points to his shirt)) >ve-az shaxaxti lehoci oto< ba-la:yla. (1.3). ditto. ((makes a face, looks at Amir))	My mother's and the:n I put him on my shirt ((points to his shirt)) >and then I forgot to take him off< at ni:ght (1.3). Ditto. ((makes a face, looks at Amir))
6	Oded:	(2.9) u:::[::] ((puts his hands on his face in mocked astonishment))	(2.9) u:::[::] ((puts his hands on his face in mocked astonishment))
7	Amir:	[ma,] en lexa yoter et ditto?	[what,] you don't have Ditto anymore?
8	Gadi:	hu axshav ba-kvisa.	He's now in the laundry.
9	Oded:	(1.6) o o:h ((his hands on his cheeks, laughing and covering his mouth. Walks around Gadi, who is smiling.))	(1.6) o o:h ((his hands on his cheeks, laughing and covering his mouth. Walks around Gadi, who is smiling.))
10	Gadi:	(5.9) tov nu ha-xulca shel pokimon sheli ba-kvisa. (1.2) hi tacil et ditto. ((laughs))	(5.9) O well my Pokémon shirt is in the laundry. (1.2) It will save Ditto. ((laughs))

Example 3 offers a much more sophisticated case of story entry. The children are standing near a drawing table and looking at a booklet with stickers. When Gadi takes the booklet in his hand, Amir notices that one of the stickers is missing. At this point Gadi turns to Alon with a question containing several devices signaling a story alert. These include a habitual story opening discourse marker (*'by the way'*) projecting a conversational shift, a direct appeal to the audience (*'have you noticed'*) and a closed question inviting a 'yes' or 'no' response, either of which could have served as story turn allocation. But turn 2 offers no ratification: instead Amir volunteers to look for the lost sticker, apparently, as witnessed by turn 3, misinterpreting the previous turn as a bona fide appeal for help. In turn 3 Gadi raises his voice to emphatically reject the offer for help (*NO*), reestablishes the background for the story (*'DITTO IS NO LONGER IN THE BOOKLET'*), appeals to his audience yet again (*'y::you know'*), and then launches into the story (*'once he got stuck to my mother's leg ... and the::n ..'*).[4]

These two examples show some of the difficulties children may have in negotiating story entry in peer interactions. The two phenomena noticed – namely the overextended use of textual embedding devices like lexical cohesion (often accompanied with sound play) and momentary failures in having the audience appreciate attempts for story entry, are quite recurrent in our data. Yet it should be noted that other aspects of the telling-performance are fully supported, and teller and audience bring the 'Ditto' episode successfully to full completion. Once the story gets under way, Amir fulfills his role as the supportive audience, asking a clarification question for disambiguating an un-clear reference ('*WHOSE?*') in the same way parents have been noted to do in response to children's stories at dinner (Blum-Kulka & Snow 1992). On the other hand, in his second question ([*what,*] *you don't have Ditto anymore?*) Amir displays support for both teller and tale as a peer who is in a position to fully appreciate the loss of a Pokémon sticker. The second child in the au-dience chooses to show his appreciation for the anecdote more dramatically, by using gesture, movement, face expression and laughter, all working together to display his high involvement with teller and tale. Such high involvement occurs in adult conversation when, in Goffman's definition, a person displays an appropriate level of engagement with a social gathering, giving "his con-certed attention to some activity at hand" (1963:43). The 'Ditto' episode, as many others from the peer-talk encounters observed, show young children as capable of matching their attention to the *involvement contour* (Goffman 1961) required by the activity at hand.

Tales: The joint co-construction of imaginary worlds

Considering the last two stories in terms of their *tales* highlights some of the unique features of young children's peer talk narratives. While the 'swimming episode' is no different from anecdotes of self-aggrandizement that could have been told in an adult conversation, the story of the Pokémon sticker 'Ditto' belongs firmly to childhood culture. It assumes a close familiarity with the ma-terial, visual and verbal manifestations of the multi-media popular culture of Pokémon series (films, books, stickers, playing cards) and it is from this famil-iarity that it draws both its value as worth telling and its humour. In Martin and Plum's terms this story would be considered an anecdote. The point of anec-dotes is to "invite the listener to share a reaction, a laugh, a groan, a tear and so forth." Anecdotes "negotiate solidarity by offering an emotional response to an extraordinary event for the listener or reader to share" (Martin & Plum 1997:301). The loss of the 'Ditto' sticker is an extraordinary and lamentable event only within this world, and the original resolution found to the crisis (the shirt that will save the sticker) also makes sense only within this world.

The other childhood-world related feature of this story is its shifts, in Goffman's (1974) terms, of *keying* and *rekeying* between the real and the imag-inary. In Goffman's conception of *frames* as organizers of social experience, the term 'keying' refers to the transformations applied to primary frameworks whereby their framing – and hence their meaning – changes to something different, but still connected. Goffman stressed the recursive nature of the process, whereby frames can be keyed and rekeyed indefinitely. Though Goffman uses the terms 'framing/reframing' and 'keying/rekeying' interchangeably, for understanding children's *discursive events* it is important to distinguish between external framing and internal keying. In the lifeworld of kindergartens and preschools, the external framing of the event as free-play or assembly time is institutionally imposed by the adults in charge. But simultaneously the children are actively engaged in the internal keying of the event, keying it as pretend or real, subversive or playful.

We have proposed to view children's *discursive events* as shaped through an interaction between at least four parameters (Blum-Kulka, Huck-Taglicht, & Avni 2004; Blum-Kulka 2005b). First, the institutional, external framing of the event usually determined for the children by the adults. Second, the child-initiated thematic frame of the event that provides the topics for the talk and activity. Thirdly, the child-constructed, internal keying of the event, and finally, the generic resources drawn on for the talk that unfolds, like narrative or argumentative discourse. Thus the 'Ditto' narrative-event enfolds during free-play time (external framing), is concerned with a topic of childhood culture (theme), draws on the conventions of conversational story-telling genre in telling a personal anecdote and is keyed mostly, but not entirely, as 'real'. The 'pretend' keying is already suggested by the personification of the Pokémon sticker through reference to it by the name of the character it depicts. This choice of reference allows for an ambiguity between factual or pretend keying as the story develops, and for the complete shift to the world of fantasy in the coda of the story (*O well my Pokémon shirt is in the laundry. (1.2) It will save Ditto*).

Extract 4 illustrates two further features of young children's stories: the joint enactment of a fantasy story in real time and the fine tuning of the two participants in upholding narrative coherence in the possible world created.

Extract 4. The Squirrels

Rafael (m; 6;3); Rami (m; 5;11). The children are looking together at '*The Big Book of Animals.*' They are now looking at the picture of a squirrel. The extract is selected from a relatively very long (about 20 minutes) segment of joint story enactment stemming from the same activity.
Date: 25.5.00; filename: Rafael; original transcript turns.

1	Rafael:	bo:: nagid she-asinu oto le-xayat maxmad. (3.7) nagid lakaxti nagid [hoce- ((hocenu))	Le::t's say that we turned it into a pet. (3.7) let's say I took let's say [we too- ((took out))
2	Rami:	[na]gid asinu alav kesem she-hu yehiye shtayim, she-hu yahafox le-shtayim.	[let's] say we put a spell on him that he will be two, that he would become two.
3	Rafael:	(3.5) ani lakaxti et ha-amiti.	(3.5) I took the real one.
4	Rami:	lo, ani. (1.8) lo, shte:nu, (0.9) °shtenu°.	No, me. (1.8) no, bo:th of us, (0.9) °both of us°.

((The children "take" the squirrels out of the book, pretending to hold them in their hands.))

5	Rafael:	(1.9) samnu oto be-kluv.	(1.9) We put him in a cage.
6	Rami:	(0.3) ani lo samti=	(0.3) I didn't put=
7	Rafael:	=(lo samnu), sh-lo <°yivrax lanu.°>	=(no we put), that he won't <°escape from us.°>

((8 turns omitted))

16	Rafael:	lo, ata lakax- ((lakaxta)) (0.4) <samnu otam be- be-kluv (0.6) she-hem yitraglu a[xshav.]>	No, you too- ((took)) (0.4) <we put them in- in a cage (0.6) so they'll get used ((to us)) n[ow.]>
17	Rami:	[lo], hu kvar hitragel.	[no], he already got used ((to it)).
18	Rafael:	(4.6) axshav hu hitragel (1.7) #tuti tuti tuti tuti xamud katan#	(4.6) Now he got used ((to it)). (1.7) #tuti tuti tuti tuti little darling# ((singing in a babyish voice))

((the children are singing together))

((22 turns omitted))

| 41 | Rami: | keilu ze haya shir, ze haya shir ((laughs)) ha-eres shelanu. | Like it was a song, it was a song ((laughs)) our lullaby. |

((the two children are singing))

((2 turns omitted))

| 44 | Rafael: | ze yardim gam otam, ki hem gam (0.6) gam <hem racu lishon.> | It will put them to sleep too, because they too (0.6) too <they wanted to sleep.> |

((the children are singing "tuti tuti" again))

((9 turns omitted))

| 54 | Rami: | >matay she-hem yitoreru< nagid she-hem rocim laxzor la-sefer. ((the story enactment continues)) | >when they'll wake up< let's say they want to go back to the book. |

The two boys constructing this story were standing next to the 'book corner' of the preschool, leafing through *The Big Book Of Animals*, pointing out and naming different animals in the book. In turn 1 Rafael introduces the 'pretend play' keying, marking it verbally with two devices: lexically, by *'le::ts say that'*, a phrase often used by the children as a discourse marker for a shift to fantasy, and grammatically, by the use of the *imaginary – performative past* (Blum-Kulka 2005b). As in many of children's utterances in pretend play, the past tense used in turn 1 (*'we turned it into a pet'*) and subsequently for most of the events in the story, marks a modal distancing from reality, denoting modality rather than temporality. With the use of the imaginary-past, events are described from a zero deictic center, namely from the here and now (Henkin 1991). In other words, the imaginary-past serves a performative function, bringing the events into being as told, meshing telling-time and story-time. This function is underscored by non-verbal behavior. In the 'squirrel' story all the verbs in the past tense (*'… we **made** it into a pet/ we **made** a spell on it/ I **took**/ we **took**'*) are accompanied by appropriate gestures. For instance, in the moment of magical transformation of the picture to pet, each child 'lifts' his squirrel from the book, walking away holding a virtual squirrel in his palm.

Within this new fantasy frame anything can happen, the picture of the squirrel becomes animated as a pet that steps out of the pages of the book like an actor in a Woody Allen film who steps of the screen to meet his admirer in the audience. By a further leap of imagination, realized through the double rekeying in '[*let's*] *say we put a spell on him that he will be <u>two</u>, that he would become <u>two</u>*' in turn 2, the single squirrel becomes two squirrels, so each child can have one of his own.

The fine-tuning of the children to each other in the joint enactment of the story is evident in several ways. The children not only fully collaborate as authors of the tale, but they also provide 'on line' support for each other as tellers. Rami in turn 2 provides double support to his fellow teller by fully accepting the story world suggested by Rafael, and by further developing it in a mutually satisfying way. In turn 3 Rafael challenges the harmonious world created in the previous turn, but is corrected by a further teller-supportive move by Rami in 4: the two protagonists (squirrels) are now matched by two authors of the tale – *'bo:th of us, (0.9) °both of us°.'*

With a few exceptions, the reference frame of two author-principals and two protagonists is systematically upheld through the anaphoric references used (*'us'* and *'they'*). From turn 5 to 44 the story enfolds as a coherent series of motivated events. The squirrels are put in a cage so they won't escape and will get used to their new surroundings (turns 7 and 16). Next, they are put to sleep (turn 44) and at a later stage are destined to end up back in the book (turn 54) according to their own (attributed) wishes ('>*when they'll wake up*< *let's say they want to go back to the book*').

The discursive powers of imagination

The most remarkable feat of this narrative event seems to be the way it opens up, develops, is contemplated on while it is happening, and provides closure for a magical tale-realm created entirely by the fully collaborative interactional moves of the two children. Pretend play narrative events like this one can make a highly significant contribution to children's narrative-discursive development precisely because they are a prime example of the 'double opportunity space' mentioned earlier. On the socio-cultural plane, they derive their tellability potential – plots and protagonists included – entirely from childhood culture. Hence their significance or relevance for the children, relevance that calls for and finds its expression in the children's sustained mutual involvement in such story enactments. On the discursive plane, it is this sustained involvement and shared background assumptions and knowledge that allow for the joint construction of connected discourse about displaced events. The capacity to construct connected discourse about non-current happenings, tuned to the audience's presumed state of knowledge, is, in turn, at the heart of 'literate' or 'decontextualized' genres of extended discourse (Ninio & Snow 1996). Thus pretend play becomes a major site of children's protected environment where they can gain skills and autonomy in genres of extended discourse.

Support for these ideas from a different angle can be found in recent work on pretend play in the work of developmental psychologist Paul Harris. In his book, *The Work of the Imagination*, Harris argues strongly against the tradition that treats children's early fantasy lives as primitive and disorganized, claiming that children's ability to imagine hypothetical and counterfactual worlds makes a continuing contribution to their cognitive and emotional development. To quote: "My proposal, then, for the puzzling emergence of pretend play in young children is that the cognitive capacity that underpins pretend play – the capacity to construct a situation model – is an endowment that enables children to understand and eventually produce connected discourse about non-current episodes" (Harris 2000: 194).

Harris concludes his book with what he calls the 'tantalizing speculation' that at some point in man's evolutionary history, there was an explosive fusion of language and imagination. It was this fusion that enabled mankind "to exchange and accumulate thoughts about a host of situations, none actually witnessed but all imaginable: the distant past and future, as well as the magical and the impossible" (2000: 195). Hence, from this point of view, symbolic play in childhood re-creates the historical fusion of language and imagination, the same fusion that is at the heart of all works of fiction. From a discursive development point of view, it is this fusion that allows for *intersubjective modes of meaning-making* (Bruner 1990) for relatively long stretches of time, and that possibly mediates the transition to the distanced, connected discourse of literate language in other than pretend keying.

Extract 5 illustrates the degree of sophistication and complexity in intersubjective meaning making reached in such imagined worlds in children's discourse.

Extract 5. Pika: The true story

Dani (m; 5;11); Oren (m; 5); Alon (m; 5) and two additional unidentified children. The children have been involved for a short while in acting out fights between Pokémon characters. At some point Dani apologizes for hitting Oren (whom he considers the enemy) apparently harder then intended; Oren accepts the apology and proceeds to tell the 'true story' as part of his explanation why he shouldn't be considered the enemy.
Date: 6-April-2000; filename: Daniel; original transcript turns: 39–48.

1	Oren:	=ani [esaper] lexa, et <u>kol</u> a-sipur a-amiti, (0.9) [axshav].	=I [will tell] you, the <u>whole</u> true sto<u>ry</u>, (0.9) [now]
2	Daniel:	[ken, ma a-sipur, pi-ka↑ krok?	[yes, what's the story, pi-ka↑ krok?
3	Oren:	>°a-dantilim, itxapsu elay,°< dentil exad itxapes elay, ki u- ki u- (0.9) ki ra<u>ca</u> she- she-ata tax<u>shov</u> she ani↑ asiti et ze. pashut ay<u>ta</u> lo taxposet meduyeket biglal maxshir admaya shelo.	>°The Dentils, disguised themselves as me,°< one Dentil disguised ((himself)) as me, because he- because he- (0.9) because he wan<u>ted</u> you to <u>think</u> that I↑ did it. He simply had an accurate disguise because of his simulating device.
4	Daniel:	u aya ra?	Was he bad?
5	Oren:	ra me'o::d.	Ve::ry bad.
6	Daniel:	(1.4) p<u>i</u>ka, <u>ei</u>fo u-nimca↓.	(1.4) P<u>i</u>ka, <u>where</u> is he↓ ((now)).
7	Oren:	u nimca↑, u nimca be-dira sodit. Ani lo [yode'a ei<u>fo</u> i].	He is↑, he is in a secret apartment, I don't [know <u>where</u> it is.]
8	Daniel:	[dira] sodit? [aval ani] yode'a, [ani xoshev].	[a secret] apartment? [but I] know, [I think.]
9	Alon:	[ani yode'a], [<u>ani</u> yode'a]_	[I know,] [I know_]
10	Daniel:	be-b-b-be dirat a-ru<u>xot</u>, ani yode'a.	In in in in a <u>haunted</u> apartment, I know.

11		The children start running around in the yard, looking for "Pika", while calling out his name and shouting directions at each other.	
12	Oren:	(.......) ani agid lexa et a-derex. yashar yemina ve-yashar smola. ((speaks while running))	(...) I'll tell you the way. Straight to the right and straight to the left. ((speaks while running))
13	Daniel:	eifo ze. [po?]	Where is it? [here?]
14	Oren:	[yashar yemi↑na, ya↓shar smo↑la, yashar yemina.	[straight to the righ↑t, straigh↓t to the le↑ft, straight to the right.
15	Daniel:	°yshar, smola° ((to himself, while running))	°straight, to the left° ((to himself, while running))
16	Alon:	TFOS OTO:: KR<u>OK</u>, TFOS OTO. ((while running))	CATCH HI::M KR<u>OK</u>, CATCH HIM. ((while running))
17	Daniel:	(2.2) °yasha::r,° ((while running))	(2.2) °strai::ght,° ((while running))
18	Alon:	MIT-<u>KE</u>FET KROK (......)	A KROK AT-<u>TA</u>CK (......)
19	*CH2:	<u>tfos oto</u>::	Catch hi::m
20	*CH1:	#nana banana# ((sing-song))	#nana banana# ((sing-song))
21	Oren:	<u>sham</u>. ta ro'e avanim yerukot? ze sham.	<u>There</u>. D'you see green stones? It's there.
22	Daniel:	pika:::=	Pika:::=
23	Oren:	=ata ro'e avanim yerukot? lo (xumot) [yerukot_]	=Do you see green stones? Not (brown) [green_]
24	Daniel:	[ken] (1.2) [ke::n_]	[yes] (1.2) [ye::s_]
25	Oren:	[az sham.] (0.9) a-dira a-[sodit]=	[so there.] (0.9) The secret [apartment]=
26	Daniel:	[sh::am_]	[the::re_]
27	Oren:	=be-tox avanim ayeru-[yerukot].	=Inside the gree- green [stones].

The dialogue between the children here is in the midst of a pretend play in which each is assuming a character from the Pokémon series. Our extract opens with an explicit announcement of the intention to tell (=I [*will tell*] *you, the whole true story*, (0.9) [*now*]) made from within the story-world in a pretend keying. Once ratified ([*yes, what's the story, pi-ka*↑ *krok?*]), it goes on (in turn 3) to elaborate a complicated plot of disguise. The ensuing story is told entirely from the point of view of and to the Pokémon characters played out by the children. What is noteworthy here is the degree of complexity in the children's high level of elaboration on the *plane of consciousness* (Bruner 1990). The tale involves three imaginary characters, two present and one non-present. The teller is attributing a deceptive theory of mind to one character, and intentional states to the two others: it is the non-present, third Dentil character who wanted you (in your present guise as another character) to think that I (in my guise as Pikachu) did it.

The 'Pika' example also illustrates the flexibility with which children shift between deictic centers and collaborate in co-constructing the story through talk and physical action. The story begins in a conjured imaginary world in the imaginary-past – the past tense used to sequence events *within* the story world (turn 5: *Was he bad – Ve::ry bad.*) and then moves to the here and now of the actual present (turn 6: *Pika, where is he↓ ((now))?*) without stepping out of the pretend frame (Blum-Kulka 2005b). Once this question is asked, the children start running around the yard in search of the imaginary evil character from the story giving each other clear but also highly contextualized directions, like '*straight to the right and straight to the left*' (turn 12) and '*There. D'you see green stones? It's there*' (turn 21). The high level of cooperation in upholding the coherence of imaginary worlds is manifest in several ways. First, in the way all three children (in turns 7 to 10) agree with Oren's suggestion that the evil character is in a '*secret apartment*' (a '*haunted*' one, according to Daniel) and their problem is to find it. Next, as Oren self-appoints as leader of the search party (turn 12: *I"ll tell you the way*) the other two follow his instructions carefully, (note turns 15 and 17, in which Daniel repeats instructions to himself) regardless whether they are concrete or imaginary (Oren:=*Do you see green stones? Not (brown) [green_. Daniel: [yes] (o) [ye::s]* (turns 23 and 24)). Thus though Extract 5 is even further removed from reality into the world of fiction than Extract 4, it is just as coherent for the children. This underscores the argument for the discursive benefits of pretend play: the more firmly grounded in childhood culture, the more confident the children seem to be in spinning complicated tales.

Tellers: Negotiating issues of gender identity

The next section discusses issues related to the children as *tellers* positioning themselves in relation to their tales and their audiences. This aspect tilts the balance of the discussion from the more discursive aspects of story telling towards the more sociocultural ones. The questions considered are: *what* compels children to tell in specific contexts, and *how* does what and how they tell function for them on the socio-cultural plane?

Extract 6. Tarzan (part b)

Dafna (f; 6;1); Raxeli (f; 4;5); Daniela (f; 5;8); Rafael (m; 5;11); Guy (m; 5;11);
Mixal (f; 4;1) and four unidentified children.
Date: 3.1.00; filename: Dafna; original transcript turns: 258–270.

26	Dafna:	<u>mi</u> carix bixlal et ze?	<u>Who</u> needs this anyway?
27	Child:	°rafael natan li°	°Rafael gave it to me°
28	Dafna::	(3.3) rafae↑l, ata oev et:taraza↑n?	(3.3) Rafae↑l, do you like:Taraza↑n?

5 turns omitted: the children discuss the degree of Rafael's love for Tarzan.

33	Rafael:	[lo] >ani kvar lo o°ev< (et tarazan°).	[no] >I don't anymore li°ke< (Tarzan°).
34	Child2:	ani lo oev (…)	I don't like (…)
35	Dafna:	ani l::o <u>o</u>evet (0.9) banot lo o↑avot et tarazan. tarazan <u>lo</u> oavot a-banot=	I d::on't <u>like</u> (0.9) girls don't li↑ke Tarzan. Tarzan they <u>don't</u> like the girls= ((As she pauses Dafna raises her head and looks around)).
36	Rafael:	=<u>oi</u>. #kshe-gil xilek lanu (0.2) xovrot tarzan, .h az <u>ex</u> .h <u>dikla</u> (0.3) ve-kama banot .h (0.8) e xis-#	=oi. #when Gil gave us (0.2) Tarzan booklets, .h so <u>how</u> .h Dikla (0.3) and few girls .h (0.8) e cov-#)
37	Child1:	[#ex iskamti le-ka-#] ((upset))	[#how I agreed to ta-#] ((upset))
38	Rafael:	[#xisu et a-　　　] a-<u>xo</u>veret .h shel <u>ta</u>razan be-xol, (0.4) <u>ni</u>can ve-r::on# ve-od .h .h <u>ba</u>t.	[#covered the-　　] the booklet .h of Tarzan with sand, (0.4) <u>Ni</u>can and R::on# and another .h .h <u>girl</u>.

7 turns omitted: the children discuss the names of girls who took the booklet.

45	Dafna:	<u>lo</u>. ze lo gil xi::lek, ze <u>rafi</u>. (1.1) ra↓fi xilek.	<u>no</u>. It's not Gil ((who)) ga::ve, it's Rafi. (1.1) Ra↓fi gave ((distributed)).
46	Child2:	(0.4) °naxon.°	(0.4) °right.°
47	Rafael:	(1.9) naxon. #ve-lama iskamti lekabel xoveret <u>tar'zan</u>?#	(1.9) right. #and why did I agree to take a booklet of <u>Tarzan</u>?#
48	Dafna:	(1.5) ve-LAMA ani eskamti .h lekabel x-=	(1.5) and WHY I agreed .h to take b-=
49	Rafael:	=ANI KISITI OTA BE-<u>XO:L</u>.	=I COVERED IT WITH <u>SAN:D</u>.
50	Dafna:	lama ani eskamti lexa- lekabel xoveret kazot. .h >aval atem yodim ma asiti ita she-egati abayta?<	Why did I agree to gi- to take this kind of a booklet. .h >but you know what I did with it when I got home?<
51	Child1:	ma, zarakt ota la-pax ve-=	What, you threw it in the trash and-=
52	Dafna:	=#<u>ke:h:n</u># (1.5) <u>ke::n</u>. (0.6) samti alea rotev shu::m,=	=#<u>Ye:h:s</u># (1.5) <u>ye::s</u>. (0.6) I put on it garlic sau::ce,= (laughing tone))

53	Rafael:	((laughs))
54	Dafna::	=#zarakti ota la-pax. .h keilu ze aya:: (0.2) kufsa shel a-ro[tev shum she-nig]mera.# ((amused tone))	=#I threw it in the trash. .h like it wa::s (0.2) a box of the gar[lic sauce that en]ded ((got emptied)).# ((amused tone))
55	Child:	[(...............)]	[(......................)]
56		(9.2) ((unclear speech, whispers))	
57	Dafna:	ve-ROTEV AGVANIYOT gam samti al ze.(0.9) gam samti AL ze rotev ag°vaniyot° .h tiru. tiru.	And TOMATO SAUCE too I put on it. (0.9) also I put ON it tomato sau°ce° .h look. look.
58	Child1:	(lo ....she-ayiti ben yom)	(no .... that I was a day old) ((comes from another circle of kids))
59	Dafna:	AN::I (0.2) az (0.6) tiru (0.2) ani lakaxti kol minei rotev, / (0.5) ve-gam e / yerak::ot. / (0.3) ve-asiti mi-ze xoveret ba:rbi:yo::::t.	I:: (0.2) so (0.6) look (0.2) I took all kinds of sauce, / (0.5) and also e / vegetab::les. / (0.3) and made a Ba:rb:i:::es booklet out of it.
60	Rafael:	(0.5) #xaval she-lo asit mi-ze xoveret marak.# ((amused tone)) ((All the children laugh together))	(0.5) #too bad you didn't make it into a soup booklet .# ((amused tone))

The Tarzan episode begins with negotiation around the password for entrance to the imaginary babies' cage (see Extract 1), and continues by focussing on the Tarzan theme as essential to the game. The conversational story round of the Tarzan booklet (turns 36 to 60) emerges from within the children's world: its mode of emergence, its justifiability as tellable, as well as its point are firmly grounded in the imaginary world of the 'babies' cage. Simultaneously, the stories introduce a new rekeying to the episode, meshing fantasy and reality in a way that allows for the negotiation of larger issues, in this case gender identities.

The larger issue of gender identities is reached gradually, beginning with Dafna's rhetorical question in turn 26 '*who needs this anyway*'. The exophoric reference of 26 seems to be to a Tarzan booklet one of the children is holding in his hand, so here the world of reality enters the world of fantasy established earlier. Against the norms established earlier, and the information provided in 27 (°*Rafael gave it to me*°, said very quietly) Dafna's question in 28 to Rafael has the illocutionary force of an accusation, inviting an account rather than just seeking information. Rafael's negative response at the onset of his turn (after some intervening talk by other children) bluntly denies the accusation and goes on to provide the implicitly invited account '>*I don't anymore li°ke<* (*Tarzan°*).'

The turning point in the development of this episode occurs in turn 35. The turn opens with a personal announcement, echoing similar announcements by other children, but then the speaker pauses dramatically, looks around, and goes on to rephrase her dislike for Tarzan as a general norm true for her gender at large. This change in footing (Goffman 1981) from the "I" of personal identity to the "we" of gender is indicated by the self-repair of syntactic subject from "I" to "girls" and the dramatic pause. There are two levels of discourse involved: on the first, the personal one, Tarzan booklets are being rejected on the power of local rules made up by the children. On the second, the gendered level, Tarzan is rejected by all 'girls' (presumably, and only by implication) as the ultimate symbol of machismo. The syntax used and the repetition of the general proclamation underscores the reading of Dafna's announcement as a feminist declaration on gender identities: girls are different, girls do not like Tarzan.

Once such an ideological framing is introduced into the conversation, it allows for stories that ensue to serve as moral tales, or in Martin and Plum's terms, as an *exemplum*: "Exemplums share a judgment about a noteworthy incident rather than an emotional response to remarkable event as the anecdote" (1997: 301). The incident of how several girls have covered the Tarzan booklets with sand, told by Rafael in turns 36 and 38, is one such moral tale, illustrating by a story the degree to which girls indeed do not like Tarzan.

Rafael's contribution in turns 36 and 38 opens up a story-competition between him and Dafna as to who can provide the best story to illustrate the general claim for gendered preferences. This story round is interrupted by a discussion of who gave the children booklets in the first place (for 7 omitted turns), and taken up again by Rafael's question (delivered in a mocking tone) in turn 47 '#*and why did I agree to take a booklet of Tarzan?*# 'This question, and the loud report that follows in turn 49 (*I COVERED IT WITH SAN:D*") retroactively casts a doubt on Rafael's alignment with Dafna's gendered claim. It suggests that perhaps Rafael is actually still pursuing the 'babies cage' community frame, by which the dislike of Tarzan cuts across gender lines.

For Dafna, on the other hand, there is no doubt. She uses Rafael's question (in turn 47) to occasion her story-entry. She appropriates Rafael's question '*and WHY I agreed .h to take b-*' (turn 48), interrupting his story, and then repeats it again (turn 50), building up the turn as an elaborate story-entry composed of *local occasioning* (taking the booklet) and a *direct summons* to her audience to invite recipientship. Her invitation is only partially ratified, since the child speaking next (turn 51) answers to the summons ('*what*'), but also proceeds to suggest building-blocks for Dafna's story. Dafna responds by building on the previous turn both as ratification and story opening, and proceeds to tell her version, using a series of prosodic features (note the elongated vowels, long pause and laughing tone) as turn-holding devices projecting story telling. As she recounts vividly the series of destructive acts applied to the infamous book-let (in 52, 54, 57, and 59), she remains a solo performer, with her audience supporting her telling with laughter. The amused tone, exaggerated intonation patterns as well as the choice of substances used and the surprising outcome (the booklet not destroyed, but instead transformed into a Barbies booklet) indicate that the story has no claim to factuality. It meshes fantasy and real-ity knowingly to tell a moral tale: look what I did to prove that girls do not like Tarzan.

Considering the ways Dafna positions herself vis-a-vis her audience and the story-world highlights the way the Tarzan story functions in the service of a gendered argument. Bamberg (1997) suggested three dimensions of po-sitioning in narratives. First, the way the teller positions herself vis-a vis her audience. Second, the way the protagonists are positioned relative to each other in the story-world. Thirdly, the way the story-teller positions *herself* in relation to the storyworld: on this level, it is the author and principal of the tale who can make general claims to the 'truths' derivable from the story on the basis of previous levels of positioning.

Dafna positions herself in relation to her audience as a solo performer with an entertaining tale to tell. Once she launches into narration in turn 52, she holds the floor successfully till the culmination of her story in turn 59. She speaks with assurance, using variation in pitch and rhythm to hold her audi-ence's attention. Her positioning of herself as the protagonist of the story is no less assertive: she is the doer, a female persona of strong will exercising her powers in the world of unwanted objects associated with males. Her position-ing of herself in relation to the story-world comes through, first in the nature of the acts named on the tale's plan of action: the garlic sauce, tomato sauce and "*all kinds of sauce*", poured over the booklet paint a vivid picture of destruction. Additionally, it transpires through her choice of resolution for the tale: by mak-ing the booklet into a Barbies' booklet she is reasserting her gendered position, underscoring the feminist claim she has made earlier. It is noteworthy that be-ing offered as an exemplum of this claim, the story sequentially follows its own coda (turn 35: *girls don't li↑ ke Tarzan*). Rafael's comment in 60 aligns with the teller as the powerful demolisher of the Tarzan booklet, but not necessarily with the teller as offering a gendered interpretation to the act of demolishing. This suggests that Rafael is still pursuing the former 'babies' cage' agenda, and is unaware of its possible broader implications.

The Tarzan example thus illustrates in several ways how the narrative events of preschool children can serve as a double opportunity space. It shows how story telling is occasioned within the imaginary worlds co-constructed by the children, how such storytelling can transcend the boundaries of the symbolic pretend frame and make points relevant to broader issues, like the children's gender identities, and how meanings on the sociocultural plane are negotiated and enacted on the discursive plane through complex interactional episodes rich in opportunities for discursive learning.

Summary

I have argued in this chapter that modes of meaning making in children's conversational narratives function simultaneously in two arenas: the socio-cultural and the discursive. Table 1 summarizes the argument by listing the specific contributions of each arena to narrative practice and meaning in terms of the three postulated dimensions of narrativity – telling, tale and tellers.

Table 1. Modes of meaning making in children's narratives

	The socio-cultural arena	The discursive arena
Telling	– Provides criteria for tellability – Allows for pretend keying and rekeying	– Occasions story-telling – Occasions the practice of performance skills
Tales	– Nurtures the co-construction of possible worlds	– Allows for the construction of connected discourse in distanced worlds
	– Helps determine the point of stories & their functions	– Allows for playing with genre conventions
Tellers	– Allows for the negotiation of issues of immediate concern	– Allows for reciprocal historical, psychological and conversational support and challenge in story-telling

'What a terrible horrible dream!' exclaims Daniel in one of the pretend play episodes of the Pika story (see Appendix). He is talking not about his dream, or his friend's dream as told, but establishing the *sharedness* of the dream (*'we were in the same dream because we slept comfortably'*) before co-constructing its tale. In this chapter I have argued that it is probably because young children feel so much at ease in pretend play tale realms that they can reach such high-points of intersubjective meaning-making as telling each other a shared dream. I further argued that all peer-talk conversational narratives – pretend and real, distanced or immediate, dyadic or multiparty – serve as rich resources

for providing children with opportunities to develop the discursive skills of storytelling while making sense of the world.

Appendix

What a Terrible Horrible Dream

Dani (m; 5;11); Alon (m; 5;0).
The kids are playing freely outside. They are engaged in an ongoing pretend play revolving around Pokémon. In a previous segment, Pikachu – who is played by Alon – went to the hospital to visit his sick friend Dani, who has been lying there for 3 days. Pokémons are stored in a ball called 'Pokéball'.
Filename: Daniel 6.4.00, turn 117.

1	Daniel:	(0) lo↑ magilot mamash. ve-keilu y-y- yashanu anaxnu be-oto xeder. (0) alon nu, az- az bo tishan po. ata po. (0) ken ata shaxabta po ani po	(0) no↑ really disgusting. And as if w- w- we slept in the same room. (0) Alon come on, so- so come sleep here. You're here. (0) yes you were lying here I here
2	Alon:	lo ani (…)((laughs))	No I (…) ((laughs))
3	Daniel:	(0) °alon al tinxar°.	(0) °Alon don't snore°.
4	Daniel:	(0) a- <u>lo</u>. ata yashanta po, ani yashanti ba-cel.	(0) a- <u>no</u>. You slept here, I slept in the shade.
5	Daniel:	ken aval, gam ata roce lishon ba-cel. ata yaxol.	Yes but, you too want to sleep in the shade too. You can.
6	Alon:	x:::::::: psh::::::: ((snoring))	x:::::::: psh::::::: ((snoring))
7	Daniel:	(0) alon, al tinxar, lo roce she-nix- she- ki ze lo yafe↑, alon.	(0) Alon, don't snore, don't want that- sno- that- because it's not nice↑, Alon.
8	Daniel:	(0) #A:: ma ze?# alon, keilu irgashti she-ani be-azikim, ki xalamti xalom.	(0) #A:: what's this? # Alon, as if I felt that I'm in handcuffs, because I had a dream.
9	Alon:	ken. gam ani xalamti xalom she gam ani↑ ayiti, aynu be-oto xalom blal ((biglal)) she yashanu, benoxut.	Yes. I had a dream too that I↑ was too, we were in the same dream becau ((because)) we slept, comfortably.
10	Daniel:	alon, adayin lo↑ aya be'ecem boke::↑r , ve:: gam <u>ata</u> ayita be-azikim.	Alon, it wasn't↑ morni::↑ng yet actually, an::d <u>you</u> were in handcuffs too.
		6 turns omitted: the children act out their dream, pretending to realize they are handcuffed.	

17 Alon: [A:: ma ze itorarti? (0) ua↑y ma ze, ma ze, e↑ize xalom ra↑ [aya↑ li].   [A:: what's this did I wake up? (0) may↑be what's this, what's this, e↑ what a ba↑d dream [I had↑.]

18 Daniel: [eize xalo::m] gam li aya:: (0) oto xalom. ma ata xalamta she ayta be-azikim?=   [what a drea::m] I ha::d (0) the same dream too. What did you dream that you were in handcuffs?=

19 Alon: =ken=   =yes=

20 Daniel: =ve-raita et a-raim?   =and you saw the bad guys?

21 Alon: im a-pokadur, ve gam [ata]?   With the Pokeball, and you [too]?

22 Daniel: [gam ani::   [me too::

23 Alon: uay eze (xalom ayom ve-nora). az itgalasht-   Wow what (a terrible horrible dream). So you slid-

Notes

1. Transcription conventions used: [words] – overlapping talk; = – overlatch; (0.5) – timed intervals; (.) – intervals of less than 0.2 seconds; (…) – incomprehensible words; (words) – transcription doubt; . – a falling intonation at the end of an utterance; , – a continuing rising intonation; ? – a rising intonation at the end of an utterance; ↑ – rising intonation; ↓ – falling intonation; WORD – high volume; °word° – low volume; word – emphasis; wo::rd – sound stretch; wor- – cut-off; >words< – fast rhythm; <words> – slow rhythm; {word} – unusual pronunciation; #words# – unusual tone of voice, described in a comment; word/word/word – rhythmic pronunciation; ((comment)) – transcriber's comments, including translation clarifications in the English version.

2. This study is part of a longitudinal research project tracing the development of different discourse genres, supported by Grant No. 980031 from the United States-Israel Binational Science Foundation (BSF), Jerusalem, Israel (1999–2002) and by Grant No. 832/01-1 by The Israeli Science Foundation (ISF), (2001–2004). The project was set up to track the development of two extended genres – narratives and explanations – in two age groups (twenty preschoolers and twenty nine year olds at the onset of the study) in three contexts: Peer interaction, family talk and semi-structured interviews. We used two techniques for collecting data in the preschool: first, individual recordings, carried out by having two children at a time carry small tape-recorders in a pouch around their belt with a small external microphone, and second, by placing the tape-recorder with an external mike near groups of children involved in talk and play.

3. Names of the week of Hebrew include the lexeme 'day': (e.g., 'Sunday' is literally 'first day', 'Monday' = 'second day' etc.).

4. See Blum-Kulka (2005a) for a structural analysis of this story.

CHAPTER 9

Two systems of mutual engagement

The co-construction of gendered narrative
styles by American preschoolers

Amy Sheldon and Heidi Engstrom
University of Minnesota

Introduction

Conversational interaction is the central medium through which we create our
social lives. Conversations are also the major medium in which children hear
stories from others and construct their own, well before they become literate.
Preschool children are members of communities that are rich in conversations – families, neighborhoods, nursery schools, and daycare centers. Conversations are the medium through which they get to know others, jointly explore
objects, materials and events, and create and recreate versions of the world they
know or imagine. Before children's formal schooling in literacy skills begins,
they usually already have years of experience developing textual skills through
shared talk with playmates, in which they have co-constructed far more elaborate stories than they can tell, or read or write, by themselves in first grade. That
is partly because children's co-constructed stories are emergent, developed in
the realm of physical activity and enactment with material resources.

   The study of these story texts is important not only because it informs us
about the foundational skills children bring to school instruction in the intri-
cacies of written texts, but also because it adds to our understanding of the
human capacity for story construction across the life-span.[1]

   This chapter describes how the activity of interactionally constructing and
enacting pretend play stories can be affected at its core by the community's
gender order. Cultural scripts of femininity and of masculinity are given subtly different sociolinguistic expression, which serves to index gender and make
it integral to children's process and content of co-constructed oral narratives.

This work on how gender can influence the process of interactive oral narrative construction builds on earlier findings of gender difference in story construction in this community of children (Sheldon & Rohleder 1996) and is consistent with work about gender differences in nursery school children's stories (Nicolopoulou et al. 1994), and in conversational cohesion in talk produced by young friends (Tannen 1994), among others.

The children's conversations discussed here emerged in the course of their spontaneous play together. They were not guided or interfered with by any adults. All adults apart from the camera operator, and occasionally the audio engineer recording the session were usually out of visible range. Extended, often negotiated, emplotment and enactment were interactively accomplished during pretend play. We start with two clear cases in each of a girls' session and a boys' session, and describe some of the sociolinguistic evidence that leads to a working hypothesis that, in this community of American preschoolers, when a child plays in a group with other girls or with other boys, these same-sex groups have somewhat different systems, or patterns, of mutual engagement that shape their joint development of stories. We call this the *Two Systems of Mutual Engagement Hypothesis*.

Two Systems of Mutual Engagement

The *Two Systems of Mutual Engagement Hypothesis* claims that there are sociolinguistic features in these children's conversations during play that subtly differentiate and add tonality to the all-girl and all-boy interactions. The girls' co-construction of pretend play discourse is primarily shaped by – or exemplifies – a *consistently integrated and coordinated engagement*. The boys' co-construction of pretend play discourse is noticeably shaped by – exemplifies – *parallel, disjoint, and intermittantly coordinated engagement*. The following is a summary overview of some features of these styles, which previews the data analysis that follows.

Features of these girls' narrative engagement:

- Girls move into an immediate and smooth engagement that has a mutual focus and coordinated activity
- They have a more continuous, consistent, and cohesive engagement
- They more often expand play themes in a linked manner
- They have more reciprocal turn sequences

- They more often talk about mutual activity
- The listener's activity is more often related to the speaker's
- Individual experience is often reported in a series of repetitions by members of the group, creating the effect of a choral ensemble or a duet
- When individual experiences and evaluations are presented to the group they tend to be mirrored and matched by the others.

Features of these boys' narrative engagement:

- Boys are slower to create a mutual focus and coordinated activity
- Their engagement is more episodic in a pattern of: engage-disengage-reengage
- They have shorter and more intermittent common foci of talk and activity
- There is more rapid introduction of play themes, and more rapid shift (turnover) to new play themes
- There are more attention-getting markers ("hey!") and resistance markers ("but") (not discussed here)
- They have fewer reciprocal turn sequences
- Their talk is often a report of the speaker's own activity in parallel with another child's activity or similar report
- Speakers jockey for topic rights
- The group eventually attains sustained mutual engagement and coordinated activity but does so more gradually than the girls, after some delays and derailments.

These are not mutually exclusive patterns, but rather differences in degree that give the girls' and boys' interactions different tonalities.

Gender in language practices

Our analysis of the data that lead to this formulation concludes that these are features that index gender distinctions between these groups. Previous descriptions of conversations of children in this community have shown that the conflict talk of these girls and boys is gendered (Sheldon 1990a, 1992a, 1992b, 1996, 1997; Sheldon & Johnson 1998). In addition, Sheldon and Rohleder (1996) have shown that even when this community of children interact in all-girl or all-boy groups in the same play spaces with the exact same play resources (on different occasions), the outcomes for their co-constructed narratives are strikingly different. The present study finds more differences in looking at other features of their joint narrative development.

In saying that these children's speech is gendered, we mean that they are using speech practices that make them recognizable to each other as a girl or a boy in ways that are consistent with the local gender order. (This is not to deny the fact that there are similarities in girls' and boys' use of language, which may be vaster than the differences.) These discourse practices achieve different narrative content and effects and give different tonalities to their interactionally produced stories. The girls and boys in this preschool community have the same (age-related) linguistic competencies available to them. Yet they are making some different linguistic choices, which have consequences for their jointly developed narrative texts. These different language practices, which may be small in proportion to the similarities, nevertheless have important effects on the moment-to-moment development of their joint narrative work, and on the narrative outcomes.

Method

The data studied here are part of an archive that was collected on videotape by Sheldon at a preschool, and is reported on elsewhere (e.g. Sheldon 1990a). Thirty-six three, four and five year old Midwestern American preschoolers were studied. They were long-time attendees at a high quality, anti-bias, all-day childcare center, which was staffed by a well-trained, skillful group of teachers, who had been at the center for many years. The center was located in the Twin Cities, in Minnesota. It was among the first to develop an explicit 'anti-bias' mission and curriculum. Developing the curriculum and training the staff to implement it was in progress during the time period studied.

The children were engaged in unsupervised spontaneous pretend play in same-sex triads at the daycare center. Twelve triads (6 of girls, 6 of boys) took turns on different days playing in the same playroom with exactly the same toy set-ups, for about twenty-five minutes apiece. They were the only children in the room. They were videotaped by a camera operator who stood in the doorway of the room. An audio engineer was hidden behind a curtain and was in charge of mixing the sound tracks from the children's individual microphones (attached to the lapel of a vest they wore) onto the audio track of the videotape at the time of taping.[2] This chapter describes an exemplar of a girls' group and an exemplar of a boys' group; the children are four-year-olds.

Both sessions took place in a self-contained play space down a hall from their larger group's activity in the day care center. The play room was set up primarily as a domestic setting, i.e. a 'housekeeping corner', which had a toy stove and sink, a basket filled with plastic food, a dinner table and chairs, eating utensils, a high chair, a crib with dolls, a child size foam easy chair, a telephone, dress-up clothes and a mirror, and some toy doctor supplies: a stethoscope with a blood pressure cuff, a needle-less syringe, and an ear scope.

The girls created a domestic script, that could be described as 'a day in ordinary life', with events such as preparing and eating a meal, pretending to be at a restaurant, having conversations about food, feeding baby at the table, putting baby to bed, tending to a sick baby which included calling the doctor, pretending to be a nurse, giving the baby a shot, taking its temperature, looking in its ears, getting and making telephone calls including narrating the unseen speaker's words to the rest of the group, and reporting a scary story 'told' by the person on the other end of the telephone. There were negotiations (of varying degrees of intensity) over roles, plot development, who got to do what, etc.

The boys spent much less time developing a domestic story world than the girls did, but they started out in that realm and spent time preparing food, eating it and talking about it at the dinner table, sitting some babies at the table, giving a sick baby a shot, playing doctor with each other and checking a boy's heart, stomach and blood pressure. But the main story world they constructed could be described as a 'dangerous and action filled adventure'. They eventually settled on a narrative proposed by one of the boys, that brought them on an 'explore', finding a bear, a bat, a lion and 'lumpy things' before they ran home, barricaded the door with the kitchen stove and overturned chairs, and hid from the polar bear who was trying to break in.

A more complete discussion of how the physical setting was congruent with, or was transformed into, different story worlds is reported in Sheldon and Rohleder (1996). These boys' pattern of spending some time in a domestic story construction mode but then transforming the domestic play resources to create a (usually) unrelated non-domestic story world was replicated by each of the other five male triads who played in this room set up when it was their turn. And the girls' enactment of a domestic script, which was consistent with the room set up and resources, was repeated by the other five female triads when it was their turn to play in the room. There were very few transformations by the girls' groups to play that was out of the domestic mode. When done, it was integrated into the domestic script, rather than being disjunctive.

Results

The two sessions that we will compare were about equal length (the girls' session was 25.92 min. long, the boys' was 26.33 min. long). Adjustments have been made for session length in making the following comparisons. We will compare both quantitative and qualitative features of their story constructions. We will look at: (1) total speech output, (2) features of their turns, (3) features of their topic development, and will then give (4) some short examples of discourse. The following tables present these features.

Basic measures

Table 1 shows that boys produced more speech than girls: almost 200 more utterances and their total word count was higher by about 600 words. This difference cannot be accounted for by the 25 second longer duration of the boys' session. Adjusting for this slight time difference, we found that girls produced 23% fewer utterances per minute.

Table 1. Amount of talk

Total number of utterances[3]	Girls	Boys
Raw no. of utterances	627	824
% of Total	43%	57%
Ratio of girls' utterances to boys'	76%	
24% fewer utterances (not adjusted for time)		
Utterances per minute	24	31
Ratio of girls' utterances to boys'	77%	
23% fewer utterances per minute (adjusted for time)		

| Total number of words[4] | Girls | | | Boys | | |
	-mazed	+mazed	all	-mazed	+mazed	all
Total	3045	218	3263	3525	317	3842
% of Total			46%			54%
Words per minute (wpm)			126			146
Girls' wpm as % of boys'			86%			–
Ratio of girls' total word output to boys'			85%			–
Ratio of girls' session time to boys'			98%			

Table 2 shows that although they produced less speech, girls had slightly longer utterances compared to boys, based on MLU as measured in words (4.83 ~ 4.31).

The average length of girls' and boys' turns were about the same, whether measured by number of utterances per turn (1.8 ~ 1.7), or number of words per turn (8.1 ~ 7.1).

Table 2. Length of utterances

MLU in words (excluding mazed words)		
	Girls	Boys
Range	4.04–5.4	4.28–4.37
Mean	4.83	4.31

Turn length		
	Girls	Boys
Mean turn length of utterances	1.8 utterances	1.7
Range:	1.5–2.2	1.5–1.8
Mean turn length of words	8.1 words	7.1
Range:	7.22–11.44	6.5–7.6

Boys produced more topics, at a rate of 3.1 topics per minute compared to the girls' 2.5 topics per minute. Girls produced 79% of the number of topics that boys produced.

Table 3. Number of topics

	Girls	Boys
Number of topics	64	82
Topics per minute	2.5	3.1
	(for 25.92 min.)	(for 26.33 min.)
Ratio of girls' topics to boys'	79% of boys' rate	

Topic development

Looking at topic development, we find that boys more often continued their *own* topic than they continued another boy's topic. There was more topic *shifting* in the boys' group, more self-reports, more demands, challenges, refusals

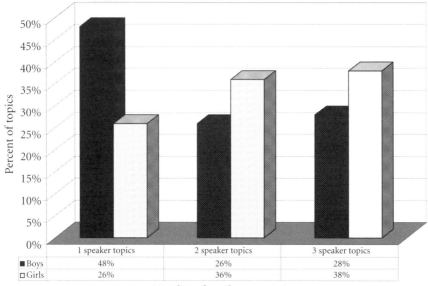

	1 speaker topics	2 speaker topics	3 speaker topics
■ Boys	48%	26%	28%
□ Girls	26%	36%	38%

Number of speakers per topic

Figure 1. Percent of topics that have 1, 2, or 3 speakers

and generally, more disputatious talk which made *joint* topic development more difficult to achieve. Girls had more *shared* topics and continued them longer in reciprocal exchanges. They had less topic shifting, fewer self-reports, fewer announcements, and less disruptive conflict talk.

These different patterns of reciprocal engagement can be seen in the two graphs, which portray gender differences in number of sequences in which all three speakers contributed to topic development.

Figure 1 shows the percentage of topics that have 1, 2 or 3 speakers. Nearly half of the topics in the boys' group had just *one* speaker. If we add to this the number of two-speaker topics, we see that nearly three quarters of the topics discussed in the boys' group involved one or two speakers. About one quarter of the boys' topics were discussed by all three boys.

The distribution goes the other way in the girls' group, however. One-speaker topics were *least* frequent. They occurred about half as often in the girls' group as they did in the boys' group. The girls had more three-speaker and two-speaker topics than the boys did, and these accounted for about three quarters of their topics.

Figure 2 compares the length of turn *sequences* when all three speakers were on-topic. When the three boys are all on the same topic, 80% of their talk on

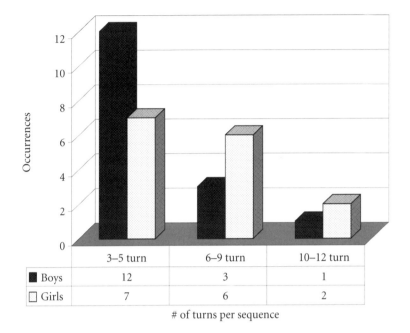

	3–5 turn	6–9 turn	10–12 turn
■ Boys	12	3	1
□ Girls	7	6	2

# of turns per sequence

Figure 2. Three speaker on-topic turn sequences

that topic is done in short turn sequences, between 3–5 turns long. Girls, on the other hand, interact in longer sequences on a single topic. 53% of their three-speaker on-topic turn sequences are longer sequences, between 6–12 turns long. As could be expected, the girls had a lower rate of topics per minute. Their topic development sequences were longer; they shifted topic less. Taken together, these facts account for our impression from viewing the sessions that these girls' discourse was more reciprocal and integrated, and that their pretend play interactions were more elaborate across the length of the session.

Figures 1 and 2 are measures of reciprocality and linguistic involvement within the group with regard to the linguistic development of topics.

Discourse examples

We now present some examples of talk in each group in order to elaborate on the quantitative measures.

Three-speaker integrated and coordinated talk

Example 1 is an example of three-speaker integrated and coordinated talk in the girls' group:

Example 1. "It's butter!" (35 seconds)

(*The girls are by the table, which they have set for a meal and have brought plastic food to. Arlene is sitting at the table. She reaches for the bread and holds a plastic knife in her other hand.*)

```
01 Arlene:  Hey, (Looks around at the table and towards the girls)
02                    where's all the stuff to spread  on      the    bread?
03 Erica:                                  Put    on- on  your  bed- bread?
04                    I don't know.
05 Arlene:           Me too. Well,=
06 Elaine:           (Sits down at the table)
07                   =It's BUTTER!
08 Erica:            (Stands near table and looks at Arlene)
                     It's butter.
09 Elaine:           It's butter.
10 Erica:               Butter.
11 Arlene: Well-
12 Elaine:           That's what mommy   putted  on          it.
13 Erica:       Yeah,
14                   wh-
15                   that's what [I-      put]
16 Arlene:           [I always] love butter        on         mine.
17 Elaine: Well,
18         I must say
19                   you cer[tainly do].
20 Arlene:           [I always] kinda have my bread cut like this. (Crosses plastic
                     knife over the bread)
21                   I always      have a je-
                     (Turns to high chair where Erica has just brought a doll to
                     put in the high chair between Elaine and Arlene)
22 Elaine:           (To Erica, about the doll) Now put her- I'm her mommy.
```

Example 1 contains conversational turns with repeated and recycled elements that create the effect of reciprocality and textual coherence. One way this is accomplished is that words and syntactic patterns are echoed by different speakers. We have put their text into a 'verse' format, following a discourse analysis technique used by Tannen (1989:72), in order to make the girls' polyphonic patterning more salient. This helps to highlight how the girls' repetition of words and syntactic structures builds a 'choral ensemble' effect. For example, Erica and Elaine repeat the same phrase, 'It's butter' in lines 7–10, and Arlene repeats 'butter' in line 16. Each girl uses a variation of V + on + NP in: 'spread on the bread' (Arlene, line 2), 'put on your bread' (Erica, line 3), and 'putted on it' (Elaine, line 12), 'love butter on mine' (Arlene, line 16). Reciprocality is also achieved through question-answer sequences. In line 2 Arlene asks, 'Where's all the stuff to spread on the bread?' In lines 3–4, Erica produces a question as a confirmation check. Explicit markers of agreement also produce reciprocal exchanges: Arlene, 'me too', (line 5), Erica, 'Yeah', (line 13), and Elaine, 'you certainly do', (line 19). Finally, there is self-disclosure and evaluation by Arlene, 'I always love butter on mine', which is confirmed by Elaine in an adult-sounding register, 'Well, I must say you certainly do'.

The features of echoic and contingent talk mentioned above reflect close listenership. The speakers are mostly facing and looking at each other when they talk. Their talk has the quality of 'mirroring', a sensitive monitoring of what each other says, in which contributions are tailored "to match what has gone before", which Coates (1996:79) notes as a characteristic of conversation among Caucasian British women friends. Tannen's (1994) study of pairs of Caucasian American girl friends notes that features of talk that build reciprocity are prominent characteristics in those dyads also. In fact, Holmes proposed a broad sociolinguistic universal that "women tend to use linguistic devices that stress solidarity more than men do" (1998:468). Although this general statement is unlikely to hold up invariantly across all situations, we note the resonance that the linguistic style of the girls described in this chapter has with talk styles found among older girls and among women in other research. We interpret this style as one way in which females can orient to a gender order that aligns them with values such as interpersonal harmony, keeping peace in groups, and attending to the needs and wishes of others. Whatever *other* agendas girls and women may choose to pursue, the gender order in English-speaking communities described in the middle class, mostly Western (United Kingdom, United States, New Zealand), Caucasian communities studied all have this prescription for females. These are discourse skills that can sustain and advance the joint activity of pretend story construction. In fact, prior research indicates that boys' more unmitigated adversarial style can disrupt pretend story construction (Sheldon 1990a, 1992a; Kyratzis & Ervin

Tripp 1999), or interaction that is not necessarily involved in story construction (Leaper 1989).

Example 2 is another example of this same kind of contingent talk that is common in the girls' session. The verse format of the text highlights the lexical repetition and structural parallelisms:

Example 2. "I need to cut up my soup!" (160 seconds)

(The girls are all sitting at the table enacting having a meal)

01	Arlene:	I'll		cut UP		the mashed potatoes.

01 Arlene: I'll   cut UP   the mashed potatoes.
02 Erica: I-
03   I   needa-
04   I   need to cut up   my CHICken.
05 Elaine: I   needa   cut up   my SOup.
06 Erica: (*Looks at Elaine*)   Your SOUP?!!
07 Elaine: (*Looks at Erica sheepishly*)   Not my SOUP.
08 Erica: (*Laughs*)
09 Elaine: I   mean   EAT   my soup.
10 Erica: (*Laughs*)
11   You   said   'CUT up'   your soup.
12   (*Laughs*)
13   You don't need to cut UP   soup.
14   Don't   cut up   soup
15 Arlene: (*Looking for an opening in the conversation to change the activity, turns her body toward the phone as if she hears it ringing and prepares to get up and answer it*)
                 Wait-
16 Erica: Don't   cut.
17 Arlene: (*Turns back as Erica continues to talk*)
18 Erica: (*Laughingly*)
           You DON'T   CUT   soup, NO=.
19 Arlene: =Oh! (*Looks at the others and raises her left hand to get their attention*)
20 Arlene: I'll get it. (*Gets up from the table, goes to the phone, and picks up the receiver. Elaine and Erica stop talking and eating and pay attention to what Arlene is saying on the phone*)
21   Yes?
22   Ok.
23   What?
24   Oh.

25		We'll be RIGHT over.
26		Do you have any other requests?
27	Elaine:	Who is it? (Arlene *continues a complex performance of telephone talk to an imaginary character. When she hangs up she tells them a story of a sick baby who needs their help, which Erica and Elaine carefully pay attention to and discuss*)

One notable feature of Example 2 is how talk itself is of interest and becomes a topic of conversation. The girls display close listenership. Interestingly, Johnson and Aries (1998) find that talk is *the* central activity between women friends, which implies the central importance of listening, as well.[5] The first example of the attention to talk is Erica's correction of Elaine's conversational misstep as she goes down the syntactic garden path of the pattern 'I'll cut up X' to produce 'I'll cut up my soup', in line 5. Elaine's blooper provides a lot of benign entertainment to Erica as she contemplates and comments on this impossibility.

Second, Erica and Elaine stop eating when Arlene 'answers the phone', an act which provides her with the opportunity to invent a conversation with an imaginary character on the other end of the line, and thus insert her own story thread. This has captured the other girls' complete interest. Arlene's new thread is woven into their joint pretend play plot, after she gets off the phone (not shown in this data, however).

A third, particularly subtle indication of how well these girls are listening to each other is the way Arlene times her phone call. She is waiting for Erica to be done commenting on Elaine's mistake. She misjudges Erica's completion point in line 15 and starts to get up for the phone before Erica is done. Seeing that Erica is still talking, she turns her body back to the table, tucks her feet back under it until the next opportunity to take a turn. Her timing is precise; in line 19 again she prepares to get up for the phone, prefacing her move with a surprise marker, 'Oh!' and at the same time lifts her hand to get the other girls' attention. Latching her talk to Erica's with these turn-initial indicators, she successfully gets a turn at talk without seeming to interrupt Erica. Once she has it, she skillfully keeps their attention fixed on her talk on the phone.

Boys' three speaker parallel talk

The following are examples from the boys' group that can be described as parallel rather than topically integrated or coordinated. Each boy is pretty much talking about his own topic although there are some overlaps. We have put their talk in columns to make it easier for the reader to follow the pattern of an individual's talk.

Example 3. "Hey, cheese!" (108 seconds)

Robert:	Connor:	Mark:
01 I got the food guys. (*Takes basket of food to table*)	(*Playing with the blood pressure cuff and a syringe in front of the table*)	(*Standing near Connor, in front of the table, holding another syringe*)
	02 Supper time.	
03 I got the food.	(*His back is to Robert and he is playing with the syringe instead*)	(*He's not paying attention to Robert, but is looking at the syringe in his hand*)
		04 Here's the shotter. (*the syringe*)
05 Look at all the food, guys.	(*He continues to play with the syringe*)	
06 I got- Give the baby a shot.		
	07 (*To himself*) And HERE'S a shot.	
08 (*To Mark*) Here, get the baby to give a shot.		
		09 (*Turns to the baby in the crib beside the table and gives it a shot*)
10 [I got ALL the FOOD.]		
	11 (*Still playing with the syringe on himself*) This [s- (*hums*)]	
12 I got a EGG for breakfast now.		
	13 (*Gets up, goes to the table and looks in the food basket*) Hey, I'm gonna have a ta- some tato.	

14 Hey, I'M gonna have a toMAto for SUPPER. (*Makes sound effect of eating*)

(*Puts his shotter down and joins the boys at the table but wanders around a bit, and goes to the food basket, then sits down*)

15 This is BREAKFAST time. (*Puts two pieces of bread on a plate and bends down to pretend to eat them, making sound effects*)

16 We're gonna have TOMATO for supper I'm like FOZZIE Bear (*Puts a tomato to his eye. Makes a sound effect*)

17 It's BREAKFAST time. (*Takes more food out of basket to his plate*)

18 (*To no one in particular*) Know what's fun?

19 Corn. (*Bends over plate and eats from it with his mouth, making eating sounds*)

20 Hey, I got a tomato- (*Puts tomato on his head then bends down to get things from the food basket*)

21 I got some MEAT.

22 Hey, could make- could make pot- pot- potatoes in it!
23 Hey, CHEESE! Swiss cheese.

24 Yes and this. (*Holding a sandwich*)

           25 I'm having CHEESE! (*Turns his back to the table ready to get up*)

26 Oh look at this! (*his sandwich*) I have a big SAMICH. (*Said in a wondrous tone. Lifts the sandwich to his mouth and makes a chomping noise*)

           27 (*Takes no notice and gets up from the table*) I'm gon- I'm gonna shot (*use the pretend syringe*). My, Robert, you're gonna have your- your shot will only hurt for a minute.

In Example 3 the boys make a number of announcements of what they each are doing or what they each have, sometimes repeating their self-report or announcement a number of times. Robert's multiple repetition that 'This is breakfast time' is ignored by Connor, who announces that *he's* having 'supper'.

Connor also prefaces a number of his turns with an attention marker, 'hey!' In this boys' session there were 46 occurrences of 'hey' in 33 turns, 21 made by Connor. The marker often prefaced an announcement of what the speaker is doing during parallel play, sometimes with as many as four occurrences of 'hey' in a single turn. Sometimes one use of 'hey' triggered a series of turn initiations with 'hey'. Other functions of the marker were to preface a question, an opposition, a suggestion, to mark surprise, and to advance the story. In the girls' group there were six occurrences of 'hey' in six turns, four by Arlene. This asymmetry in the use of 'hey' held up across all the triads in the larger corpus: In the six girls' triads 'hey' was produced 75 times, and in the six boys' triads, it was produced 298 times. The difference suggests that the boys had to do more conversational work to get noticed or to get a response and reciprocal engagement. Although the talk in Example 3 is mostly in parallel tracks of self-reports, the boys usually seem to be noticing what each other is doing and their announcements could be interpreted as competitive comparisons. There is at least one structural parallelism in the above data, in the pattern 'I got X' ,'I'm having Y', and 'I have Z', said by one or the other boys, all self-reports. Another difference between Example 3 and the two examples in the girls' group is that the boys do much more moving around back and forth from the table, compared to the longer stretches of time that the girls sit and eat and talk face to face.

Example 4. "I'll be the doctor for a minute, ok?" (90 seconds)

This next example is a spate of parallel talk that is prior to the point at which all three begin to coordinate with each other in jointly producing a story of action and adventure. Connor has invited the others to join him on 'an explore'. He is alternatively caught in the embrace of his imagination, enacting and narrating his explore, and reemerges from it to persuade the others to join him. At first, Mark and Robert make a brief effort to join him, but they quickly drop out and get interested in their own parallel activities. Robert is setting the table and will soon try to get the boys involved in a story enacted in a doctor's office. Meanwhile, Mark is looking around the room, distractedly holding a doll by one arm and the opposite leg, noticing things in his surroundings. It is Robert and Connor who are independently developing story worlds in this example, each trying to get the others involved, but not having success yet. (Overlapping utterances are in square brackets.)

01 Connor: (*Carrying a doll, wearing a military jacket and hat, and walking*
                  around the room by himself)
02   I [hear some- I see] some-
03   I see some lumpy things.
04 Mark: (*Standing by the table, holding a doll by one arm and the opposite leg,*
05   *looking around the room*)
06   [They're taking pictures of us]
                  (*Referring to camera operator in a corner*)
07 Connor: (*Goes up to the table that Robert is setting*) What are those?
08   (*Referring to silverware*)
09 Mark: They're taking pictures of us.
10 Connor: (*To the others*) We're taking- we're going- Shhh!
11   There's a BEAR!
12   Now it's time to leave=
13 Robert: (*Humming*) =dan-dan-dan- Let's eat!
14   (*Ignores Conner, sits at table*) (*Hums*)
15 Connor: (*Ignores Robert and walks away from the table into his "explore"*
                  territory)

16		Mark, [Come on, there's no bear].
17	Robert:	(*Gets up from the table and says to Mark, who is standing next to him*)
18		[I'll be the doctor now for a minute, ok?]
19		I'm gonna be the doc- ooh
20		(*Unsnaps his vest by mistake and then resnaps it*)
21	Connor:	(*Talking sotto voce to himself and twirling around, away from Robert and Mark, taking his jacket off*)
22		Number "B", and "A"
23		(*Reading the letters on their vests*). I'm "A", I'm "B"
24		(*Twirling around and taking his jacket off*)
25	Robert:	(*To Mark in a whisper*) I snapped it back. (*his vest*)
26	Connor:	(*He's taken his hat off*) Come on, quiet.
27	Robert:	(*To the group*) I'm gonna be the doctor for a minute, ok?
28		I'm gonna be the doctor for a minute, ok? (*Goes to get his doctor things*)
29	Connor:	Come on, Louie, we'll have to tiptoe.
30		(*Looks at Mark*) Louie, come on.
31		Tiptoe tiptoe.
32	Robert:	We're in the waiting room. (*Stands behind the stove, has
33		put his doctor things on the floor in front of it*).
34		(*Goes over to Connor*) You're in the waiting room
35		(*Touches Connor's hand*) Your turn.
36		(*Goes back to the 'waiting room' but Connor backs away*)
37		(*Encouragingly*) Your turn.
38		Your turn.
39	Connor:	(*Goes up to Mark and says*) We're tiptoeing in the woods, remember?
40	Mark:	(*Is standing by the 'waiting room' also, and whispers to Robert*)
41		There's a bear nearby.
42		(*Whispers*) I don't know who's behind that person.
43		(*Looking at the audio engineer behind a partition*)
44	Connor:	(*To Robert, in a whisper*) Be careful, Betty.
45		(*Hums and walks away to talk to his doll*)
46		(*Whispers to his doll*) Don't speak.
47	Mark:	Look behind-
48	Connor:	(*Speaks aloud in the voice of his doll*) Eh, eh!
49	Mark:	Look behind there. (*Behind a curtain where the engineer is*)
50	Connor:	(*Looking at his doll*) Don't speak!
51		(*Turns to Mark and whispers*) There's a lion in the front. (*Points*)

52		(*Whispers to Mark*) And he's saying "rrraaarrr" to us.
53		And we better run home. (*Runs away from Mark, and sits in a chair by the kitchen table*)
54	Mark:	(*Walks over to the table*)
55	Robert:	(*Goes over to the table*) I'll be the dad for a minute, ok?
56		I'll be the da-=
57	Mark:	(*To Connor*) =No that's my chair.
58	Connor:	(*Gets up from the chair, hums a tune*) de-de-de-de de- de-de-,

The boys eventually did develop the story of the 'explore'. What is missing in the above text is the creation of involvement through joint verbal negotiation of the story. In lines 10–12, each one announces their own story theme in progress, to the others. Connor announces 'We're taking- we're going- Shhh! There's a BEAR! Now it's time to leave='. In lines 27–38, Robert begins his story line with the announcement, 'We're in the waiting room'. (*Goes over to Connor*) 'You're in the waiting room.' (*Touches Connors hand*) 'Your turn.' (*Goes back to the 'waiting room' but Connor backs away*). (*Encouragingly*) 'Your turn. Your turn.' The other boys do not respond to either Robert's or Connor's invitations, and instead continue in their separate story worlds. All three girls, on the other hand, move into the joint discussion and enactment of their story world quickly at the beginning of their session. Competition for 'story rights' between Robert and Connor delays story development and enactment, both their own and as a group activity.

Discussion

We have described two sessions that are representative of what we claim to be two gendered systems of mutual engagement, which are operating in girls' and boys' spontaneous pretend story construction. These are not mutually exclusive processes in the girls' and boys' groups, but they are noticeable in their effect on the quality and outcomes of the interactions, both social and narrative. The girls' joint construction of pretend play stories have a strong quality of continuity, smooth development, mutuality, and cohesion, where listener and speaker are engaged in interrelated activities that advance jointly constructed pretend play stories. The boys are slower to develop a mutual focus and coordinated activity in a single story world. Their mutual engagement takes the form of numerous announcements of their own side-by-side activity, attempts to get each other involved in their own story worlds, resistance or absence of uptake interspersed with episodes of short mutual foci of talk and activity. They have more of an *engage-disengage-reengage* pattern of imaginary play, until the group finally sustains a shared imaginative focus.

The girls' talk has a 'dialogue' quality, a sense of duetting, or turn-by-turn coordination of content and form. All speakers' activities seem to be on-topic.

Grounding

Two phases are needed for a complete conversation, or for it to be 'grounded': the 'presentation phase', in which messages are sent off to be considered, and the 'acceptance phase', in which a speaker is assured that the message has been understood as it was intended to be (Clark & Brennan 1991).

The two groups seem to be producing their discourse as a collective activity somewhat differently. The boys are issuing utterances, spending a lot of time in the presentation phase, e.g. self-reports of their own activity, repeated attempts to get their own topic picked up by the others, or introductions of a new topic. But they are not always receiving a response that indicates that their utterances have been received, or understood, i.e. the acceptance phase. Competing for attention and pursuing individual activity apparently does not move a group into an elaborate jointly developed narrative for the time spent together. The girls, on the other hand, seem to be giving more positive evidence of understanding to each other, i.e. providing the acceptance phase, providing evidence of attending to what is being said and incorporating it into their own next utterance. This may be one source for the impression of greater positive reciprocality in the girls' group. The differences in the organization of conversations in these two groups probably reflect the speakers' interactional goals at the time, e.g. the importance placed on independent activity vs mutually coordinated activity, and would change as those goals changed.

Conclusion

The research reported here describes some characteristics of children's discourse that have consequences for the joint construction of pretend play stories. It is intended as a first step toward studying a larger body of data.

We are claiming that the narrative practices of these friends in same-sex groups contain interesting differences – whatever similarities they *also* contain. Pointing out gender differences in how language is used in this particular context does not mean that these practices 'belong' to one sex in some essentialist fashion, or that their linguistic practices are invariant across all situations and with different interlocutors, e.g. in mixed-sex groups. The linguistic practices used in one group are available to all the children and can be used by girls and boys alike. Speech style is variable because it is situated behavior.[6] One area for further investigation would be to learn more about how children's discourse may vary in their displays of gender as a response to situational constraints. There is evidence that children are attending to gender differences in how language is used, and can talk about it, at around six years of age, or when meta-linguistic abilities emerge (Sheldon 1990b). Thus, a fruitful avenue for research would be to compare the process of co-construction of stories by the same children as a function of being in same- and in mixed-sex groups, in the same play spaces.[7] To echo the position articulated by Eckert and McConnell-Ginet, "... gender is not part of one's essence, what one is, but an achievement, what one does. ... gender is also about managing social relations" (2003: 305).

Story-telling is a key way in which we create social relationships and make sense of the complex world in which we live, until the end of our lives. It is a major way in which we display aspects of our identity to others, and read their identities. The preschool years are rich with exciting story-telling accomplishments, which are primarily communal. They are opportunities for the construction of often complex, shared, oral texts (Sheldon in press). The joint construction of stories is an opportunity for children to be fully engaged in the embrace of imagination as tellers *and* recipients, as they give the tale linguistic and interactional shape. They can be involved in every aspect of the craft – from inventing, to deciding, to editing and rearranging – developing characters, providing suspense. Hopefully, this research is a step toward the goal of knowing how the production of co-constructed story worlds also connects their individual minds and bodies to a symbolic gendered social order.

Acknowledgements

Research assistance was provided by Jessica Franklin, Matthew Wolf and Lisa Rohleder, at the University of Minnesota. Special thanks to Professor Jennifer Windsor for assistance with the SALT program.

Notes

1. These issues are explored further in Sheldon (in press).

2. Taping was done before digital equipment. VHS tape was used and each child was additionally taped on an individual audio cassette in a back pocket on a vest each one wore.

3. A measure based on all words spoken, including undeterminable words or pharases. Determinable utterances are ones which coders could determine what the child was speaking about. An undeterminable utterance is a false start, e.g. 'one ba-', which could not be interpreted from context, or an unintelligible word or phrase that was untranscribable and appeared in the transcript as 'XXX'. The girls' utterance total includes 39 undeterminable utterances and the boys' total includes 21.

4. Two word counts were taken in the SALT Program (Miller & Chapman 1998). SALT allows one to separate out words that are false starts, repetitions and reformulations. Those are coded as a 'maze' and the word count can contain them or not. An 'unmazed' word count contains all words that are not in a maze, which are considered the main content of the discourse. Thus, a mazed plus an unmazed word count are all words spoken. The boys had somewhat more tokens of mazed words. This may be due to more repetition, reformulation due to overlap, trying to get attention, individual differences in overall speakers, or it may be random.

5. "The women we interviewed isolate talk as the most important aspect of the relationship [with women friends]" (219). "... Through extensive talk about the most routine daily activities to the most private of personal problems and crises, women friends establish connections with one another that function significantly in their lives" (221).

6. Although it is beyond the scope of this chapter, it is worth mentioning that the children in this study already have learned a variety of speech repertoires, as shown by their use of different speech registers: e.g., speaking like a parent when they were in that role, using child-directed speech to the dolls, using robot speech, using a military register to issue commands, etc.

7. For some work on mixed-sex groups, see Kyratzis and Guo (1996).

CHAPTER 10

Narrative and the construction of professional identity in the workplace

Janet Holmes and Meredith Marra
Victoria University of Wellington

Introduction[1]

In this paper we examine one of the many functions of narratives in the work-place, namely their contribution to the construction of the professional identi-ties of managers. In different workplace contexts, and even at different points within the same interaction, participants emphasise particular facets of their social identities and different dimensions of social meaning – institutional or organisational affiliation, professional status, collegial solidarity, authority re-sponsibilities, gender category, ethnic affiliation, and so on (see Meyerhoff & Niedzielski 1994). Narratives provide one resource for producing or enacting particular aspects of an individual's social identity, and may serve, in particular, as discursive strategies for reconciling contradictory aspects of an individual's complex social identity at work.

In addressing our topic, we first briefly describe the dataset and method-ology of the large project from which the material analysed in this paper is taken. We then discuss in some detail the issue of how to identify workplace narratives, or 'workplace anecdotes' as we label them, and, in particular, how to distinguish them from reports and descriptions with which they share many structural features. Finally, we turn to an examination of some specific work-place anecdotes, exploring their function in relation to the 'display' of partic-ipants' social identities (Goffman 1981), and especially in the construction of the complex professional identities of managers in two contrasting workplaces.

The dataset

The Wellington Language in the Workplace Project (LWP) aims to analyse features of interpersonal communication in a wide variety of New Zealand workplaces (Holmes 1998a, 2000a). The methodology has been designed to record workplace interaction as unobtrusively as possible (Stubbe 1998, 2001). Typically, with the explicit knowledge and agreement of all involved, and using unobtrusive recording equipment, volunteers tape-record a range of their everyday work interactions over a period of time. In addition, wherever possible, workplace meetings are video-recorded.

The dataset we have amassed in this way includes workplace interactions recorded in a number of government departments and commercial white-collar organisations, as well as in small businesses, and in blue-collar factory environments. It includes social talk as well as business or task-oriented talk, and the length of recorded interactions ranges from short telephone calls of less than a minute, to long meetings which last more than four hours. The LWP corpus currently comprises more than 2000 interactions. The excerpts analysed in this paper are taken from anecdotes told during 'business talk' or in the course of normal workplace interaction in three contrasting work environments, namely, a government department, a soap powder factory, and a private, commercial sector organisation.

Business talk

Before addressing the issue of how we define a workplace anecdote it is useful to distinguish task-oriented, or 'business talk', from social talk and phatic communion.[2] Core business talk is relevant, focussed, usually context-bound, on-task talk, with a high information content. *Relevant* here means relevant to the organisation's core business: the underlying assumption is that the 'proper' focus of workplace discourse is the business at hand. Business talk directly serves the organisation's interests. *Informativeness* is another useful criterion: core business-talk is well-focussed, referential talk with high information content. A third criterion is the extent to which talk is *context-bound*: a full understanding of core business talk typically involves a great deal of background knowledge. There is also, typically, a specific agenda for core business talk, though this may not be written or even explicit. So, talk which qualifies for classification at the core business end of a continuum running from business talk through social talk to phatic communion is crucially informative, highly focussed, and 'on-topic' in terms of the agreed meeting agenda for that particular meeting in that

CORE BUSINESS TALK -------------- PHATIC COMMUNION
SOCIAL TALK

Relevant 'on-topic' talk   Off-topic talk
Maximally informative   Minimally informative
Context-bound   Context-free
Transactional   Social

Figure 1. Criteria for distinguishing business talk from phatic communion (from Holmes 2000b: 37)

particular workplace, and it directly serves the organisation's goals. (Figure 1 summarises these points in diagrammatic form.) This is useful background for a consideration of what counts as a workplace anecdote, the focus of our analysis, since workplace anecdotes, as we define them, are specifically digressions from core business talk.

Defining narrative: What counts as a 'workplace anecdote'?

Many researchers have confronted the problem of defining what constitutes a narrative, but none has resolved it satisfactorily. Goodwin (1990: 231), for example, states that she "will not attempt to provide a precise answer to this question", but uses the issue as a framework for examining alternative approaches to narrative analysis. Labov's definition of narrative – "a method of recapitulating past experience by matching a verbal sequence of clauses to the sequence of clauses which (it is inferred) actually occurred" (1972: 359–360) – has been widely adopted (e.g. Polanyi 1985; Johnstone 1993; Linde 1993; Rymes 1995; Coates 1996). Nevertheless, this definition raises a number of problems, as various researchers have noted (e.g. Edwards 1997; Linde 1993; Holmes 1998b; Coates 2003; Herman 2001).

Firstly, the crucial role allocated to temporal sequence has been questioned. Herman, for example, examines the role of spatial reference in narrative domains.[3] While researchers have generally agreed that "the temporal juncture characteristic of the minimal narrative has to be present in a text that [realizes] the narrative discourse type" (Virtanen 1992 as cited in Herman 2001: 535), Herman's analysis suggests that "temporal sequence is a necessary but not a sufficient condition for narrative" (2001: 535), and that spatial reference is also a core property of stories. His analysis of a number of narratives demonstrates that the boundary between description and narrative text types is a fuzzy one, an issue very pertinent to our attempts to characterise workplace narratives. Thus, he notes that "features that have been centrally associated with the prototype *description* may be core properties of narrative as well" (2001:535). He concludes that the boundaries between *narrative* vis-à-vis *description* are "fuzzy instead of sharp" (2001:535).

This exactly coincides with our experience in attempting to distinguish in our workplace data set between descriptions of past events or reports, on the one hand, and narratives or anecdotes on the other. The criterion of temporal sequence could not distinguish them, and even adding Herman's criterion of spatial reference did not exclude many instances of texts which we were confident did not function as 'stories'. Moreover, both temporal sequence and spatial reference were often implicit rather than explicit in the typically very brief workplace anecdotes which punctuated the business talk in our dataset. So, while we could intuitively identify 'workplace anecdotes' and distinguish them from reports and descriptions with almost 100% inter-rater reliability, the criteria we were using were certainly not exclusively structural. Hence, Example 1 was identified as a minimal workplace anecdote, while Example 2 was not.

Example 1.[4] *Near miss*

Context: Regular policy group meeting of large team in government department. The group is discussing procedures for dealing with accidents at work.

Pre-amble

a Max: you're also required to um record near misses
b   like if (the) you know shelf falls or something
c   and and um + doesn't cause any injuries
d   but it (will then be) a near miss
e   so that they can be um followed up and corrected

Anecdote

1 Josh: Bob Dickson had a near miss on the plane with some seagulls
2 Ed: yeah /[laughs] that's right]\
3 Max: /[laughs]\ yeah
4 Sel: did he?
5 Max: (yeah he'll) + have to ask Air New Zealand
6   what they're gonna do about it yeah
7 Sel: [softly]: wow:

Example 2.

Context: Regular project meeting of a large team in a corporate organisation. Individual team members are updating the group on the tasks for which they have been responsible.

```
1  Rob:  but um no it's come a long way
2        I've been really happy with it
3        Harry's um er it hasn't just been me doing this
4        Harry's done a lot of those maps and stuff like that
5        and and he's been like really um involved in you know
6        (importing) all the procedures and that sort of stuff
7        so come a long way [tut] okay?
```

Both of these excerpts from workplace meetings recapitulate past experience by matching a verbal sequence of clauses to the sequence of clauses which (it is inferred) actually occurred. In the first case, however, we have a very brief narrative or workplace anecdote, while in the second we do not. What distinguishes them?

Labov's analysis of narrative focusses on the various components of the internal structure of a narrative (abstract, orientation, complicating action, evaluation, resolution, coda). Edwards (1997: 274ff.) claims these categories are "idealized as well as empirical... they define the kinds of things a story *ought* to contain, theoretically, in order to count as a story" (1997: 276). He argues that they are very difficult to apply to particular examples, and suggests they impose structure rather than reveal it. Nevertheless, some researchers have explicitly or implicitly used these as a guide to what counts as a narrative (see Bamberg 1997). However, because, technically, the only essential or core element is the complicating action – what Toolan (1988: 153) labels the "obligatory nucleus" – this approach is also ultimately unable to assist in distinguishing report from narrative.[5] In Example 1, for instance, the anecdote compresses into one clause (line 1) the abstract, orientation and complicating action, while lines 5–7 could be interpreted as expressing the evaluation, resolution and coda. In Example 2, we could interpret line 1 as the abstract, line 2 as the evaluation, lines 3–6 as the complicating action and line 7 as the resolution and coda. Yet we know, firstly, that Example 2 does not fit our intuitions about what constitutes a narrative, and secondly, that almost every one of the structural categorisations we have made could be challenged.

In practice, most researchers have assumed that evaluation is also an integral and essential component of a narrative. Charlotte Linde claims, for instance, that narratives "crucially contain evaluations" (1993:71), and describes the evaluation as "socially the most important part of the narrative" (1993:72). And Labov and Waletzky (1967:33–39) comment on the significance of the evaluative component in determining what constitutes a "complete narrative". Hence, if Example 1 had consisted only of line 1, we might consider it an incomplete narrative. But, in fact, the wide variety of means by which evaluation may be conveyed – including the possibility that it is implicit in the contextual placement of the narrative, or even that its identification is the responsibility of the recipient – results in this too being unhelpful as a definitive criterion.

Livia Polanyi (1989) notes that reports are typically contextually *required* in a sense that stories are not: "A *report*, unlike a *story*, is most typically elicited by the recipient ... or in response to circumstances which require an accounting of what went on. The context of reporting supplies a framework in which the relevance of the states and events reported can be ascertained" (Polyani 1989:20).[6] This proved a useful guide in distinguishing anecdotes from reports in business meetings, though, of course, the borderlines were not as clear-cut as the definition suggests. So, for instance, colleagues often demanded a re-telling of a good story, or elicited an account of an event, such as a party, which they knew had occurred in the recent past.

Polanyi also comments on the difference in the impact of a report compared to a story: a report is "often linguistically identical to the story in terms of event and state information, but [differs] dramatically in impact" (1989:20). The relevance of dramatic impact is also suggested by the notion that a story entails some kind of conflict. In a recent discussion of the problem of distinguishing narrative from description or report, David Herman (personal communication) suggests "narratives involve conflict, disequilibrium, transgression of expectation, etc., in some fundamental way, whereas descriptions do not – or do not prototypically speaking ... In narrative, goals are thwarted, often because of interfering motivations and goals associated with *other* characters. Descriptions would prototypically be less rich, in this respect." He also notes that the boundaries will inevitably be fuzzy because some descriptions may indicate bases for potential conflict, while some narratives could imply, rather than elaborate upon, conflicts or thwarted goals. The relevance of conflict is also implied in Johnstone's suggestion that plots "center around disturbances in the usual flow of events, which must be overcome or lived through" (1993:62).[7] Herman's suggestion also echoes comments by Schiffrin (1996), who analysed family narratives and noted that stories are often told "to justify one's own actions" both during overt family conflicts, and during "subtle disputes over rights and obligations" (1996:171). The narrative serves to highlight and resolve tensions. This notion that a narrative involves some element of conflict or transgression of expectation proved a useful additional guideline in our identification of what we finally labelled 'anecdotes' in the workplace business talk data, and seems a promising direction for future research on this problem.

A final problem with most definitions of a narrative, which is raised explicitly by Goodwin (1990), concerns the restriction of the term 'narrative' to accounts of past events. She argues that "limiting narrative to reports of *past* events is far too restrictive" (1990:231). The narratives she examines include "future and imaginary events as well as past occurrences" (1990:279). In other words she includes what Hay (1995), in her analysis of humour, labels "fantasy sequences" (1995:68). There are a number of such sequences in our data which in terms of their *function* certainly seem to contribute to the interaction in ways that are identical to the anecdotes or narratives we analyse (see Example 13 below). However, for reasons of comparability with other research in this area, we have not included fantasy sequences in our quantitative comparisons of workplace anecdotes vs. reports and descriptions.

After considering the various criteria which had been proposed and critiqued by those engaged in narrative analysis, we developed the following guidelines for identifying workplace anecdotes which occurred during the business talk in our dataset. These guidelines served, in particular, to distinguish workplace anecdotes from reports and descriptions.

Guidelines for identifying a workplace anecdote occurring during business talk:

– primary function is to entertain/interest/amaze (rather than to inform)
– not institutionally ratified 'on task' core business talk
– not 'required' accountings, strictly redundant to current business
– minimally includes complicating action and (implicit or explicit) evaluation
– involves conflict or transgression of expectation (loosely interpreted)

We have indicated the basis for each of these guidelines explicitly or implicitly in the discussion above. Typically the anecdotes we identified were produced as entertaining or interesting, if typically brief, digressions from core business talk. Moreover, they did not contribute to the completion of a task, or the realisation of an institutional objective, even if, inevitably, they related indirectly to workplace business, or arose out of a business topic that was being discussed, as illustrated by Example 1.

Finally, it is worth noting two features of those workplace anecdotes which occur during core business interactions which tend to differentiate them from narratives told in more social contexts, such as those produced at tea breaks or lunchtimes, or in out-of-work contexts. Firstly, they are typically very brief, and often seem truncated, a reflection of the fact that they are strictly digressions in task-oriented workplace or business talk. Example 1 illustrates this point, as do Examples 3 and 4.

Example 3. *Christian and the cops*

Context: Manager Ginette and supervisor Russell are discussing the draft of a newsletter Ginette has written. The newsletter includes a reference to speed regulations in the area of the factory. Christian is the factory manager.

Preamble
a Gin: you read the road patrol +
b Russ: yeah that's the one that's the one I like

Christian and the cops
1 Gin: that's Christian he got pulled over by the cops
2 Russ: [voc] +++

Example 4. *Ronny and the video*

Context: Manager Ginette and supervisor Russell are discussing the draft of a newsletter. The newsletter includes a reference to the random air tests Ronny performs outside the factory.

1 Gin: Ronny found a video down the road
2 Russ: yeah I know +

Sometimes, as in Example 4, the story is already known by the addressee; we are presented with just the abstract. However, as we all know, this is not a sufficient reason to inhibit many raconteurs from repeating what they consider a good story.[8] A second point worth noting about the workplace anecdotes in our dataset is that they are sometimes joint constructions, collaborative achievements by more than one speaker, as illustrated by Example 1.

Workplace anecdotes and professional identity

We turn now to a consideration of the role of workplace anecdotes in the construction of the professional identity of managers. Specifically, we focus on workplace anecdotes and exchanges which provide insights into the different management styles of managers from two different workplaces comprising very different communities of practice, or workplace cultures. Sociolinguistic researchers have pointed out that:

> The fine-grained analysis of speaker turns and utterances [can] shed light on such general notions as institutional identity and the ways in which participants orientate to institutional settings. So doctors, for example, take on their doctoring identity as they present themselves as questioners of patients. Or the prosecutor designs her turns in such a way to implicate the defendant or witness. The social facts of workplace life such as decisions, institutional roles, standards or what counts as 'success' are not givens or simply the product of external variables but are interactionally accomplished.
>
> (Sarangi & Roberts 1999:7)

This is equally true of the professional identities that managers construct in their everyday interactions at work. And as Coates, points out, narratives are an important resource in identity construction: "Through the exchange of stories, we share in the construction and reconstruction of our personal identities, our 'selves'" (Coates 1996:94). An examination of the ways in which workplace narratives may contribute to the construction of professional identity provides a productive link to research on institutional discourse, whilst also throwing light on the complexity of the achievement involved (cf. Dyer & Keller-Cohen 2000). Narrative analysts have argued that it is precisely in narrative that people's individuality is most clearly expressed (Linde 1993:98; Johnstone 1996:56; Schiffrin 1996). The analysis which follows illustrates the varied ways in which individual managers make use of narrative (or not) to express their individuality within an institutional context.

Leila: Manager in a government department

The first workplace we discuss is a government department organised on very democratic lines, and oriented to the interests of women. The interactions we examined occurred mainly in the policy development section, and the meetings we recorded were chaired by the section manager, pseudonymed 'Leila', who is our main focus here. Leila was a capable and efficient manager as assessed by the performance criteria of the department she worked for, as evaluated by her colleagues, and as evidenced by our ethnographic observations (see Holmes 2000c). She was firm and authoritative when appropriate, but in her everyday workplace interactions, Leila most frequently presented herself as a concerned and caring manager, sensitively oriented to the needs of her staff. She paid attention to their professional development needs, their personal problems, and their positive face needs in interaction. In one meeting, for example, she indicates awareness of the state of one of her staff's teeth, and jokingly threatens to provide her with healthy food to improve them. In various sections of her recorded interactions, she constructs herself in a very 'motherly', nurturing role – benevolent but nonetheless an authority figure (see Holmes 2000c; Holmes & Stubbe 2003). In the following workplace anecdote, however, she presents another aspect of her identity, an aspect which surfaces repeatedly throughout her workplace interactions.

Example 5. *The Flying Filing Squad*

Context: Planning meeting attended by six women in government organisation.

1 Lei: mm /[voc]\ didn't you hear my little story=
2 Em: /oh\
3 Lei: =about coming back from somewhere and seeing this little dirty
4 Em: I haven't actually seen it (   )
5 Lei: v van I saw this little dirty v van
6   and on the back it had flying filing squad=
7   /and I was trying to drive\ round to [laughs]: see who it was
8 XF: /I think I have seen them\
9 Lei: and I was cos: they didn't have their phone number
10   on the back only on the /side of the van\
11 Zoe: /yeah that's there's\ a lot that do that
12 Em: (for)=/
13 Lei: /=mhm no well they were in front of me [laughs]: you see:
14 Lei: /so just at our corner\ you know like
15 Ker: /flying filing squad\
16 Lei: just at the point they were going up Brooklyn hill
17   and I was proceeding up Aro [laughs]: Street: or into Willis
18   and I was trying to sort of edge round
19   and I was [laughs]: stretching this way in the /car: [laughs]\
20   /[General laughter]\
21 Lei: /I was a wee\ bit like (   ) [laughs]
22 Em: /(they must have) thought you were a maniac\
23 Lei: you must have been away the day that I told this
24 XX: [laughs] /[laughs]\

25 Lei: /that I'd found\ these funny people
26   and er Zoe tracked them down

Leila clearly labels this contribution to the discourse as a 'story'. Moreover, she indicates that at least some of her audience, other than Emma, have heard her tell the story before. The most overt point of the story is that Leila managed with some difficulty to identify the name and telephone number of a firm that offered a potential solution to a problem the team was facing – relating to keeping records and getting their filing up-to-date. One could see this work-place anecdote, then, as an example of a good manager finding a solution to an on-going problem faced by the team.

What is most interesting, however, is the manner in which Leila tells the story. She adopts a self-deprecating style, casting herself as a bit of a clown for the purpose of making the story amusing. Note, for instance, her tongue-in-cheek use of a phrase stereotypically associated with police accounts in court: 'I was proceeding up Aro Street' (line 17); her accompanying laughter signals her awareness of the formal echoes. She then repeats the syntactic pattern twice more 'I was trying....I was stretching..' (lines 18–19). She paints a ludicrous and amusing picture of herself stretching her neck to see the side of the van. Emma's laughing comment 'they must have thought you were a maniac' (line 22) picks up exactly Leila's tone, thus nicely constructing a collaborative floor (see Holmes in press), an appropriate response to the slightly ridiculous image that Leila has presented.

A range of linguistic devices personalise the story and make it appealing. Leila describes her account of how she found the firm as 'my little story' (line 1), using a personalising possessive pronoun 'my' rather than an article such as 'a', a diminutive 'little', and choosing the friendly lexical item 'story', rather than a more objective word such as 'account' or 'description'. She uses a number of addressee-oriented, pragmatic particles eg. 'you see', 'you know', appealing to the audience's understanding, and attenuating phrases such as 'sort of' (line 18), 'a wee\ bit like' (line 21). Particular adjective choices give the story life and colour, suggesting it is an amusing and interesting one: e.g. 'this little dirty van' (lines 3, 5); 'these funny people' (line 25). Members of the team who have heard the story before also cooperate by chiming in with supportive comments: e.g. Zoe contributes a supportive comment 'yeah there's a lot that do that' (line 11), and Kerry helpfully repeats the amusing name of the firm 'the flying filing squad' (line 15).

Although in the management of her department section and the running of meetings, Leila was a firm and capable manager (see Holmes & Stubbe 2003), this self-deprecating presentation was by no means unusual. At a later point in the same meeting, and, significantly, after a number of problems which have caused considerable tension had been resolved, Leila made a similar comment that placed her 'one down', and suggested that she had only limited skills. Specifically, she asserted that the only thing she might be awarded a good performance on was making coffee. By such strategies, she mitigates the authoritative style she has necessarily needed to adopt during the meeting to assist the team resolve conflicts and reach decisions.

This approach was consistent not only with Leila's personal leadership style, which was consultative, collaborative, which emphasised negotiation, and which paid careful attention to the face needs of others, but also with the wider workplace culture or community of practice within which this team operated and which, at the time of our study was very consensus-oriented, egalitarian, and democratic in style at all levels (see Holmes & Stubbe 2003). It is also of course consistent with the observations of a number of researchers that women "often create and display their authority in ways that downplay rather than emphasize it" (Tannen 1999: 226; Kuhn 1992; Kendall 1993; Smith 1993). However, it is important to note that in this respect Leila's style contrasted markedly with that of the two other women managers whose professional identity displays we examine below.

Example 5 is also interesting from another perspective. It highlights the fact that Schiffrin's claim (which makes use of Goffman's analytic concepts of *figure* and *author*) that stories present an 'idealized' view of the narrator and/or experience may be rather more context-dependent than she suggests and may even be restricted to stories told to support a particular argumentative position:

> The audience gains an idealized view of the experience (through the author), and an idealized view of the narrator (through the figure). And the narrator's hope is that these idealized views will lead the audience into acceptance of the position being argued for. (Schiffrin 1990: 253)

As we have indicated, Leila most certainly does not paint an 'idealised' view of herself in any conventional sense. Moreover, it seems to us that Leila's goals with the 'flying filers story' are at once simpler at one level, and more complex at another. At the point she recounts the story, she is not using it implicitly or explicitly to support any particular argument. Rather she seems to be using it to entertain the team, with an underlying goal, perhaps, of assisting them relax and relate to each other more easily. By making fun of herself, Leila emphasises that she is just an ordinary team member; her story builds cohesion and constructs group solidarity. At another level, in the light of the way discussion in the meeting subsequently develops, it is interesting that she ends her story by noting that Zoe did the required follow-up to track down the flying filers (line 26). This finale suggests both that she and Zoe worked together smoothly on this task, and more subtly, that she and Zoe are in agreement about the potential value of the flying filers. It subsequently emerges that Zoe has a number of serious reservations about the use of the flying filers. From this perspective, Leila's story can be seen in hindsight as a politically astute strategy for emphasising positive team relationships, and her final line as a skilful pre-emptive alignment of Zoe and herself (see Holmes 2000c for fuller discussion of this meeting). However, there is no evidence in the transcript or tape at this point to indicate that Leila anticipated the direction in which Zoe subsequently developed the discussion.

Even in more social contexts within the workplace (e.g. the tea-room), many of the stories Leila tells have this distinctive self-deprecating style. One such story begins with her describing how she was summoned to see the Minister unexpectedly and, since she was dressed in an inappropriately casual style, she had to borrow a jacket from someone else in a colour (green) which did not suit her: 'I mean a really non-my-colour GREEN jacket [laughs] you should have seen me.' Again, she emphasises the ludic elements of her story, presenting herself as a slightly comic figure, firstly in being inappropriately casually dressed, and then in having to wear a jacket that did not suit her and made her feel slightly ridiculous. Interestingly this story leads into a collaborative humorous fantasy, discussed in some detail in Holmes (in press) and Holmes and Marra (2002a) about an all-purpose Ministry suit, a nice example of a narrative about an 'imaginary event' using Goodwin's (1990:279) classification mentioned above. It is also worth noting that Leila shares a good deal of her personal life with her staff, a practice which has the effect of reducing power differentials and constructing a more egalitarian work ethos. From various workplace interactions, we learn such personal information as the fact that she is married with children, has a cat, has regular visitors staying with her, and admires the comedian, Victoria Wood.

In this consensus-oriented, egalitarian, and democratic workplace, then, Leila, the capable and efficient manager of the policy team uses workplace anecdotes, even in business meetings, to complexify the professional image she presents. Interestingly, Schiffrin (1996) and Dyer and Keller-Cohen (2000) similarly identify narratives as a means by which speaker's manage contradictory aspects of their self-presentation. Analysing the lecture-room narratives of two professors, Dyer and Keller-Cohen draw a parallel with the narratives told by Jewish mothers and analysed by Schiffrin, noting that in both cases:

> The narrators are figures of authority attempting to construct selves both by displaying their authority and at the same time downplaying it, because of the democratic nature of the society they live in. Such dilemmatic discourse may therefore characterize the construction of self in a situation where the speaker is in a position of authority in the narrative, but is cautious about how this should be presented.   (Dyer & Keller-Cohen 2000: 300)

In a similar way, Leila's self-deprecating anecdotes attenuate the authority of her managerial position; her self-mockery has the effect of 'democratizing' the more managerial discourse of the surrounding text. Her anecdotes are strategically positioned, and, like humour in meetings, they enhance team cohesion, strengthen collegial solidarity, and reduce attention to status differences and power imbalances.

Ginette: Manager in soap powder factory

The second workplace from which we have selected a typical narrative told by a manager is a factory, here pseudonymed Tallows. Tallows is very hierarchically organised with clearly demarcated professional roles for staff at different levels. The interactions we examined in this workplace focussed on a particular production team, pseudonymed the Power Rangers, whose manager Ginette was universally recognised within the factory as outstandingly good at her job (see Stubbe 2000a), a recognition well supported by our detailed ethnographic observations, and which has resulted in several promotions since we collected the data analysed in this paper. The Power Rangers was equally recognised as a high-performance, strongly-motivated team with high morale and a very distinctive sparky communicative style. They had a well-deserved reputation at the factory for uninhibited swearing, and constantly joking around and 'having each other on' (see also Stubbe 2000a; Holmes & Marra 2002a).

Ginette's authority as team leader was unquestioningly accepted by her team. She was a straight-talking and authoritative manager who provided direct and ungarnished criticism when the team failed to meet its targets or made errors, but who also provided positive and encouraging feedback, especially to individuals, when the team performed well. She often expressed particularly positive feedback on the way team members worked together cooperatively and supported each other in reaching a high performance standard (see Stubbe 2000a, 2000b) but she did not suffer fools gladly, nor tolerate slack work, or lateness. So, for instance, dressing down a late-comer at the early morning team meeting, she calls out humorously, but mercilessly, '*nice of you to join us, were you busy making babies last night?*' Her humour often has this kind of raw edge, and this is also typical of interaction among all her team members – jocular abuse is the normal coinage of their everyday workplace interaction. Hence, in the following workplace anecdote, Ginette presents an important facet of her professional identity as a team manager:

Example 6. *David and the vacuum cleaner*

Context: Ginette, the team manager is working in the scales are of the packing line and talking to other members of the team.

```
1   Gin:  yesterday + afternoon Christian and I were standing at the end
2         by the elevator over there talking
3         and David was coming round with the vacuum by the two kilo elevator +
4         and just along the wall there on the (   )
5         there's a trail of powder just went right along +
6         we were standing away talking
7         and David had the hose and had that long thing connected t-
8         hosing um vacuuming by the two k g elevator +
9         and then he went over to clean that trail of powder + along side the
10        wall + what he did h- he disconnected the hose off + off the end piece
11        and then he walked over
12        and he swept [voc] + the trail [laughs]:of powder up with that:
13  Hel:  how stupid
14  Gin:  [laughs]: with that metal bit:
15  Hel:  yeah
16  Gin:  when he finished that he connected the hose back on
17        and then he vacuumed it up +
18        the pile of powder that he'd swept up with just (the end)
19        me and Christian were just cracking up laughing
20        and (he turns to me) (   ) said + this is very [laughs]: embarrassing:
21  Hel:  [laughs]
22  Gin:  I thought what a dick + you know
23        all he had to do was go along with this thing /and suck it all up\
24  Hel:  /(   )\ and suck it up + it's actually easier + ( ) for that one +
25  Gin:  [said to someone in distance]: that's a nice one: eh
26        (6)
27  Gin:  dumb eh
```

Ginette here entertains team members, and particularly Helen who is her immediate neighbour on the packing line, with a story which exposes a third (absent) team member David to ridicule for stupid behaviour. The story is told with little embellishment. First the context is set, establishing how Ginette came to observe David as he vacuumed the floor (lines 1–3). Then Ginette describes how David first manually brushed up a trail of powder with one of the vacuum cleaner attachments, before then using the vacuum cleaner to suck up the pile he had made (lines 4–12). The story is a simple one, and its point appears to be to amuse others at David's expense.

Again, however, it is worth examining in more detail just *how* the tale is told. This is a concisely presented narrative; the 'complicating action' (in Labov & Waletzky's 1967) terms is sparely described (lines 9–18) with no wasted words. The only strictly redundant words in this whole section are the words 'what he did' (line 10), a phrase which serves to draw attention to the crux of the stupid behaviour Ginette is parodying. By contrast, the evaluation is much more fully elaborated. The ridiculousness of David's behaviour is emphasised by three different devices: firstly, we are told that it evoked a paroxysm of laughter from those watching 'me and Christian were just cracking up laughing' (line 19). Secondly, Ginette indicates explicitly how simple the alternative sensible behaviour was: 'all he had to do was go along with this thing /and suck it all up' (line 23), and Helen signals she has taken the point by using an echoic phrase 'suck it up' (line 24), and a confirmatory evaluation 'it's actually easier'. Thirdly, and most tellingly, Ginette provides two no-punches-pulled evaluations of David's behaviour, 'I thought what a dick you know' (line 22) emphasised in the coda, 'dumb eh' (line 27). The accompanying addressee-oriented pragmatic particles 'you know' and 'eh' are solidarity markers, indicating her confidence that she and others share the negative evaluation (as clearly signalled by Helen in lines 13, 24).

Ginette's story provides a strong contrast to Leila's story. It focusses on arguably the weakest team member and exposes his stupid behaviour for others' entertainment. In team meetings, too, Ginette provides ascerbic evaluations of unintelligent behaviour, and indicates that she will not tolerate mistakes, especially those which could damage the teams' record or adversely affect their productivity. She presents herself as a hard taskmistress with very high standards, 'a bit of a tartar' who is intolerant of errors and expects perfection from team members. In her interactions with individual team members on a one-to-one basis, her behaviour is quite different (see Stubbe 2000a; Holmes & Stubbe 2003), but when dealing with the public image of her team and its members, she is merciless. Her direct, focussed, unelaborated narrative style, with no hedging, no mitigating devices, and no spare adjectives is an interesting discoursal instantiation of her direct, no-fuss, authoritative managerial style.

This story provides insight into one facet of Ginette's professional identity at work. Another anecdote which provide a similar picture involves a story about a team member Sam banging a huge thick pipe rather than the appropriate hopper in which powder has got jammed. She also tells anecdotes which emphasise a different aspect of her professional image, namely her well-integrated status as a member of the team, and especially as a practical joker, a pervasive team trait. One story, for example, describes a practical joke which she successfully played on a number of team members on April Fools Day, persuading them to phone the number of the zoo (without their realising where they were ringing) and ask for Mr. Lion. The use of humour to express and construct team solidarity was a very salient feature of this community of practice (Holmes & Marra 2002a), and Ginette's status as a core member of the team was well-reflected in the content as well as the narrative style of such anecdotes.[9] Moreover, it is also worth noting that, as with Leila, Ginette fully engages in the personal and social chat which takes place in workplace interactions in the factory. She is fully integrated into the close relationships between team members which are reflected in many shared social activities outside work, as well as in social spaces such as the lunch and tea room. We know, for instance, from her recordings of her workplace interactions, that her husband also works at the factory, and that he works different shifts to assist with childcare. Also on the basis of the chat she shares with her co-workers, we know a good deal about her extended family, about the movies she does and does not like, and the outings she has organised and enjoyed with other team members.

Again Ginette's style of narration, as described in relation to the recounting of Example 6, is an interesting reflection of the very different community of practice and workplace culture which the factory constitutes compared to Leila's government organisation. Whereas language, including talk, is the main output of the government department, the primary currency, and the major means by which the work gets done, this is not the case for the factory. The main output of the factory is a material product, soap powder; talk is a secondary activity and is only justified to the extent that it facilitates productivity. Ginette's direct and focussed style – even in her workplace anecdotes – is an interesting verbal instantiation of this difference. Secondly, while the government department team members work together in many respects to achieve their work objectives, much of their work involves independent thinking and writing after periods of discussion. By contrast, factory team members are highly interdependent in their work. One person's task typically provides the input for the next person's. Hence David's stupid behaviour, while not immediately a threat to team productivity, could easily, when he was engaged in another task, cause problems to fellow team members. Ginette's focus on a team member's less than intelligent way of approaching a task thus has an important underlying message, one which is consistent with her message and her self-presentation as a demanding team manager in other contexts.

Linde makes the point that narrative is "an extremely powerful tool for creating, negotiating, and displaying the moral standing of the self" and that "the most basic moral proposition, which is contained in some form by all first-person narratives, is 'I am a good person'" (Linde 1993: 123). If this is true of the workplace anecdotes in our dataset, then it applies at a subtle, and perhaps deeper, analytical level. The most obvious basic moral propositions for the workplace anecdotes told by Leila and Ginette are considerably more complex. The proposition underlying many of Leila's stories appears to be something like 'I am the boss, but I am also an ordinary, fallible person'. In other words, she plays down any basis for status distinctions and emphasises her fallible humanity. In Ginette's case, the propositions might be 'I am a tough boss, but I am also one of the guys, a regular joker'.[10] Each manager constructs their professional identity and the position of authority they hold somewhat differently in their workplace interactions. Moreover, these differences can be related to the attitudes and values which characterise the contrasting communities of practice and workplace cultures in which their verbal practices are embedded.

Conclusion

Workplace anecdotes clearly constitute a special kind of narrative. They are often compressed and structurally minimal, reflecting their essentially marginal status in an institutional context. Unlike many other types of institutional discourse, workplace anecdotes typically contrast with and complement the more focussed business talk which constitutes the ratified 'core' of workplace interaction. In this role, they often complexify and humanise the standard professional identity constructed by workplace managers, for example, providing a more personal perspective than the standard institutional discourse allows. Similarly, workplace anecdotes may relieve the tension created by the ideological dilemma between authority and equality; they 'democratise' the discourse, providing a means for speakers to manage contradictory aspects of their self-presentation.

Exploring these issues, we first discussed the problems of distinguishing workplace narratives from more routine workplace reports, which are structurally very similar, though functionally relatively distinct. We suggested criteria for identifying the kinds of workplace anecdotes which are the focus of the analysis in this paper. Functionally, these anecdotes de-formalise the workplace environment since they are, by definition, digressions from work-oriented discourse: i.e. NOT core business talk. Their function is typically to entertain. They could be regarded as instances of resistance to what Fairclough (1996:71) describes as the "technologisation of discourse".

Workplace anecdotes may also contribute to the construction of "the professional self" (Dyer & Keller-Cohen 2000), and an analysis of such anecdotes suggests that people's workplace identities are typically complex and multi-faceted. We focussed in the second section on examples of workplace anecdotes produced by managers in the course of their everyday workplace interactions. The analysis suggested that, while some managers use anecdotes to complexify and modify the authoritative stance required of their position, different managers achieve this in different ways. Moreover, the different emphases of different anecdotes tend to reflect the different interactional practices and workplace cultures in which they are embedded and from which they emerge.

The discourse of Leila, the manager of a unit in a government organisation, typically constructed her as a concerned and caring manager, sensitively oriented to the needs of her staff. Her anecdotes complexify this 'motherly' identity, however, by suggesting that she is also a capable but fallible human being, with similar interests and concerns to those of her colleagues. This represents one possible response to the tension between her leadership role and the egalitarian ethos of her community of practice, a tension described by a number of researchers as a widespread ideological dilemma between authority and equality in modern (western) society (Billig et al. 1988; Dyer & Keller 2000; Fairclough 1989, 1993). Thus Leila's stories typically assume or subtly emphasise the collegiality, democratic values and egalitarian philosophy of the community of practice to which she belongs. The stories told by Ginette, the manager of a very effective and productive factory team, also indicate her awareness of her authority and status, as well as her willingness to exercise that authority. In addition, however, her anecdotes construct her identity as a fun-loving joker, 'one of the boys' with an abundance of humour and willingness to participate in practical joking. Her stories emphasise her solidarity with her team, and capture well the good-humoured but verbally abusive interactional style which characterises this community of practice, with its emphasis on team spirit and high performance. This paper has indicated how the analysis of workplace narratives may contribute to the construction of contrasting and complex professional identities at work. We have illustrated one way in which individuals "produce, negotiate, modify and use their social identities in social interaction" (Widdicombe & Woofitt 1995: 73).[11] The workplace anecdotes of managers in the two communities of practice on which we have focussed complement other discursive strategies they use to construct their complex professional workplace identities. The styles in which these managers issue directives (Holmes 2000c; Vine 2001), respond to an initiate humour (Holmes et al. 2003; Stubbe 2000a; Holmes & Marra 2002b), and conduct their regular staff meetings (Holmes 2000a; Holmes et al. 2003) are generally consistent with the picture portrayed by this analysis of their workplace narratives. Narrative analysis clearly offers researchers an additional source of insight into the ideological significance of the way people talk at work.

Appendix

Transcription conventions

=	Speaker's turn continues
[voc]	Vocalisation
[laughs] : :	Paralinguistic features in square brackets, colons indicate start/finish
+	Pause of up to one second
(3)	Pause of specified number of seconds
… /......\ …	Simultaneous speech
… /.......\ …	
(hello)	Transcriber's best guess at an unclear utterance
( )	Indecipherable utterance
?	Rising or question intonation
–	Incomplete or cut-off utterance
=/\=	No discernable pause between turns
XM/XF	Unidentified Male/Female

All names used in examples are pseudonyms.

Notes

1. The research described in this paper has been funded by the New Zealand Foundation for Research, Science and Technology and the International Science and Technology Linkages Fund (ISAT) to whom we express our gratitude. We also express our appreciation to other members of the Language in the Workplace Project Team, and especially Rowan Shoemark, George Major and Fleur Findlay, for their contributions to the research on which this paper is based. We also gratefully acknowledge the support supplied by the University of Wales,

Bangor, and especially Professor Jenny Thomas, and to the University of Freiburg, and especially Professor Christian Mair, which facilitated work on this paper. The paper will serve as a foundation for one aspect of further planned collaborative research with these institutions.

2. This definition was first developed in Holmes (2000b: 36).

3. Herman defines a narrative domain as "a spacetime region built by a storyteller, who uses discourse clues to enable recipients to reconstruct the same spatiotemporal zone" (2001: 519).

4. Transcription conventions are supplied in the appendix. All names are pseudonyms. Some minor editing of examples has been undertaken to eliminate irrelevant detail and improve readability.

5. See Holmes (1998b) for discussion of the problems of using the components in Labov and Waletzky's model of the internal structure of narratives as a means of defining what counts as a narrative.

6. Heath (1986) uses a similar criterion in distinguishing factually-based *recounts*, *eventcasts* and *accounts* from fictional *stories*.

7. This formulation also usefully broadens the notion of 'conflict' which, if interpreted narrowly, could be regarded as a potentially gendered criterion (Coates personal communication).

8. Buying vegetables in a rural shop in Anglesey, another customer and I were regaled twice, in almost as much detail each time, with a story about how the shopkeeper had stood on a wasps' nest with horrible consequences. The story was so compelling for the shopkeeper that she obviously felt it deserved to be repeated so that we could fully appreciate the horror of her experience. It struck me that the length of time she felt justified in devoting to the story while we waited to be served would not have been tolerated in a more urban environment, and certainly not in the task-oriented workplaces in which we had collected our meeting data.

9. See Hay (1994) for a discussion of the relationship between humour and group integration.

10. The term 'joker' in New Zealand English is equivalent to the term 'guy' in American English or 'bloke' in British English. Since it can also refer to someone who plays jokes, its ambiguity in this proposition is an advantage.

11. See Holmes (1998c) "Why tell stories?" for a discussion of the ways in which stories told in conversational by Maori women in our Wellington Corpus of Spoken New Zealand English (Holmes, Johnson, & Vine 1998) often focussed on power and authority in the workplace. The Maori women tended to construct strong and assertive identities, presenting themselves as women with authority, and as effective managers. Their stories contrasted with those of Maori men who tended to construct themselves as subversive anti-heroes.

CHAPTER 11

Telling stories and giving evidence
The hybridisation of narrative and non-narrative modes of discourse in a sexual assault trial

Sandra Harris
Nottingham Trent University

Introduction

Courtrooms have provided a fruitful context for research on the narrative, particularly in recent years, and the importance of narratives in courtroom discourse has long been recognised. (From legal studies, see Bennett & Feldman 1981; Jackson 1988; Robertshaw 1998; Amsterdam & Bruner 2000; and from linguistics and discourse see Penman 1987; Stygall 1994; Jacquemet 1996; Lakoff 1997; Conley & O'Barr 1998; Matoesian 1999, 2001; Harris 2001; Heffer 2002; Hobbs 2003.) There is clearly a widespread perception that witnesses and others who take the stand 'tell their stories' while giving evidence in court. Bennett and Feldman (1981) conclude that the process of 'storytelling' is a crucial one in criminal trials, and that "the storytelling perspective answers the question of how jurors actually recognise and analyse the vast amounts of information involved in making a legal judgement" (p. 5), likening jurors to readers of a detective novel or watchers of a mystery movie. Fictional and drama representations of the courtroom often foreground a powerful narrative aspect, strengthening this view in the popular imagination.

Indeed, Amsterdam and Bruner (2000) recently state that "law lives in narrative, for reasons both broad and deep" (p. 110). Not only do they maintain that "the law is awash with storytelling" (p. 110) but, perhaps more importantly, narratives are 'embedded' in the very way law is constructed, interpreted and intermeshed in culture itself. The literature on legal discourse and narrative is now a very large one (see for example Engel 1993; Sherwin 1994; Symposium 1994; Brooks & Gewirtz 1996; Feiner 1997; Troutt 1999), stimulated perhaps in particular by the huge interest in the O. J. Simpson trial in the USA (Lakoff 1997 and Cotterill 2002).

However, anyone who examines the text of an actual trial will discover that the presence, purpose and structure of narratives in courtroom discourse is not nearly so obvious or straightforward as some of this literature suggests.[1] Particularly in a lengthy trial, even where there are strongly perceived over-arching and competing narratives of guilt or innocence (such as the cases of O. J. Simpson and Louise Woodward provided), examining the strategic use of narratives in trial language proves a complex and challenging task. There are several reasons for this, which it might be useful very briefly to examine.

Paul Robertshaw (1998), working with judges' summations to juries, points out what he calls the 'anti-narrativity mode of trial narration', and this sums up a number of features of trial language which create what Stygall (1994) considers to be a significant disjunction between discourse coherence and the narrative expectations of jurors. One of these features is the fact that the structure of trials, and in particular the ordering of witnesses, does not reflect a chronological ordering or, indeed, any easily discernible relationship to the events in question which are at the centre of the trial itself, i. e. what actually happened. Legal coherence appears to take precedence over discourse coherence in trials, and jurors must come to terms with this. A second feature which creates such a disjunction is the fact that not only are there the primary competing narratives of the defence and the prosecution but in most trials there are also a number of supplementary narratives which can be very substantial in themselves. For example, in the O. J. Simpson trial the issue of whether the Los Angeles police had racist motives in charging O. J. Simpson with his ex-wife's murder consumed a huge amount of witness testimony, as did the question of whether baby Matthew Eappen died of injuries sustained long before he was allegedly shaken by Louise Woodward and how he might have come by these.

Not only is the structure of a trial an 'anti-narrativity mode', but this 'anti-narrativity' is, arguably, at the very heart of the presentation of evidence by witnesses and defendants, once again in a number of ways. First of all, evidence must be presented through question and answer sequences, involving multiple tellers and the inevitable fragmentation of their narrative accounts (Harris 2001). Witnesses are hugely constrained in 'telling their stories' in a courtroom. Secondly, witnesses are also substantially constrained by the rules of evidence, which seek to eliminate those very qualities which are often most closely associated with personal narratives in ordinary life, i.e. hearsay, belief, speculation, opinion, etc. And, thirdly, there are significant differences in narrative strategies and the use of narrative modes of discourse between direct and cross examination and between different types of witness evidence, for example, the testimony of expert witnesses and the police.

However, one thing does seem clear: that practising lawyers as well as researchers recognise that the narrative is a powerful and compelling mode of discourse in the courtroom on a number of different levels, from the account of an individual witness to the construction of the over-arching and shared cultural narratives referred to by Lakoff and others. Despite the constraints on narrativity, it has long been recognised by legal practitioners as well as researchers that achieving narrative coherence can be one of the most effective ways of convincing a jury. Hence, cross-examining lawyers most often focus their questioning either on subverting any such narratives put forward in direct examination or in constructing alternative narratives of their own.

The primary aim of this chapter, then, is to examine the various narrative types and structures generated in a single trial, in this instance a sexual assault case, with a view to exploring both:

1. the presence of hybridisation and the intermingling of narrative and non-narrative modes of discourse across the trial as a generic type of discourse, contrasting the explicit narrativity of the opening statements with the complex hybridity of witness and defendant testimony and, following on from this:
2. the strategic pressure, particularly on prosecuting lawyers, to construct witness narratives as a powerful and persuasive way of achieving a measure of discourse coherence in the giving of evidence by such witnesses in what is otherwise in many ways a non-narrative generic type.

The data

The data base selected is the *Marv Albert Sexual Assault Trial*, which took place in Virginia in the United States in 1997. This case involved a well known NBC sports broadcaster (Marv Albert) who was accused of sexually assaulting a woman with whom he had had a ten year sexual relationship (Vanessa Perhach), i.e. biting her back and forcing her to perform oral sex against her will. Like other well-publicised cases, this case too was televised and was the subject of immense coverage in the press. Since there was no essential disagreement over the 'facts' of the case, the competing narratives of the prosecution and defence centred on the *interpretation* of the 'facts', i.e. whether the sex was consensual or sexual assault, especially given the longstanding nature of the relationship.

The case was not chosen on the basis of its subject matter (sexual assault) but primarily because of its relative brevity. The case lasted four days, which heightened the feasibility of examining the complex interweaving and layering of the multiple narratives constructed within the trial. In addition, the *Marv Albert Trial* was brought to a premature conclusion by a process of plea-bargaining after the defendant unexpectedly changed his plea to 'guilty', largely in response to the testimony of a female witness who corroborated, in the form of her own narrative, the narrative account of the plaintiff. Thus, the focus of the remainder of this chapter will be on the two aspects identified above, illustrated by extracts from this single trial.

Narrative vs. non-narrative discourse

In two recent papers, Georgakopoulou and Goutsos (2000a and 2000b) argue that studies of narrative and non-narrative discourse have become artificially separated, with a resulting and unhelpful fragmentation. While the narrative mode has been extensively researched, generating a large, wide-ranging and multi-disciplinary literature, there is no comparable research on non-narrative modes of discourse. In these papers Georgakopoulou and Goutsos refer to and make use of Bruner's influential foregrounding of the narrative not so much as a means of storytelling, but rather as a mode of discourse which "operates as an instrument of mind in the construction of reality" (1991:6) and the structuring of human experience. In his earlier work (1986, 1990) Bruner identifies two major modes of thinking, which are realised as *narrative* and *paradigmatic* (*logico-scientific*) modes of discourse. The former is categorized by Bruner as a way of encoding subjectivity, the nature of human reality, experience, beliefs, and emotions, while the latter is concerned with rationality, the observation and analysis of (physical) reality, i.e. how things are in the world. Bruner sums up their differences in function as *verisimilitude* (narrative) versus *verifiability* (paradigmatic or non-narrative). The implications of Bruner's description of modes of thinking and their differences are particularly interesting for trial language, a point which will be taken up presently in some detail.

Equally important, however, is Georgakopoulou and Goutsos's (2000a) contention that the two ways of 'knowing' which Bruner identifies are often not separated in many real life contexts and that what is perhaps most interesting for current researchers may be their conjunction. What is missing, they argue, is "a systematic study of the hybridization and inter-mingling of the narrative and non-narrative modes" (p. 76), especially in institutional and 'public' discourse. Legal discourse is undoubtedly one of those contexts where it is especially fruitful to explore this conjunction of narrative and non-narrative discourse.

However, before this is possible, it is crucial to be able to distinguish narrative and non-narrative discursive modes clearly enough to be able to recognise their occurrence in the trial data. Even though it was written over thirty years ago, Labov's (1972) canonical work on narrative structures still provides a useful starting point for this task. Although Labov's definition of the narrative is almost wholly concerned with structure and is a very restricted one, it nevertheless is particularly well-suited to the analysis of trial language, given its emphasis on both *the referential* (narratives match verbal sequences of clauses to sequences of events) and *the temporal* (the clauses in a narrative are characteristically ordered in a temporal sequence). These very qualities, which have often proved troublesome to researchers analysing personal oral narratives, lend themselves more easily to the more formal context of a trial, with some modification. I have proposed certain modifications of Labov's work on narrative structure elsewhere (Harris 2001), and these are reproduced here.

Narrative structures in courtroom discourse

Orientation	establishes the circumstances which surround the narrative account, i.e. who, when, where, etc.
Core Narrative	establishes what happened. Often involves what was said and sometimes what was seen as well as what was done, i.e. the actual events which occurred
Elaboration	provides further details, clarification, explication, etc. of aspects of the Core Narrative
Point	establishes the significance of the narrative account for the larger trial narrative, i.e. the guilt or innocence of the defendant in criminal trials, and addressed directly to the jury

In addition, in order to refine the distinction between narrative and non-narrative modes, I have further identified certain features which are incorporated into narratives as they are manifested in a courtroom, making use of a modified version of what Labov calls a *minimal narrative.*

Textual features of narratives in trial language

Narratives in trial language incorporate the following features:

1. they involve a re-capitulation of past events, including speech events;
2. they contain a predominance of past tense verbs which are often simple past tense;
3. events are temporally ordered, though this temporal ordering often includes an elaboration of an event which is itself non-temporal;
4. at least two independent clauses are present.

Opening statement narratives

Perhaps the clearest instance of the narrative mode in a trial occurs in the opening (and closing) statements of both prosecution and defence lawyers. Such statements are often explicitly characterised as narrative accounts as in the following two extracts:

Extract 1

(PL: Prosecution lawyer)

PL: This trial is going to be the first time that Vanessa Perhach will *tell her tale* in public of what this man did to her.............. and *she'll tell you*............ Let's *tell a different story*.........

Extract 2

(DL: Defence lawyer)

DL: Mr. Trodden says that *their story* has not come out. I disagree with what he says. But whatever it may be, the first time that *Marv Albert's side of what happened* on February 12th will be heard here today.

The extracts from the opening statements above specifically refer to what takes place in the trial as 'telling her tale' and 'a story', hearing a 'side of what happened.' Moreover, in his address to the jury after the presentation of opening statements, the judge makes a clear distinction between the nature of the *opening statements*, which have been characterised in this way (as tales, stories), and *evidence*, which is factual and presented by witnesses who testify under oath to tell the truth, the whole truth and nothing but the truth. Bruner's distinction here between modes of thinking/knowing is clearly applicable – opening statements are in the narrative mode, oriented to how speakers tell their stories; and the testimony of witnesses is in the paradigmatic (or non-narrative) mode, oriented to evidence, fact, truth.

Extract 3

Judge: The purpose of this opening statement is designed to give you an idea of what he *thinks or intends the evidence to be presented to you will be...* When all of the evidence is in, the Court will instruct you on the law to be applied to *the facts* of this case. You will decide what *the facts* are.

Extract 4

Judge: Now, you're going to have the benefit of some very skilful and very, very good lawyers. But let me caution you now. What the lawyers say in *the opening statements and the closing arguments is not evidence.* And you shall not receive their statements as evidence. *The only evidence that you will consider in this case is evidence that you hear from witnesses* who testify before you in open court under oath and any exhibits that are introduced through various witnesses.

The essential narrativity of the opening statements is clearly manifested. They 'fit' the modified version of Labov's narrative structure, with the *point* in the extract below framing the core narrative itself, having been established initially and re-iterated at the end of the statement.

Extract 5

Extract from opening statement of prosecution: Narrativity
(PL: Prosecution lawyer)

PL: May it please the Court, counsel, ladies and gentlemen.
On February 12th, a coarse and crude abuse of a human being took place. It took place at the hands of that man. And it took place and was accomplished by his physical domination of a 41-year old woman, a woman who had been his friend; a woman who had been his lover; a woman who he knew for ten years; a woman who had cared for him. But it was a woman whose human dignity he chose to ignore on this night in his egocentric quest for sexual gratification.

Point

This trial is going to be the first time that Vanessa Perhach will tell her tale in public of what this man did to her. And the evidence will be that Ms. Perhach has known the defendant since about 1986.

At that time, Ms. Perhach <u>was living</u> in Florida, in Miami. She <u>was undergoing</u> the stress and beginnings of the break-up of a marriage. She <u>had</u> two children. And she <u>began to try</u> to get herself back on her feet by seeking employment. And she <u>found</u> employment at a hotel, the Airport Hilton in Miami. And she <u>was working</u> as a telephone operator when she met the defendant. The defendant and she <u>met</u> in 86, and the relationship <u>took off</u> rapidly.......

Orient-
ation

She <u>began to get</u> up, shocked, dazed, and <u>began to gather</u> her items together She <u>took</u> the panties and <u>put</u> them in her pocket. Then she <u>put</u> them in her purse, <u>gathered</u> her things and <u>said</u>, I'm leaving. He <u>said</u>, what, so soon? She <u>walked</u> out of that hotel room. She <u>went</u> down to her car, which was parked on the street, absolutely stunned, <u>looked</u> for a police vehicle in the neighborhood, <u>started up</u> her car and <u>started driving</u> to look for a police car, [because she knows that sometimes there are police cars down there in the Crystal City area,] <u>saw</u> a police car, but no one was in it. She then <u>pulled over</u> about a block away and <u>called</u> 911 and <u>told</u> the police what had happened. The evidence will show that Officer Hanula <u>responded</u> to the place where she had placed the phone call, and there she <u>was</u> leaning out of the side of her car, gagging and retching into a pool of liquid outside of car, wincing as she <u>felt</u> her back.

Core
Narrative

It was a crude use of a human being. And the evidence will show that it was done by this man for one purpose. He wanted a scenario that night. And the dignity of a human being that was with him did not matter. She was his property, and that's a crime.

Re-iter-
ration
of Point

Moreover, the core narrative exhibits all of the textual features of a narrative account: temporal ordering, a series of clauses linked to past events, and the predominance of past tense verbs (underlined in the transcript). The prosecutor sees his role as producing a narrative monologue on behalf of the plaintiff, drawing heavily on those very resources of belief, opinion, intent and subjective evaluation which the rules of evidence prohibit. As further evidence of their narrativity, both opening statements in this trial (prosecution and defence) make extensive use of the historical-present tense (shown underlined and italicised).

Extract 6

(PL: Prosecution lawyer)

PL: ...He <u>called</u> her again that day, about 1.30, this time on her cell phone as she's shopping, again trying to make arrangements for when are we going to meet, got somebody to take the tickets, and, oh, by the way, do you have somebody for the threesome? There <u>were</u> at least two or three more telephone calls. Sometimes I think the last two actually, the last one <u>was</u> just before the victim got to the hotel. But in the afternoon I believe she <u>called</u> him to talk about picking up tickets and making arrangements for these tickets, and again the subject matter <u>came</u> up. And I believe he <u>called</u> her one last time from the Arena, saying, hey do you have somebody lined up? She <u>kept saying</u>, I don't have anybody right now. About 11.38, she *has left* her home, and she'*s* on her way to visit the defendant after the game, as she had planned to do. She *calls* him up on her cell phone in her car, saying, I'm about 20 minutes away, or 10 minutes away, and, again, the subject *is brought up* one last time. But this time *there's* a bit more insistence. Each time *it's* a bit more insistence for this threesome. She *says*, no. She *goes* up to his hotel room. It's about midnight, *knocks* on the door, he *opens* it, *says*, ah, I see you have nobody, Come in. You look great. How you been doing. They *sit* down and they *sit* on the sofa, and they *do* what old friends do. They *talk*. And they *talk* about their families, they *talk* about their children, they *talk* about their love lives. And they *do* what they have done many times in the past, they *get* comfortable... She *goes* to the bathroom, *brushes* her teeth. And by this time, she has removed her pants. She *is wearing* her panties and a camisole and a pair of socks. And she *goes* into the bathroom, *thinks* for a minute, and she *puts* on a robe, one of these real fluffy, fancy robes that they have at the Ritz... she *comes out* of the bathroom, and Marv Albert, the defendant, is in the bedroom... she *takes off* the robe. He *grabs* her by the arms, and he *throws* her on the bed, and he *says* to her, you've been a bad girl... But he *grabs* her and he *throws* her on the bed and he *jumps* on her back. She *is* shocked. He then *begins* to bite her back. The first bite is a complete shock. But as she *realizes* what is going on, she *says*, stop, it hurts. But he <u>did not stop</u>. He <u>continued</u> to bite her on the back in a painful way. In fact, he <u>mocked</u> her. He <u>said</u>, aw, come one, you know you like this. She <u>said</u>, stop, it hurts.

Schiffrin defines the Historical-Present tense as "the use of the present tense to refer to past events" (1981:45). She further argues that the HP is almost

totally restricted to (Labovian) complicating action clauses (rather than orien-
tations, abstracts, codas, etc.). What I have labelled the 'core narrative' is the
closest equivalent to Labov's 'complicating action' in narrative structure, and
in opening statements too the HP is restricted to the core narrative. Schiffrin
also proposes as a 'typical pattern' one where past tense verbs switch to HP near
the beginning of the narrative and back to past tense at the conclusion, which is
precisely what occurs in the extract above. Schiffrin sees the HP as an 'internal
evaluation device', allowing the narrator to present events as if they were occurring at that moment for dramatic effect, and it is the switch itself which creates
this effect. In this extract, the speaker switches to the HP at the point where the
plaintiff leaves home and approaches the hotel where the alleged assault takes
place. Not only a heightened sense of drama but also of narrativity is surely in
this instance both intended and strategic, and the use of the HP is pervasive in
this opening statement.

Narrative, non-narrative and hybridity as evidence

As has been mentioned, in his address to the jury the judge clearly distinguishes
between the opening statements (characterised as stories) and the testimony of
witnesses (characterised as factual evidence). His emphasis (in Bruner's terms)
is clearly on evidence as *verification* rather than as verisimilitude; the narratives
of the prosecution and the defence as presented in the opening statements can
only be *verified* by means of witness accounts which are based on 'fact'. But
this characterisation of the nature of evidence as essentially factual and truth
oriented creates in the evidential portions of trials a profound tension between
narrative and non-narrative modes of discourse which goes well beyond their
surface manifestations to the very heart of precisely what it is that is being verified. Few lawyers would deny the power of narrative forms in the evidential
portion of a trial, or that the prosecution in particular is under pressure to create coherent witness narratives which will corroborate its opening statement.
Though narratives are necessarily fragmented in testimony through the use
of questions and answers and most often subject to construction by multiple
tellers, narrativity itself is crucial, and it's possible to identify clear instances of
narrative structures, even in the fairly restrictive Labovian sense.

The following testimony relates to the moment when the plaintiff realises that the man she met earlier in the hotel (the defendant) is a celebrity
sportscaster, and her account takes the form of a *minimal narrative:*

Extract 7

Minimal narrative
(PL: Prosecuting lawyer; P: Plaintiff)

PL: How did that come about

P: My ex-husband was watching a foot ball game I believe on a   **Orientation**
Sunday afternoon. And I just came from work. And I heard
this voice which sounds familiar. And I walked out from my
bedroom back to the living room, and there was a voice and
there was a game. So I asked my ex-husband who that
person was. He said the announcer, but he did not know the   **Core Narrative**
name. So then I got interested and started watching the
game, which it was almost half-time. At that point when half
time came in, he was there for some commentaries. And I
said, oh my God. That's what he does. That's when I realized.   **Point**

This extract exhibits all the features, both structural and textual, of a minimal narrative, including speech events, i.e. what was said as well as what happened. Indeed, what was said becomes a significant part of what happened. There is also a predominance of past tense verbs, often in the form of simple past tense; events are temporally ordered and there are at least two independent clauses. There are also other markers of temporality in the use of connectors such as 'and', 'so', 'so then', 'at that point', etc.

But there are significant and substantial (probably predominant) parts of witness testimony which are very clearly non-narrative in mode. The following is an extract from the cross-examination of the plaintiff:

Extract 8

Non-narrative discourse. Cross-examination of the plaintiff.
(DL: Defence lawyer; P: Plaintiff)

DL: You talked about your old times together. Is that correct?
P: Yes
DL: Talked about your kids?
P: Uh-huh, yes
DL: There was certainly no anger exhibited during this conversation. Correct?
P: That's correct.
DL: This was a very friendly kind of conversation?
P: Yes.
DL: It was very nice?

P: Yes.

DL: Marv was a gentleman. Correct?

P: Yes.

DL: In your ten-year relationship, he's always been a gentleman. Correct?

P: Yes.

DL: He doesn't even swear?

P: No.

DL: He never even says a bad word. Is that right?

P: That's true.

DL: Always been gentle with you?

P: Yes.

DL: Always exhibited himself as a gentleman. Is that correct?

P: Yes.

This extract, taken from a longer cross-examination sequence, cannot be described as a recapitulation of past events, though it seems to start out as such. A number of past tense verbs are present, but they don't correlate directly with a series of events; there is no obvious temporal ordering, and the independent clauses present are not related in temporal ways. The purpose of the interrogation is not to produce a witness narrative account, a representation of what happened, but rather to get the plaintiff to *verify* a particular version of the defendant's character. The fact that it is the lawyer putting forward propositions for the witness to confirm or deny is significant but not in itself necessarily an anti-narrativity mode. Lawyers, particularly in direct examination, can put forward a series of propositions which are clearly structured as narrative accounts, as will be demonstrated presently.

   An even more obvious example of a non-narrative mode of discourse is the following extract from the testimony of an expert witness:

Extract 9

Non-narrative discourse: Expert witness (forensic scientist) testimony

PL: Just a few background questions. What is DNA?

W: DNA stands for Desoxyribose Nucleic Acid, the chemical substance found in our body. And it's basically responsible for determining every aspect of a human being. It determines such things as body functions, body size, body structure, as well as our own individual uniqueness.

PL: And where do we get it from initially?

W: DNA is an inherited substance. And we receive half of our DNA from our mother and half from our father. And therefore our overall DNA make up is a composition of our parents.

PL: And where do we find it in the body?

W: DNA is found in all cells in the body that contain nucleus. And nucleus is basically a control center for a cell. And some cells in the body contain white blood cells, sperm cells, skin cells, saliva cells that might be present. All the cells that make up the different organs and tissue in our body contain a nucleus and DNA would be present in those.

PL: And the cells in our body which have DNA, is the DNA the same from one cell to another cell?

W: Yes, it is. Regardless of our body fluids tested and analysed within one person, all the DNA would be the same.

PL: And how about between people, different people have the same DNA?

W: No two people except for identical twins have the same overall DNA composition.

The primary purpose of this testimony is to establish that it is the defendant's saliva which has been extracted from the bites on the plaintiff's back. Indeed, the prosecutor characterised his questions as 'background' ones, and this account lacks both the structural and textual features of a narrative, though clearly such non-narrative testimony can and does contribute to the overarching competing narratives of guilt and innocence which are constructed in the trial at the highest level. Much of the 'evidence' put forward in this, and indeed most trials, can be characterised as non-narrative in mode, despite the variety of types.

However, what I want to argue is that not only do trials comprise a hybridisation and inter-mingling of narrative and non-narrative discourse (opening statements versus the presentation of evidence) but that evidence itself represents a similar hybridity. Moreover, instances of narrative and non-narrative discourse only cohere (if indeed they do cohere at all) in complex ways. Narrative passages can occur in discourse which is essentially non-narrative and vice versa. The following is one of the more interesting examples.

Hybridisation and intermingling of evidence narratives

Extract 10

(DL: Defence lawyer; W: Police officer)

| 1 | DL: | Detective Morris, you are the investigating officer in this | **Orientation** |
| 2 | | case; is that correct? | |

3   W: Yes, I am.

4	DL:	And I take it that you *were assigned* that role in the early
5		morning hours of February 12th?

6   W: Yes, sir.

7   DL: And you *undertook* your investigation at that time?

8   W: Yes.

9   DL: You *began* your investigation at that time?

10 W: Correct.

11 DL: After – and I assume one of the first things you *did was debrief*

12   the officers who were at the hospital, *asked* them what happened?

13 W: Right.

14 DL: And you *said* you *had* a short conversation with Ms. Perhach: is

15   that correct?

16 W: That's correct.

17 DL: Now, after that, did you go to the Ritz Carlton?   **Point?**

18 W: No, I did not.

19 DL: How long after that did you go to the Ritz Carlton?

20 W: It was months later.

21 DL: I'm sorry?

22 W: Months later.

23 W: Uh-huh.

24 DL: That night you did not go to the room of Marv Albert;

25   is that correct?

26 W: That's correct.

27 DL: And you didn't go to the Ritz to interview any witnesses?

28 W: No, I did not.

29 DL: And you didn't get a search warrant for his room?

30 W: No, I did not.

31 DL: And you didn't search his room?

32 W: No, I did not.

33 DL: Didn't take any photographs?

34 W: Not at that time, no.

(The DL continues to elaborate on what the witness didn't do.)

In this extract, the defence lawyer is cross-examining a police witness, putting forward a series of propositions for the witness to confirm. The beginning of this extract is structured explicitly as a narrative account which is ordered temporally with a predominance of past tense verbs. However, from line 17 the questions of the lawyer move from what happened, i.e. what the police officer did, to what *didn't* happen, i.e. what the police officer *didn't* do. It's interesting to note that what the witness *didn't* do actually becomes the *point*, which is more elaborated than the initial narrative of what *did* happen and that even this account of what didn't happen has a strong element of the temporal and sequential. Clearly the *point* of the account, which is not made explicit, is that the assault wasn't taken seriously enough for the police to examine the scene of the crime or attempt to gather further evidence by questioning the hotel staff or indeed anything usually associated with serious criminal behaviour. The non-narrative takes on a quasi-narrative form, with a view to the explicit verification of what didn't happen.

Another example of hybridity of a different type is manifested in the following extract, once again a cross-examination:

Extract 11

(DL: Defence lawyer; W: Plaintiff Vanessa Perhach; PL: Prosecution lawyer)

1	DL:	Well, let me ask you then about the beginning. The beginning is
2		in September of 1986. Correct?
3	W:	Yes.
4	DL:	When he checks into the Miami Airport Hilton. Is that right?
5	W:	Yes.
6	DL:	And you were working at the Airport Hilton at that time. Is that
7		correct?
8	W:	Yes. Orientation
9	DL:	You said that at that time you were having problems in your
10		home life. Is that correct?
11	W:	Yes.
12	DL:	As well as you were just finishing up a four-year relationship
13		with a man named Jack Reynolds. Isn't that correct?
14	PL:	Objection.
15	Judge:	Sustained.
16	DL:	And you say that you were working as a telephone operator.
17		Is that correct?
18	W:	Yes.
19	DL:	Now, of course, you found out from this registration form that
20		Mr. Albert worked for NBC. Isn't that correct?
21	W:	Yes.
22	DL:	And you knew that NBC was a television network. Isn't that

23		correct?
24	W:	Yes.
25	DL:	Isn't it a fact – did you stop by his room?
26	W:	Yes, I did.
27	DL:	Is that after you found out that he worked for NBC?
28	W:	Yes.
29	DL:	And did you knock on his door?
30	W:	He asked me to come up.
31	DL:	You're telling us that he calls up on the phone and talks to
32		you and likes your voice, so he asked you to come up to his room.
33		Is that correct?
34	W:	Yes.
35	DL:	Isn't it a fact that you just went and knocked on his door after you
36		found out that he was employed by NBC?
38	W:	Absolutely not.

Narrative fragmentation is present in this extract as well, again with propositions put forward in cross-examination which aren't strictly temporal, after the Orientation. What happens here is that the defence lawyer attempts to subvert the plaintiff's narrative account, summarised in lines 31–33, by posing an alternative narrative (lines 35–36) which also becomes a version of point. He also suggests that his alternative narrative is 'a fact' (line 35), in clear contrast to what the plaintiff is 'telling us' (line 31). Both of these extracts thus exhibit a high degree of hybridity and an awareness of the tension between narrative and non-narrative modes of discourse through their deliberate contrast between what happened and what didn't happen (Extract 10), and what is 'a fact' from what is 'a telling' (Extract 11).

Corroborating narratives as evidence

This takes me to my second argument, i.e. the strategic pressure, particularly on prosecuting lawyers, to construct witness narratives as a powerful and persuasive way of achieving a measure of discourse coherence in the giving of evidence by witnesses despite the constraints of the rules of evidence, the characterisation of evidence as 'fact' by judges and the basically anti-narrativity mode of much of the discourse in a trial. This is an interesting case, which the prosecution eventually wins largely because the defendant changes his plea to guilty after two corroborating narrative witness accounts. Up to this point in the trial, the defence has managed effectively to subvert most of the plaintiff's own testimony, i.e. that she was a victim of a sexual assault and not a partner in consensual sex. Also, the defence has introduced a supplementary narrative whereby the plaintiff is taped apparently trying to bribe a witness, which also serves to undermine her testimony. No sustained and coherent narrative has been elicited from the plaintiff, and the case only turns clearly in her favour after the testimony of two prosecution witnesses who produce explicit narratives which do effectively corroborate the prosecution's opening statement 'story'. I shall conclude by presenting, very briefly, these two examples of coherent and powerful narratives, though both are fractured through a series of questions and answers. These two accounts serve to corroborate the prosecution's narrative of sexual assault rather than consensual sex, despite much evidence to the contrary. In both cases, the defence fails to subvert or create a convincing alternative narrative.

The first is the testimony of the plaintiff's sixteen-year-old daughter, which includes both direct examination (PL) and cross-examination (DL).

Extract 12

Plaintiff's daughter's testimony: Narrative as evidence

1	PL:	Would you please tell the Court and the jury your name?	
2	W:	Elaine Perhach.	
3	PL:	Elaine, how old are you?	
4	W:	Sixteen.	
5	PL:	Do you go to school?	**Orientation**
6	W:	Yes.	
7	PL:	Where do you go to school?	
8	W:	James Madison High School.	
9	PL:	Is your mom Vanessa Perhach?	
10	W:	Yes.	

11	PL:	Elaine, I would like you to think back to the night your mom was	
12		attacked. On the day before, did you have an opportunity to	
13		speak to the defendant, Marv Albert?	
14	W:	Yes, I did.	**Core Narrative**
15	PL:	How did you speak with him?	
16	W:	He called asking for my mother.	
17	PL:	He asked for your mother?	
18	W:	Yes.	
19	PL:	And did there come a time that night that your mom went to	

20		the defendant's hotel?
21	W:	Yes.
22	PL:	Approximately what time was that?
23	W:	Eleven o'clock. She has to take my boyfriend home.
24	PL:	She took your boyfriend home?
25	W:	Yes.
26	PL:	Did you then go to bed that night after your mom left?
27	W:	I didn't go to bed exactly after she left. I waited for her to come
28		home for a little while. Then I went to sleep.
29	PL:	Were you awakened later that evening?
30	W:	Yes, I was.
31	PL:	What woke you up?
32	W:	My mom. She was in the bathroom and she was crying, and her
33		crying woke me up. And I asked her –
34	PL:	Where were you when you woke up?
35	W:	I was in my room.
36	PA:	What did you do?
37	W:	I went to the bathroom to see what was wrong with her.
38	PL:	Was she standing or was she –
39	W:	She was sitting.
40	PL:	What was she doing?
41	W:	She was crying.
42	PL:	What happened next?
43	W:	And then I asked her what had happened to her.
44	DL:	Objection. Hearsay.
45	PL:	Your honor, it certainly goes to corroborate her prior testimony.
46	DL:	It's still hearsay.
47	Judge:	Overruled. Go ahead, Counsel.
48	W:	And then I asked her what happened and she said, don't worry about
49		it. Don't worry about it. And I said, Please tell me what happened.
50		And she pulled up her shirt and she showed me her back, and it was all
51		messed up and had bruises and marks on it. And I said, Who did this
52		to you, and she said, Marv.
53	PL:	Would you please answer any of Mr. Black's questions? **Cross**
54	W:	Yes. **Examination**
55	DL:	Miss Perhach, do you know George Papal?
56	PL:	Your Honor, I object. It's beyond the scope of direct examination.
57	Judge:	Sustained.
58	DL:	Have you told what you testified here today – have you told this

59		to any lawyers?
60	W:	Yes.
61	DL:	Other than the Commonwealth's Attorneys here?
62	W:	No.
63	DL:	And that night when you talked to your mother, what she said, she
64		pulled up her shirt and showed you her back. Is that correct?
65	W:	Yes.
66	DL:	And when you said why she was crying, that's what she said,
67		is that correct?
68	W:	What do you mean?
69	DL:	Well, you said that when you went into the bathroom and you
70		asked her what happened, what she did is pulled up her shirt and
71		showed you her back, is that correct?
72	W:	Yes.
73	DL:	And she said nothing else, is that correct?
74	W:	She told me – like after she showed me her back and after she
75		told me who did it, she told me briefly what had happened.
76	DL:	That it was Marv – is that correct?
77	W:	Yes.
78	DL:	I have nothing else, Your Honor.

There is an essential narrativity about this testimony, even though it's fragmented. The prosecutor controls the discourse but in a collaborative way. The narrative voice shifts between the witness and the lawyer, who incorporates most of the narrative propositions into his series of questions. However, there is very clear temporal sequencing, with little elaboration, and a predominance of simple past tense verbs within a highly visible narrative structure. Indeed, the narrative coherence of this testimony is such that there is no need for an explicit *point*, and the testimony concludes instead with a climactic account (lines 48–52) of what happened. This witness account demonstrates clearly the power of testimony in the form of a coherent, if highly restricted, narrative which manages to corroborate an important component of the prosecution's 'story'. The narrative structure and textuality are unambiguous.

The cross-examination is also interesting, in that the defence lawyer attempts to do two things. Firstly, he tries to establish that the witness's mother (the plaintiff) has engaged a lawyer for purposes of a civil suit to extract money from the defendant, who is a wealthy celebrity (alternative point lines 55–62). Secondly, he attempts to call into question the daughter's evidence, i.e. that Marv Albert is guilty (subverting her narrative, lines 63–77). Neither of these strategies is successful, and the defence lawyer doesn't persevere with his cross-examination.

However, it's the testimony of another witness which ultimately brings about the defendant's change of plea to guilty. This account is that of a woman who testifies regarding her own encounter with the defendant. She too works in a hotel and, like the plaintiff, met the defendant in that context.

Extract 13

Patricia Masten, the corroborating witness: narrative as evidence
(PL: Prosecution lawyer; W: Witness)

1   PL: Did you ask him to do a favor for you while he was there?
2   W: Yes, I did.
3   PL: What was that?
4   W: I asked him if he had any plans for lunch and he said no. I asked him if
5   he would like to join the general manager for lunch and he said yes
6   he would.
7   PL: Did you go to lunch with them?
8   W: I met him in the lobby and I introduced him to the general manager
9   and they asked me to join them but I figured they would talk about sports
10   because my general manager was a sports fanatic. I mean,
11   I had plenty of work to do. So they went by themselves to lunch.
12 PL: After lunch did you see the defendant again?
13 W: I saw him in the lobby when lunch was concluded and
14   he took the elevator up to his room.
15 PL: Did you hear from him after that?
16 W: About 15 minutes later I got a page on my pager and there was
17   a call waiting and I responded to the call and it was him.
18 PL: Why was he calling?
19 W: He called to say that he needed a fax sent and could I send a fax
20   and help him with a fax. And I said sure.
21 PL: Is that something that you do as part of your job?
22 W: All the time I send faxes, and I deliver Fed Ex packages. That's part of
23   my job.
24 PL: What did you do?
25 W: I went up to the suite and the door was – the bolt was open on the door
26   so it wasn't shut; it was ajar.
27 PL: What kind of suite was it?
28 W: It was a two-room suite with a bedroom off to one side and a
29   living room and a bar area.

30 PL: And when you found the door ajar, what did you do?
31 W: I knocked on the door and I said, It's PJ – and – that's the name I go under.
32   And he said, come on in. And he wasn't in the room, so I just walked over –
33   He called from the bedroom and said he would be right out.
34 PL: Where did you go when you got into the room?
35 W: I walked over to the window and I was looking out the window, because
36   the hotel was right at the airport and I was watching the planes land.
37 PL: What happened after that?
38 W: I heard the door close behind me and I turned around I saw him
39   standing there.
40 PL: What did you see?
41 W: I saw him standing in white panties and a garter belt.
42 PL: And what else did you see, if anything?
43 W: He was exposed and he was aroused.
44 PL: What did you do at that point?
45 W: I was in shock. I didn't know what to do. I was in shock. I just stood there.
46 PL: And what did he do then?
47 W: He came over to me and he said he was tense and that he needed some
48   relief and he started rubbing up against me and he leaned over and he
49   bit the back of my neck.
50 PL: What happened then?
51 W: And I tried to push him away and he put his hand on my head and tried
53   to push my head down.
54 PL: To where?
55 W: To his crotch area.
56 PL: It was still exposed?
57 W: Yes, it was.
58 PL: And then what happened at that point?
59 W: I tried to push him away from me, and I was pushing and then I went to
60   grab his hair to pull his hair and his hair lifted off and he immediately
61   went his – put his hand on his hair and I ran out of the room.
62 PL: Thank you.

This narrative in fact brings the case to a close. It effectively corroborates the 'story' narrative of the prosecution's opening statement, since this witness has no previous sexual relationship with the defendant. She goes to his room in the performance of her professional duty as a hotel manager and unambiguously rejects his sexual advances so that the case for sexual assault is not in doubt. In addition, the account has a powerful narrative force, and unlike the account of the witness's daughter, the narrative propositions are almost all put forward by the witness herself rather than the prosecutor, who utilises mainly the 'what happened then' kind of prompt along with some occasional but fairly minimal elaboration. Once again, temporal coherence and chronological sequencing are much in evidence. There is no explicitly expressed *point*, and this narrative changes the course of the case, since the defence subsequently fails to subvert this narrative and is unable to offer an alternative account or version of *point*.

Conclusions

Trial language is undoubtedly a fruitful context for examining narratives on a number of different levels and over the past two decades a substantial amount of literature has been generated. What has not been explored in the same depth is the conjunction of narrative and non-narrative modes of discourse, and Georgakopoulou and Goutsos' call for further study on "the hybridization and inter-mingling of narrative and non-narrative modes" (2000a: 76) in institutional and public discourse is a timely one. Most interesting, perhaps, is the profound tension in the evidential portions of trials, in particular, between witness and defendant accounts, which are 'characterised' by judges as primarily the verification of the factual, i.e. what happened, and the strong pressure on both the prosecution and the defence to construct such accounts as coherent and convincing narratives. It is significant that Bruner, who distinguished so insightfully between the two primary modes of thinking (narrative and paradigmatic) in the context of education, should in his most recent book choose to collaborate with a leading civil rights lawyer to explore how narrative structures and modes of thinking permeate legal decision making and the interpretation of the law (Amsterdam & Bruner 2000).

In summary, then, this chapter has attempted to demonstrate:

1. that trial language represents in complex ways the hybridisation and intermingling of narrative and non-narrative modes of discourse, both across sub-generic types of discourse relating to the trial as a whole and, more specifically, in the presentation of evidence by witnesses;
2. that, as a consequence, what counts as a narrative in a trial is 'characterised' in different ways by the participants (judges, lawyers, witnesses), and there is a crucial distinction between, in particular, the opening and closing statements by prosecuting and defence lawyers as a generic type of discourse, which contains a high degree of 'narrativity', and the presentation of evidence, whereby witnesses are subject to the rules of evidence

and 'narrativity' is fragmented both by question/answer sequences and multiple tellers of the narrative; and

3. that despite the 'anti-narrativity mode' of much trial language, the power of the narrative in court is indisputable. The prosecution, in particular, is under pressure to create persuasive and coherent witness narratives as evidence which will corroborate opening statements explicitly characterised as 'story telling' narratives, and one of the primary objectives of the defence is either to subvert the narratives of the prosecution or to establish credible alternative versions.

Note

1. There are a number of websites which display transcripts from American courtroom trials. For example, the *O. J. Simpson Trial* transcripts are available at (http://www.cnn.com/US/OJ/trial/index.html). The Court TV website (http://www.courttv.com) also contains the transcripts of a number of trials, including the *Marv Albert Trial* used in this chapter and extracts from the *Winona Ryder Trial*. British courtroom data is still much more difficult to obtain.

CHAPTER 12

Television news and narrative
How relevant are narrative models for explaining
the coherence of television news?

Martin Montgomery
University of Strathclyde

Introduction

It is something of a truism that news is a narrative form. For one thing, it
chimes with our common-sense description of news in terms of 'news stories' – a way of thinking shared alike by analysts, producers and consumers
of the news. As Allan Bell writes at the beginning of his article on press journalism – significantly entitled *Telling stories* – "Journalists do not write articles.
They write stories" (1994: 100). And certainly his analysis of press journalism as
narrative is illuminating, demonstrating not only how narrative forms of the
news have changed but also how professional pressures (sub-editing to meet
the constraints of space, etc.) have helped to mould and re-mould those particular versions of narrative that dominate the press. In this he shares common
ground with Caldas-Coulthard (1997) and Van Dijk (1988a and 1988b) who,
in specifying the discourse structure of news stories, draw upon schemata as
well as, in Caldas-Coulthard's case, Labov's work on 'natural narrative' (Labov
1972; Labov & Waletsky 1967) to account for the coherence that news discourse
displays.[1]

 Although the discourse of television news has received much less attention
than that of print journalism, the well-established sense of news as narrative still provides a dominant model (see, for example, Hartley 1982; Graddol
1994). Here, for instance, is Graddol:

> TV news tells stories about the world and the dominant narrative technique
> for such storytelling is what is called *realism*. Realism of the kind I am referring
> to here first arose as literary convention [...]

> The cinema adopted and adapted the realist narrative techniques of the novel
> [...] Realism thus provides a powerful visual technology for cueing narrative
> modalities. The regime of camera work and editing is so naturalized that we
> rarely stop to think about its artifice. [...] Indeed, the realist technique is so
> naturalized that TV news cannot avoid drawing on its resources when telling
> its own narratives.   (1994:140–142)

This is a very strong claim about the way pre-existing cinematic codes have
determined a narrative tendency in TV news discourse.[2]

Despite the firmness with which such perspectives are advanced, several
problems arise when notions of narrative are applied to television news. Firstly,
on closer inspection it is not at all clear – despite what Graddol says – that TV
news footage bears much (or, indeed, any) resemblance to the narrative forms
of fiction cinema. At a very obvious level the pervasive and habitual mode of
address of TV news, involving direct visual address to camera, is hardly ever
seen in fiction film. More fundamentally, perhaps, the guiding principle of
mainstream narrative cinema is to unfold an action in which identifiable protagonists are engaged, so that the task of continuity editing, as evidenced in
classic Hollywood cinema, is to develop character and action in a trajectory that
leads to a resolution (Kuhn 1985; Bordwell & Thompson 1979; Bordwell 1985).

Television narrative, however, as Ellis (1982) persuasively claims, is more
diffuse, more fragmentary, more episodic and iterative than cinema. This is
particularly true of news. Even in an area where comparisons are often made –
the depiction of war – television news coverage conspicuously lacks the narrative coherence of the Hollywood war movie, even of those films where '(documentary) realism' is a much declared production value (such as, for example,
the opening scenes of Saving Private Ryan). For, unlike cinema, where the
structure of editing is devoted to following the fate of a character (or characters) to some kind of closure, television news presents actions which are often
incomplete and where no identifiable character or protagonist is offered to help
structure the subjective identification of the viewer.[3]

A second and more serious difficulty is that much television news in its
textual particulars quite simply fails to exhibit story-telling characteristics.
On the contrary, the core principle of intelligibility in television news reports
might be summed up as the convincing deployment of pictures – and, in this
respect, narrative is only an occasional discursive resource even when the notion of an event or happening provides an important background element in
news coverage.

Indeed, as many have noted, news as a system is uncomfortable for various reasons with the unfolding complexities of abstract social and historical

processes such as economic change or international diplomacy. These become foreshortened in routine news coverage to the most recent action/event and its consequences. Examples abound: labour unrest becomes condensed to a strike, visualised as picket lines, and its consequences for the public. The democratic process becomes condensed to the election campaign. Parliamentary policy-making becomes condensed to a crucial vote, or Prime Minister's Question Time. The invasion of Iraq by a Western coalition takes place as bombing raids, firefights and overturned statues. Television news coverage, in the face of complexity, seeks out the iconic and emblematic incident.

In this foreshortening, however, even those events that are reported may lack a narratable structure. More crucially, perhaps, many news reports – although they may take the background of events for granted – set out to tell no story but to do some other kind of discursive work. Indeed, attempts to conceptualise television news primarily in terms of narrative distort our understanding of the prevalent characteristics of journalism as a textual system – especially in its televised manifestations.

Instead of assuming from the outset, therefore, that the intelligibility of television news is grounded in narrative, it is arguably more revealing to identify some pervasive characteristics of the texts of television news and then to elaborate from these characteristics some core principles of their discursive intelligibility. In what follows, therefore, I will lay out some recurring elements of the verbal texts of television news reports in order to suggest some crucial principles of non-narrative coherence that the discourse of TV news reports relies upon, before returning to the question of narrative in TV news.

Some textual features and principles of intelligibility of television news reports

Tense

Despite variations depending on the time of day and the 'house style' of the broadcaster, television news reports often rely heavily on the present tense. In particular, daytime (rather than evening) television reports and the BBC (as opposed, for example, to ITN) tend to favour the present tense. (All examples come from extracts given in full in the Appendix.)

> | Bad weather *cloaks* the mountains above Kaprun | *bringing* yet more warnings of avalanches. | [ASRA][4]

| Heavy snowfalls *are* only *adding* to the risks. Warmer temperatures at | this time of the year *make* the fresh snow unstable – more liable to move. |
[ASRA]

| For now, most of the ski slopes here *are* shut. The authorities | *aren't taking* any chances. |
[ASRA]

| The friendly society which commissioned the survey *says* grieving | relatives rarely *get* a | true picture of the funeral costs | before committing themselves. Its spokesman *says* funeral directors *are giving* them cheap initial quotes which typically *double* before the funeral's over, an issue *being investigated* by the Office of Fair Trading. |
[RCF]

| No-one *knows* how many stars are in our universe. And so far no-one *knows* if | – like our sun – they can support life on nearby planets. But by *using* the | Araseevo radio telescope at Puerto Rico – the largest of its kind | in the world – astronomers *are trying* to find out if there is intelligent alien life outside our solar system. |
[SETI]

The wounded *are* brought here to a bar…Hygiene *is* minimal. Standards low. This *is* how they sterilize surgical instruments. But what they *lack* in perfection, the medical team *makes up for* in determination, desperately trying to save the life of yet another comrade-in-arms   [WIC]

This is not the historic (or conversational historic) present – the use of the present to describe past events – noted by analysts of narrative (see, for example, Wolfson 1979, 1982); 'She reached into her bag. She *feels* for her mobile phone. *Realises* with a shock it's missing….'. In examples of the historic present, sequence is recoverable as well as a sense of the events having been completed in time before the moment of telling. This is not the case with the present tense of news, of which various uses may be distinguished.

First of all, the action may be projected as contemporaneous with and projecting beyond the moment of utterance. Thus, examples such as 'most of the ski slopes are shut' (ASRA), or 'heavy snowfalls are adding to the risks' (ASRA), refer to an ongoing state of affairs at the time of broadcast utterance. Secondly, a version of the customary present may be used to refer to an action that is routinely repeated or a state of affairs that endures: for example 'The wounded are brought here to a bar' (WIC), 'Funeral directors are giving them cheap quotes' (RCF), 'Astronomers are trying to find out…' (SETI) or 'No-one knows how many stars are in the universe (SETI). Thirdly, the present tense is used to refer to an action that could still apply even though it is completed: thus, 'the friendly society says grieving relatives…' (RCF) refers to an action that has been completed but since the proposition that it governs ('grieving relatives rarely get a true picture of funeral costs') is taken as continuing to apply after the moment of utterance, then the act of saying can be taken as reiterated as long as the proposition still applies.

In part this salience of the present tense is driven by the news value of 'recency' (Galtung & Ruge 1965; Golding & Elliott 1979). The news has to be new – dealing with *The Day Today*, as the satirical parody of a news programme was called. But the common use of the present tense in news reports does more than project the news as right up to date and dealing with 'the now'; it also helps to create a sense of referring to a present reality. The frequent selection of the present tense helps to collapse the distance between the event and its telling in such a way that it undermines chronology. In addition, the present tense, in as much as it is unmarked for modality, contributes to the routine 'facticity' of televisual news discourse.

Textual cohesion in television news reports: The interplay of the visual with the verbal

If the choice of tense emphasises the 'present-ness' of the reality depicted in the report, images of that reality serve as a visual back-up to the words. The presence of these images ensures that the way textual cohesion works in the verbal track of a news report is somewhat different from the way it works in standard written text. Consider the following extract from the verbal text of a report:

> Another motorist is pulled over by the police as part of their crackdown on drink-driving.
> "A good strong blow please an ah'll tell ye when to stop. Keep blowin'. Keep blowin'. Keep blowin'" [fade out]
> This man hadn't been drinking. He was simply lost. But last year one in six deaths on our roads were drink-related. And across the UK the figures are edging upward.
> A new survey suggests half of Britain's drivers admit drinking before getting behind the wheel. And many have little idea about the potency of alchohol.
> Anything over two units will put you over the limit. Each of these drinks represents one unit of alchohol: that's a glass of wine, a half-pint of beer and a measure of spirit. But what happens if your wine comes in a large glass or the lager you're drinking happens to be a strong continental type. Each of these on their own will put you over the limit and merely adds to the confusion.
> "This a Stella Artois which ah know is quite strong. It's heading towards a

whole one and a half to two units. So again it's probably a pint is as much. But the best thing is not to do it."   [PCDD]

If this were standard written text the reader would be puzzled in the first instance by who/what is the referent for 'another motorist'. They would equally be puzzled by unassigned quotations. Who, for instance, is saying "a good strong blow please"?

    This text, of course, is part of a package assembled from material collected on location, at the roadside, in a pub and so on. The visual and verbal elements are edited together along with the reporter's 'voice-over'. So the passage in quotation marks, transcribed above, for instance, is not introduced by reporting clauses such as 'The Strathclyde Police Officer said:…'. The package merely shows the police officer, the drinker in the pub, the reporter – and simply uses the visual depiction (sometimes supported by caption) to identify them. Indeed, there are several points in the transcribed verbal track where the verbal text makes sense by reference to what is visible in the visual track:

> *Another motorist* is pulled over..
> *This man* hadn't been drinking..
> Each of *these drinks* represents one unit of alchohol..
> *This* is a Stella Artois..

Broadly what is at stake in this, and most TV news reports, is a presumption of shared reference between the verbal track and the visual track so that for any single report there will be at least some overlap for some of the time between word and image. This is reinforced verbally by a specialised use of spatial deixis:

> | If you're hoping for proof of an alien civilisation then the best place to be in the UK is *here* at the Jodrell Bank Observatory *here* in Cheshire. Because its radio telescope is so sensitive it could detect *one* | *of these* from 220 million | miles away. | [SETI]
>
> | Few of the people buried *here* in Highgate Cemetery have endured a |
>   [RCF]
>
> | Not *everyone here* seems aware of the danger. | [ASRA]
>
> | For now, most of the ski slopes *here* are shut.   [ASRA]
>
> | Relatives of those who died in the accident have also been arriving *here* |
>   [ASRA]
>
> | The number of avalanches *here* has increased sharply during the last few years.   [ASRA]

In addition to this kind of deixis there are related patterns of usage of demonstrative reference:

> *This* man hadn't been drinking..   [PCDD]
> In *this* demonstration of a typical funeral..   [RCF]
> It could detect one of *these*   [SETI]
> *Each of these* drinks   [PCDD]
> *Each of these* on their own   [PCDD]
> *This* is as far as Russian patrols dare go   [WIC]
> *This* is one section of the front line   [WIC]
> *This* is how they sterilize surgical instruments   [WIC]

In these examples, and commonly elsewhere in TV news reports, deixis and demonstrative reference is proximate rather than distal and, in some cases at least, it seems to refer not simply to 'near' rather than 'far' but to what is visible in the visual track of the report. These sentences cue a close connection between what is being said in the verbal track and what can be seen in the visual track of the report.

Indeed, there is a general sense in TV news reports of co-reference along the two tracks so that what the verbal dimension of the text refers to is also seen to be referred to in the visual track. So a clause like:

> | *Flashing lights* tell skiers and snowboarders there's a serious possibility of avalanches.   [ASRA]

is accompanied by a shot of a flashing light.

> | *Bad weather cloaks* the mountains above Kaprun | [ASRA]

is accompanied by a long shot of a snow grooming vehicle obscured by wind-driven snow. And a clause such as

> | For now, most of the ski slopes here *are shut*.   [ASRA]

is accompanied by a shot of an empty set of ski-lift chairs swinging in the wind.

Accordingly, whilst expressions such as 'one of these' or 'most of the ski slopes here' function to cue a connection between the verbal and visual tracks, there is a more generalized sense of co-reference at work. It is important to note, however, that identifying a visual correlate of a verbal referring expression is the outcome of sometimes quite complex and cumulative inferential work: in other words, although it may seem transparent on casual viewing that the visual track refers to the same things as the verbal track, the connections depend upon an inferential accomplishment. For instance, a group of three adults huddled together is seen as a group of mourners precisely because – against the background of a presumption of a connection between word and image – the verbal track tells us in voice-over to the shot:

> | *Relatives of those who died* in the accident have also been arriving here | mourning their sudden loss. | [ASRA]

Principles of intelligibility in TV news reports

The supposition of co-reference between the verbal and visual tracks should, therefore, be seen as an effect of the discourse, in which sentences including proximate deixis and demonstratives ('here', 'this', 'these') cue us to see an overarching relationship between word and image. In practice, of course, the relationships between the verbal and visual components of a news report prove to be uneven and erratic. Meinhof (1994), for instance, notes three main kinds of interrelationship which she describes as 'overlap', 'displacement' and 'dichotomy'. Overlap is where the visual footage and the verbal text share the same action component. Displacement is where the footage and the text represent different action components (e.g. the effect of a disaster depicted in image, with its cause described in words). Dichotomy is where footage and text represent action components of different, if related, events. There is obviously a cline or gradient between extremes and it is important to note that different economies of exchange between word and image can obtain at different moments within the same news report. Nonetheless, despite the potential for shift and variation, a primary principle of intelligibility of the televisual discourse of news reports may be formulated as follows:

> Rule 1:
> For any referring expression in the verbal track, search for a relevant referent in the image track.

Conversely, however, a secondary and complementary principle might be formulated thus:

> Rule 2:
> Treat any element depicted in a shot in the visual track as a potential referent for a referring expression in the verbal track.

It is the operation of these twin rules of interpretation (or principles of intelligibility) that achieves a kind of closure between what we can see and hear represented in televisual news discourse. This might be called 'the effect of simultaneous (verbal and visual) reference'. It is this effect that explains a problem noted by Meinhof (1994). She observed that the same shot of a man with a container on the back of his bike included in both a German news programme and a British news programme was interpreted by viewers respectively as transporting water or petrol. The variable reading of the image was prompted by alternative wordings in the two reports: the German programme referred to food shortages whereas the British programme referred to petrol shortages (Meinhof 1994: 217–221). Underlying the discrepant interpretations are the twin rules of interpretation, noted above: viewers were predisposed to find the container on the back of the bike as either petrol or water on the basis of the presumption of simultaneous overlapping reference.

The presumption of overlapping reference is reinforced not just by cueing sentences (for example, 'the best place to be in the UK is *here at the Jodrell Bank Observatory here* in Cheshire. Because its *radio telescope* is so sensitive it could detect *one | of these* from 220 million | miles away.|') where proximate deixis and demonstratives reinforce the relationship between word and image. It is also reinforced by synchronized editing in which the transition from one shot to the next coincides with clause and sentence boundaries, though the degree of synchronization varies. In cases of close synchronization as many as two-thirds of the cuts between one shot and the next within the body of the report will occur at clause and sentence boundaries. And it is rare to find less than one third correspondence between shot boundaries and the boundaries of clause and sentence. On average there is close to a 50% correspondence between shot boundaries and those of clause or sentence.[5] Synchronized editing helps to reinforce a sense of mutual assembly of the words and images and hence of their reciprocal relevance: the words seem to be driving the pictures at the same time as the pictures seem to be driving the words.

Finally, the presumption of overlapping reference is supported by the notion that the words and the pictures in news reports emanate or issue from a defined and visualized space. In each of the reports used as data for this chapter (see appendices) the speaker delivers their wording for the most part as unseen voice-over; but at some point in the report this same speaker will be featured in direct address to camera – even if only momentarily – and thereby situated in the space from which the report (in part, at least) is projected. And routinely, of course, the voice of the report 'signs off' with some kind of locational formulation: 'Brent Sadler, CNN, Grozny'; 'Andrew Verity, BBC News in Highgate Cemetery'; 'Jonathan Charles, BBC News, Kaprun'. Thus speakers in voice-over not only identify themselves by name but simultaneously situate themselves in the space of the broadcast.

report signs off with the routine reference to the identity of the reporter and a specification of where the report is from.

It is crucial to stress, however, that the presumption of simultaneous reference is an effect of the text and of the inferences which it prompts. If we consider the opening of the news report transcribed in its entirety above, most viewers will make several perfectly routine and commonplace assumptions about what they can see. They will assume, for instance, that:

- the two men in uniform wearing yellow jackets and peaked hats visible on either side of a stationary car are police officers;
- the two men (police officers) have stopped the car that is stationary;
- the driver of the stationary car is suspected of drink-driving;
- the man seen blowing into an instrument in the second shot is the driver of the stationary car in the first shot;
- he has been asked to blow into the instrument because he is suspected of drink-driving;
- the instrument into which he blows is for measuring quantities of alcohol on breath (a breathalyser);
- we see part of this from the vantage point of a policecar.

It would be difficult to account for these inferences on the basis of the pictures alone. Without the verbal track to guide and prompt them, other conclusions could be drawn. Indeed, as the report itself reveals 'This man hadn't been drinking. He was simply lost'. Elsewhere, for example, the report asserts 'And many have little idea about the potency of alcohol.' This assertion is accompanied by a shot consisting of a low angle close up profile shot of male drinking from a pint glass labelled Guinness.

A routine assumption will link these elements by means of the inference that the man drinking Guinness (an assumption in itself) is one of the many who have little idea about the potency of alcohol. These assumptions arise in a matter of fact way (reinforced by the reporter pointing up the confusions surrounding units). They are little disturbed by the ensuing shot of 'an ordinary drinker' at a bar giving a very precise estimate of the units at stake in the Stella Artois which he's drinking.

This is not to claim that some kind of deception or *trompe l'oeil* is at stake in news reports – only that such packages invite routine assumptions dependent upon co-referencing between word and image. And two kinds of assumption are present in this routine co-referencing:

1. that there is a reciprocal connection between word and image of the kind stipulated above;
2. that what is visible in the image has a kind of documentary status. Unless marked to the contrary, the image depicts an element found in reality, not staged for the camera. The image may be 'illustrative' or 'representative' but it is 'real', not 'faked' or 'staged'.[6]

In many ways the processes at stake support Andrew Tolson's comment: "This illustrative use of the image is one way in which the news gives the impression of 'fact' – that is say, factuality is a produced consequence of this text's particular structure" (Tolson 1996: 18). Or in other words, the reality depicted in the pictures of television news is treated as indexically real. It is a reality which pre-exists the act of reference and it endures. It is not summoned into existence for the purpose of the news. Rather the news constantly seems to index a reality presumed to pre-exist it. The news merely reports what is there, which in a compact between producer and viewer is found over and over again in routine acts of inference.

Conclusions: Narrative or commentary?

Considering news as a system in its entirety ("*the* sense-making practice of modernity" as Hartley 1996: 32–33 calls it), one can of course find examples of narrative, just as one can reveal the narrative elements implicated in therapy, drama, gossip, fine art, cinema, historiography, conversation, court-room cross-examination, or jury deliberation. But news on television only intermittently relies on narrative. It nearly always, however, relies on pictures. And in doing so it has evolved a quite distinctive discursive posture within the overall practice of news. Although news as a whole admittedly does involve events, television news is not so much about telling their structure as about showing where such incidents are located. It is about referencing the familiar parameters of a world taken-for-granted but which most of us rarely see at first hand. Indeed, it defines the significant parameters of that very world which it makes familiar and goes on to people it with faces or types which it makes familiar: Trafalgar Square and demonstrators/supporters, the House of Commons and the Prime Minister or the Leader of the Opposition, Cardiff Arms Park and football supporters, traders gesticulating on the New York stock exchange, lawyers arriving at the Old Bailey. Even where the spaces, the people and the incidents are highly particular, television news invests them with a representative status. Individuals and settings cannot be shown without them becoming iconic or emblematic. A portly man in glasses blowing into a breathalyser at the roadside becomes 'the motorist (who may have drunk too much)'. A tall thin man sipping a pint of Guinness becomes 'one of the many (of us) who don't understand units of alcohol'.

Only occasionally are these reports 'history in the making'. Routinely they cover broadly what might be called 'public information': a toll Motorway is opening parallel to a busy section of the M6 – motorists will be able to pay to avoid congestion; using a mobile phone while driving will become illegal from tonight; the police will crack down this Christmas on drink-driving; a new scientific assessment casts fresh doubt on the possible link between the MMR vaccine and autism; the government is proposing an 'honesty box' to make credit agreements more transparent; house prices are still rising in most parts of the country; obesity is on the increase in young people. These announcements ratify or produce a world held in common with particular structures of concern – with health, with property, with life-style, with transport, with the law. Those of us who watch the news, it is implied, are concerned about our children, take package holidays, want to observe the law, enter into credit agreements, have mortgages and so on. The news in its iterative fashion refers us repeatedly to this world which it produces and reproduces as a normative order. For this reason, it would seem fair to say that much of what is spoken by news reporters as voice-over to news reports is better described as 'commentary', or maybe as a species of public announcement, rather than narration. And while some news events and some genres of news give rise to storyable forms, television news generally is best understood in other terms. In television news, word is to image as commentary is to illustration. That, rather than narrative, is its core principle of intelligibility.

Appendix

Data and transcription

The data on which this chapter is based are drawn mostly from news reports broadcast by BBC television either at 1.00 p.m. or during the late evening (usually 10 p.m.) news programme. One report is from CNN. They were selected at random from the main body of their respective news programmes. In other words none of them were broadcast as part of the lead or the closing news item. As such they would seem to be fairly typical of routine, unmarked news items. They were transcribed and punctuated as if they were written text (except where, as in the first, there is strong presence of vernacular forms). In addition several of the reports include information about shot transition, indicated by |. Information about the nature of the accompanying shot has been included where appropriate within curly brackets thus: {Mid shot of same man flanked by two police officers}.

(1) **Police Crackdown on Drink Drivers [PCDD]**
Pre-recorded news report:
| Another motorist is pulled over by the police as part of their crackdown on drink-driving. |
{Long shot from interior of one stationary car – a police car – towards two police officers on either side of stationary car ahead.}
| "A good strong blow please an ah'll tell ye when to stop. Keep blowin'. Keep blowin'. Keep blowin'" {fade out of voice of policeman and diegetic sound}
| This man hadn't been drinking. He was simply lost. |
{Close up shot of man blowing into instrument}
| But last year one in six deaths on our roads were drink-related. |
{Mid shot of same man flanked by two police officers}
| And across the UK the figures are edging upward. |
{Shot of police car roof with flashing lights from behind}
| A new survey suggests half of Britain's drivers |
{panoramic shot of (pub) interior}
| admit drinking before getting behind the wheel. |
{close up of Christmas decoration}
| And many have little idea about the potency of alchohol. |
{low angle close up profile shot of male drinking from a pint glass labelled Guinness}
| Anything over two units will put you over the limit. |
{close up profile shot of man drinking from pint glass}
| Each of these drinks represents one unit of alchohol: |
{mid shot of reporter speaking from behind bar or table in direct address to camera}
| that's a glass of wine, a half-pint of beer and a measure of spirit. |
{close up of three glasses}
| But what happens if your wine comes in a large glass or the lager you're drinking happens to be a strong continental type. Each of these on their own will put you over the limit and merely adds to the confusion. |
{mid shot of reporter speaking in direct address to camera producing a

large wine glass and a continental beer from behind bar or table.}

| "This a Stella Artois which ah know is quite strong. It's heading towards a whole one and half to two units. So again it's probably a pint is as much. But the best thing is not to do it." |

{close up of man speaking in profile}

| "Everybody is different innit they? (....) It's what ye limitations are, I suppose, or what ye think are yer limitations." |

{Close up of another man speaking to camera}

| Every year government sponsored adverts ram home the dangers of drink driving. It works for many motorists but for others the police are the deterrent. |

{Reporter speaks over a sequence of seven shots from a Government sponsored advert}

| "The core message is 'don't drink and drive'. You can see the results behind me. If ye are gonna drink and drive, we're gonna do our damnednest to catch ye." |

{Mid shot of police officer in front of damaged car}

| The results of ignoring the warning, say the police, are more wrecked cars and wrecked |

{Panning shot up and zoom close on front of damaged car}

| lives. Andrew Cassell. BBC News. Glasgow |

{close up from beside car on some kind of cloth material draped over front seat and steering wheel}

(2) **Austrian Ski Resort Avalanche [ASRA]**

News reader's studio presentation:

AF: Rescuers have abandoned the search for two snow-boarders missing after yesterday's avalanche in Austria because of dense fog and the risk of further slides. Eleven people died near the ski resort of Kaprun and as our correspondent Jonathan Charles reports this morning most of the ski runs were closed.

Pre-recorded news report:

JC: | *Bad weather cloaks* the mountains above Kaprun |

| bringing yet more warnings of avalanches. |

| Heavy *snowfalls* are only adding to the risks.

Warmer temperatures at | this time of the year make the fresh snow unstable – more liable to move. |

| For now, most of the ski slopes here *are shut*.

The authorities | aren't taking any chances. |

| *Flashing lights* tell skiers and snowboarders there's a serious possibility of avalanches.

Yesterday's tragedy appears to have been triggered by a group that were skiing | away from marked paths right in front of a massive wall of snow. |
| Not everyone here seems aware of the danger.
Interview clip....
| Few of the skiers appear to have been deterred by the avalanche though. |
| *One British group* told us the risks are minimal
as long as you stick to slopes which are properly prepared and monitored. |
Interview clip....
| *Military helicopters* were called in earlier today
to help in the search for two snowboarders |
who are still missing after the avalanche.
But the operation | is now being abandoned because visibility at the top of the | mountain is too poor. |
| *Relatives of those who died* in the accident have also been arriving here |
mourning their sudden loss. |
Reporter to Camera:
| The number of avalanches *here* has increased sharply during the last few years.
That's not just dangerous.
It's also bad for the tourist industry.
The Austrian authorities are now trying to persuade people that it's still safe to ski.
Jonathan Charles, BBC News, Kaprun |

(3) **The Rising Costs of Funerals [RCF]**
News reader's studio presentation:
AF: The cost of a burial has risen by a quarter since 1998
and has more than doubled since 1990.
The annual survey of funeral costs in Britain shows a large increase in bills for both burials and cremations.
The average burial service now costs more than £2000.
Pre-recorded news report:
AV: | *Funerals* are a distressing time for a family even without
| the fear of excessive costs.
In this demonstration of a typical funeral the real life cost |
would be two thousand and fifty pounds
up twenty five per cent from two years ago. |
| According to today's survey
the price of an average cremation went up by a tenth
to one thousand, two hundred and fifteen pounds.
| *Funeral directors* say they shouldn't be held to blame for the rising prices.

....Interview clip....

| The friendly society which commissioned the survey says grieving |
relatives rarely get a | true picture of the funeral costs |
before committing themselves.

Its spokesman says funeral directors are giving them cheap initial quotes
which typically double before the funeral's over,

an issue being investigated by the Office of Fair Trading. |

....Interview clip....

Reporter to camera:

| *Few of the people buried here in Highgate Cemetery* have endured a |
pauper's funeral.

But the fear is that, if burial and cremation costs continue to rise more
and more,

relatives | of the dead will find it hard to give their loved ones a dignified
send-off.

Andrew Verity, BBC News in Highgate Cemetery |

(4)   **The Search for Extra-Terrestrial Intelligence [SETI]**

News reader's studio presentation:

NR1:   Now, one of mankind's greatest questions must be: "Are we alone
in the universe?".

And for the last four decades scientists around the world have been trying
to find out the answer.

NR2:   Well, so far, human beings appear to be unique.

But, who knows? E-T could already be out there.

It's just that we haven't picked up his call.

But for forty years now scientists working for SETI,

"The Search for Extra-Terrestrial Intelligence",

have been listening out for his number.

Pre-recorded news report:

SN: | No-one knows how many *stars* are in our universe.

And so far no-one knows if | – like our *sun* – they can support life on
nearby planets.

But by using the | *Araseevo radio telescope* at Puerto Rico – the largest of
its kind | in the world – astronomers are trying to find out if there is intel-
ligent alien life outside our solar system. |

Reporter to camera

| If you're hoping for proof of an alien civilisation then the best place to be
in the UK is *here at the Jodrell Bank Observatory* here in Cheshire.

Because its *radio telescope* is so sensitive it could detect *one* | *of these* from
220 million | miles away. |

| *This 76 meter radio telescope* is used in conjunction with the dish at Araseevo.
They're conducting the most sensitive and comprehensive search ever undertaken | for extra-terrestrial radio signals. |
| It's part of Project Phoenix – a privately funded research programme with the SETI Institute.
….Interview clip…
Extract from BT ET advert
Astronomers have spent forty years looking for *ET*. |
| For the last eleven months | people with home computers have joined in the search using *a SETI 'at-home | screen-saver'* to help analyse all the signals |
received from the sky. |
| But *one woman* takes the amateur approach more | seriously.
Jenny Bailey is a computer consultant | specialising in radio systems |
and a member of the SETI league. Her search for extra-terrestrial intelligence incorporates a *two metre dish in her Cambridge back-garden*, | with *equipment in the kitchen for processing the signals* |
….Interview clip…
Radio signal noise
| And if E-T ever | does phone home, Jenny will be | waiting. |
Sue Nelson, BBC News.

(5) **War in Chechnya [WIC]**[7]
The Russians were supposed to conquer Grozny in one day – a simple operation lasting a few hours. But now – a month after launching one of the most devastating attacks on a city since the Second World War – their troops are bogged down.
The capture of the Presidential Palace – now a skeletal ruin – failed to break the resistance.
This is as far as Russian patrols dare go.
A few more yards beyond the palace and they'll be targeted by rebel rockets or gunfire.
The civilian catastrophe engulfed the population of 400,000 in just a few weeks.
This is the heart of the capital – torn apart.
It looks as if civilisation died here decades ago.
There are too many bodies to count: Chechen fighters entombed in a car; a soldier incinerated beyond recognition.
The survivors barely notice the corpses or the smell anymore.
Living conditions are subhuman.

Carrying a chunk of ice an old woman said sarcastically:

"This is the kind of water we have. Not bad is it?"

Those who are fit enough to escape plead with soldiers to take them out – any way they can.

Too few places for too many people.

Moscow's troops were presented with a mission impossible – take Grozny and kill few, if any, civilians in the process.

Unless there is a ceasefire and a mass evacuation of civilians, Russian forces may in the end have no choice but to storm the city regardless of the appalling consequences.

So far the military has been neither able to do its job quickly nor quietly.

In the old Red Army days it would have been different – a free hand to crack down in dissent; no international scrutiny, and no open condemnation of their own side.

"One of our planes – a MIG – dropped two bombs on us in a house", said a soldier. "Thirteen of us died."

At Grozny's command headquarters – marked by a graveyard of destroyed armour – the Russians are supposed to be on the verge of completing military operations.

This is one section of their front line.

Soldiers don't believe what Moscow claims and condemn their own officers for incompetence.

"We shoot at each other," said this Russian.

"It's a mess. There are no commanders: they're drunk every day."

Chechen fighters are slowing down their advance.

Here an anti-sniper squad uses old tricks to locate a source of incoming fire.

The Russians have convinced themselves that women sharpshooters like this – with experience in the Yugoslav War – are fighting as mercenaries in Chechnya.

"The snipers are doing most of the killing", said this Captain. "They're very hard to see, and even harder to eliminate."

They work at night, striking fear into Russian ranks, inflicting many casualties.

The wounded are brought here to a bar converted into a makeshift field hospital.

Hygiene is minimal.

Standards low.

This is how they sterilize surgical instruments.

But what they lack in perfection, the medical team makes up for in deter-

mination, desperately trying to save the life of yet another comrade-in –
arms.

Moscow's official account of the numbers of troops killed in action is less
than a thousand.

Those on the ground who say they know better believe their losses are
much higher – at least two, maybe three thousand and rising – a high price
to pay for a war which Moscow promised would be over before it started.

Brent Sadler, CNN, Grozny.

Notes

1. As Caldas-Coulthard (1997) puts it: "One of the explanations for the domination of news
in the discourse of the media is that news is **narrative** or story telling and therefore the
most attractive and vivid representation of experience through language…Like any other
narrative text news is centrally concerned with past events which develop to some kind of
conclusion" (Caldas-Coulthard 1997:45).

2. A rather different argument, though one that still involves issues of realism, is suggested
by Scannell (1996) who sees radio and television news as the successors to great historical
novels of the 19th century as exemplified by Scott, Stendhal or Tolstoy. Radio and television
bring to fulfilment a process begun with the daily press in which the two worlds of everyday
life and public events are brought together (Scannell 1996:160–164).

3. As Kuhn makes clear the 'staging' of scenes for the camera/audience and the construction of character as a point of subjective identification are perhaps the two most important
constraints on cinematic codes: "The conventions of classical editing constitute a particular
mode of address to the spectator. In, accepting a certain kind of verisimilitude in the spatial
and temporal organisation of the film narrative the spectator becomes witness to a complete world, a world which seems even to exceed the bounds of the film frame. In looking
at the faces of characters in close-up, and in identifying with characters in the text through
taking on their implied point-of-view, the spectator identifies with the fictional world and
its inhabitants, and so is drawn into the narration itself. Consequently, a resolution of the
narrative in which all the ends are tied up is in certain ways pleasurable for the spectator"
(Kuhn 1985:214–215). It is the absence of character as a point of identification and the pur-
ported avoidance of staging as a way of suggesting a world in its fictional totality that most
marks out television news as quite different from the narratives of mainstream cinema.

4. These abbreviations refer to the titles of the five extracts given in the Appendix, as follows:
ASRA Austrian Ski Resort Avalanche; PCDD Police Crackdown on Drink Drivers; RCF The
Rising Costs of Funerals; SETI The Search for Extra-terrestrial Intelligence; WIC War In
Chechnya.

5. These figures deliberately exclude major transitions within the news items between, for
example, studio intro and report or between report and interview.

6. Sky News, for example, suffered a major crisis of credibility over a news report during the Iraq war which apparently featured a Royal Navy submarine engaged in firing a cruise missile in support of the invasion. The report failed to make clear that the footage was archive material gathered during exercises and did not feature the submarine in action at the time. Sky News held an internal inquiry, the reporter lost his job and subsequently took his own life.

7. Further analysis of this report, including the matching of still images from the visual track with referring expressions in the verbal track, may be found in Edginton and Montgomery (1996:98–104).

Chapter 13

Performing theories of narrative
Theorising narrative performance

Terry Threadgold
Cardiff University

Introduction

In the chapters collected here, a wide range of different kinds of social activity have been analysed under the rubric of 'narrative': 'storied worlds' are elicited to understand how identities and generational knowledge are constructed as ways of managing traumatic social change and upheaval; the stories women tell about themselves are explored for what they tell us about the ability to 'tell' serious illness as part of a stable, coherent life story; stories embedded in anti-narrative genres in courtrooms are explored for what they contribute to cross-examination, evidence and legal process; children's collaborative conversational stories are studied as both enactments of childhood culture and 'pretend' strategies for the learning of social story/discourse conventions; or for what they tell us about gendered forms of storying behaviour; stories are explored for their tellability, their well-formedness and as recognisable performances of cultural identity; and finally television news is argued to be 'non-narrative'. Across the range of this work, storying seems sometimes to be embedded within other forms of discourse or discursive practice such as interviews, cross-examination, counselling, play, television news. Sometimes stories seem to stand alone. Many different theoretical paradigms are referenced in the process: the work of Fishman, Bruner, Todorov, Ricoeur, Haydn White, Hernstein Smith, Chatman, Goffman, Bauman, Labov and Waletzky, to name just a few.

Why do we analyse all this storying activity? Arising from this primary question are the following related issues: is narrative itself a theory of the world and of our place in it? Is there some (or several) theoretical basis (-es) for our interest in the practice of storying as 'narrative'? On what grounds do we include all these heterogeneous phenomena under the rubric 'narrative'? Is there in fact any real commonality between the various kinds of 'performance' that are described here? And if narrative is not a genre (because it is embedded in so many other kinds of genre (Swales 1990)) are there nevertheless different genres of narrative? These are some of the questions I want to address in this concluding chapter.

What is the relationship between theory, method and narrative? In this collection they are certainly not always related in the same way. Sometimes narrative is 'elicited', that is, used as a method to produce, and then also as a theory to investigate, a particular area of social reality or social practice. This, as in the case of interviews during the course of which narratives emerge, involves the researcher in the co-production of the narratives, which are then the object of narrative analysis. In other cases, narrative is used as a theory to explain what goes on in an existing institutional, workplace or everyday setting. Here the researcher observes practices which involve the individual or collaborative telling (sometimes seen as the performing and usually as the constructing) of stories in order to understand how these practices function to construct selves and realities and to manage 'crises' in the daily living of those selves and realities. In each of these cases there is a constructionist and functionalist theory at work, which assumes that stories, as everyday linguistic performances, are both contextualised and framed by the contexts in which they occur and in turn contribute to the construction of those wider institutional and social contexts. The stories in this collection are also in many cases theorised and analysed as contextually situated practices, practical actions which are the "ongoing accomplishments of organised artful practices of everyday life" (Garfinkel 1967: 42). There are both socio-linguistic and ethnomethodological approaches and theories in evidence here. There is also a good deal of influence from the literatures on the narrative construction of identity and memory (Harre 1998). Clearly the work of Labov and Waletzky plays an important role in terms of the structural identification of narratives (what are the parts it must have to be well-formed) while structuralist narratology, of which more below, is less in evidence. In all cases however, the narratives that have been explored here are oral, embodied performances which are then transcribed for analysis. Narrative structures are recognised and then interpreted as having particular kinds of social function in very specific contexts or locations. Narrative here seems to be identified as the denotative level of analysis while the interpretations of social function are connotative readings: a metalanguage in each case whose "plane of content is itself constituted by a signifying system" (Barthes 1964/73: 90), in this case 'narrative'. It is important I think to explore what Barthes has to say about connotation. He argues that the signified of connotation is:

> ... at once general, global and diffuse; it is, if you like, a fragment of ideology: the sum of the messages in French refers, for instance, to the signified 'French'; a book can refer to the signified 'Literature'. These signifieds have a very close communication with culture, knowledge and history, and it is through them, so to speak, that the environmental world invades the system.
>
> (Barthes 1964/73: 91–92)

Thus the process of narrative analysis and interpretation involved in this collection would be one which, at a theoretical level, sought to understand, empirically, how it is that the objective world becomes a part of subjective, lived reality in much the same way as Bourdieu attempts to understand that relationship in the theory of the habitus:

> The habitus is a spontaneity without consciousness or will. ... the habitus, which is constituted in the course of an individual history, imposing its particular logic on incorporation, and through which agents partake of the history objectified in institutions, is what makes it possible to inhabit institutions, to appropriate them practically, and so to keep them in activity, continuously pulling them from the state of dead letters, reviving the sense deposited in them, but at the same time imposing the revisions and reactivations that reactivation entails. (Bourdieu 1990: 56, 57)

Narrative, telling stories, seems to be an important part of the way in which the habitus is negotiated and thus of the way in which the social is embodied, enacted and remade. I want to suggest here that this is one way of theorising and understanding the work that is being done in the papers in this collection.

Narrative politics

The whole notion of habitus, and of ideology, of the ways in which institutions and practices become corporeal for example, introduces other questions about the significance of narrative. Narrative has not always been researched as a primarily oral, everyday activity. The whole long tradition of structuralist narratology began with oral tales and myths and ended focussing much more on written literary narratives. Narrative was seen as fiction, not fact; primitive or play, not cultured and rational, and certainly not scientific. Deconstructing these kinds of binary oppositions has been an essential part of the work done in cultural studies and in various kinds of poststructuralist theory and

to describe the 'performance' of everyday life as well as the enactment of ritual, ceremony and so on (Goffman 1959; Schechner 1985; Turner 1987). *Performativity* in Butler's work derives from the work of J. L. Austin (1976) and is a philosophical/linguistic concept. However Butler's use of the term is mediated by Austin's encounter with Derrida (1982) and her own with Althusser, Foucualt and Bourdieu. Derrida insisted *not* that the speech act would be 'infelicitous' if the context did not remain the same (as Austin had argued), but rather that "the locution would go on meaning in radical disregard of the proper or appropriate context" (Derrida 1982: 320). The fact that the mark/locution can be cited (and made to signify) in any context at all, its *iterability*, is, according to Derrida, precisely what ensures instability and the possibility of change. These concepts of *citation* and *iterability* are central to Judith Butler's understanding of the way change in meaning, resignification, which cannot in her work be separated from radical changes in the performance of the body, takes place.

She has argued that it is the speech act as performative which both *materializes* (*has material effects on*) and *makes bodies matter* (Butler 1993). Her work has challenged the hegemony (the compulsory performance of heterosexuality) which banishes certain ('lacking'/deficient – e.g. women's, racialised, gay and lesbian) bodies to an abject and excluded realm, the realm of matter or nature. Butler is working here with Irigarayan ideas, specifically the notion that radical alterity (woman) has always been associated with the 'outside of language', the inarticulable, nature/matter – or, to put it another way, with stories that can neither be told nor performed in the context of other hegemonic narratives.

Butler's work 'makes visible' the hegemonic and heterosexual 'gender hierarchy' and its performative mode of production: the speech act produces the things of which it speaks, it has effects on bodies. She links speech act to body through her understandings of Althusser's concept of the materiality of ideology (it is practice, regular and regulated modes of embodiment, not words, which make us believe), Foucault's work on the discursive disciplining of the body, and Bourdieu's theory of habitus. Thus she will argue that: "Gender is the repeated stylization of the body, a set of repeated acts within a highly rigid regulatory frame that congeals over time to produce the appearance of substance of a natural sort of being" (Butler 1990: 33).

Resignification of these performative regularities, for Butler, involves first, recognising the power of the speech act as citation (the fact that it is repeated in the same conventional forms) to produce stable hegemonies (e.g. heterosexuality as norm) and then understanding that the very fact that citation also involves *iteration* (possible interaction with new contexts) produces the possibility of change.

Butler's work has been criticised for being elitist, theoretical, and insufficiently based in empirical evidence (Sedgewick 1995; Kirby 1997). She does not, for example, ever really explore the way in which oppression may actually craft and shape the materiality of the body, something which performance in its literal theatrical forms would enable us to do (Threadgold 1997). To perform in theatrical, rehearsal or acting contexts is always, in attempting to articulate the other's words, to live and embody an*other* narrative, to struggle with the substance, the matter of the body. Her work is nonetheless important because of the ways in which it changed the theoretical narratives then current in feminist theory, in cultural studies and in a whole range of disciplines. In doing so it pointed us again in the direction of the reasons for studying narrative in its empirical mode as both performative speech act (a speech act which has corporeal and material effects) and as a performance which is always originally oral and everyday and inherently 'dialogical' (McLean 1998). Performativity, in Austin's original formulation, mattered for the reasons Derrida saw so clearly. It alerted us to the real, material effects of language, and therefore of narrative, and explains the extraordinary power stories have to change worlds and lived realities (Wilentz 2000; Bromley 2000; Ochs & Capps 2001; Farrell, Kamler, & Threadgold 2000). As Kamler et al. (1994) have also pointed out, it matters how narratives are performed and embodied. They do affect the ways bodies are lived and imagined, how selves and identities are crafted in everyday interactions, and how those interactions construct and craft in turn the hegemonies and the regularities of the social. This is why the work we do with and on narrative in sociolinguistics and in other contexts *matters*, because it is in the end investigating how it is that bodies of knowledge are narratively constructed, and how they come to make only certain bodies *matter*. This work provides much of the empirical evidence, if we but saw it this way, to argue Butler's case much more convincingly than she herself was able to in theory alone.

Rewriting: Theory as narrative and intertextuality

The consequences of the kinds of work and theory that I have been discussing here did not just result in rewriting stories or embodied practices, it also worked at rewriting the theories themselves, especially linguistic theory, because these too came to be seen as 'narratives' which told only part of the story. Perhaps the most important consequence of this work for this chapter was the recognition that most textual or discursive activity involved narrative (so that, on narrative grounds at least, there was no easy distinction to be made between literature and science, or science and myth, or theory and practice for example); that intertextuality played an important role in the construction of all texts and that narrative was one of the important resources for intertextual activity.

All of this work, like the work in ethnomethodology and sociolinguistics, owes something to the academic study of narrative (narratology), which derives from the much earlier traditions of formalism (Propp 1968) and structuralism (Levi-Strauss 1963; Barthes 1979; Genette 1980; Greimas 1966, 1970; Todorov 1969). Propp's work on the Russian fairy-tale involved a typical kind of narrative grammar or poetics. He was able to show that the abstract system which made possible the generation of a wide variety of stories was in fact very simple, consisting of a small number of roles (character types) and functions (actions or events significant to the plot) and ways of combining these. Levi-Strauss (1963) in his structural study of myth took this much further, focussing not just on the poetics, or grammar, that made myths possible but also beginning to understand their functions as ways of story-telling which resolved social contradictions, becoming, as Barthes (1957) later understood even more explicitly, 'common-sense' (myth) or naturalised ways of constructing and understanding the world. He anticipated Lyotard by quite a long way in arguing that "the same logical processes operate in myth as in science" (229–231) and in recognising that that logic is narrative.

These distinctions between apparently timeless (creative, oral) narratives of the mythical or fictional kind, and the legitimating, time-and-history-bound (factual, written) grand narratives of e.g. history and science (see also Levi-Strauss 1963; Barthes 1957, 1973) became the focus of Lyotard's work on the condition of knowledge in postmodernism: "Science has always been in conflict with narratives" (1984:xxiii). "... I will use the term *modern* to designate any science that legitimates itself with reference to a metadiscourse of this kind making an explicit appeal to some grand narrative, such as ... the emancipation of the rational or working subject ..." (1984:xxiii). The 'grand narrative' here is recognised only by reading against the grain, by refusing the rules of the genre or discourse of science, and looking for 'fables' where there is supposed to be only logic and science. But even once we have set aside the grand narratives which structure scientific endeavour, Lyotard will argue that "the little narrative [*petit recit*] remains the quintessential form of imaginative invention, most particularly in science" (1984:60). Lyotard's work recognised the centrality of narrative to all human activity and communication. It also identified the constructive aspect of narrative, the fact that narrative is a way of constructing, not just representing, realities and selves (Fulford 2000; Kirkman, Maher, & Souter 2002).

All of this work contributed to and supported the development of theories of intertextuality. The theories of intertextuality which were dominant came from the work of Bakhtin, Barthes and Kristeva and constituted a serious critique of ideas of authorship and originality in literary contexts. Texts were now conceived as being constructed not word by word (as in the work of de Saussure), but chunk by chunk (rather more like the way Propp and Levi-Strauss imagined the construction of fairly-tales and myths respectively). They were, as Barthes put it in one of his accounts, 'tissues of quotations from the corners of the culture'. When critical discourse analysts turned to trying to define the resources that made this approach to the construction of texts possible, genre, narrative and discourse loomed large as possible categories (Kress & Threadgold 1988; Fairclough 1995). The process by which chunks were mapped into texts in the making of them, and recognised in the reading of them, was very similar to the processes of denotation/ connotation described above. Readers would map from the material traces in one text to whole text structures (genres or narratives) or discourses familiar from other textual encounters, or they would draw on chunks of such structures and meanings as the paradigmatic resources for making new texts with. Again the relations between the denoted and connoted systems were 'general, global and diffuse': the units of the two systems do not necessarily have the same size. "Large fragments of the denoted discourse can constitute a single unit of the connoted system, e.g. all of the elements in a text which might connote its 'tone'" (Barthes 1964/73:91). And in the same way, small units of the denoted text – a phrase or a couple of sentences – can connote a whole genre or narrative or discourse. The theoretical significance of intertextuality was huge because it explained the heteroglossia and dialogism of textual structure (Bakhtin 1981), the polysemy and complexity which could never be contained by genre or authorial intention (Threadgold 1997), and indeed how it was that narrative versions of events could circulate as common sense or myth without analysis or question. It also gave a central role to narrative in the construction of all text and explains why narrative is likely to be found across a range of otherwise diverse and heterogeneous kinds of social practices.

In such poststructuralist contexts, structuralist narratology was largely lost in favour of the more subjective and interpretative strategies involved in recognising 'global and diffuse' intertextual relations, some of them narrative in kind, and all of them demonstrating the dialogic nature of all texts, and the ways in which myth/ideology/common sense (depending on your theoretical perspective) circulated and were, to use a Derridean/Butler formulation, citationally and iteratively reproduced and changed. Story logic is in fact an "unreplaceable resource for structuring and comprehending experience, a distinctive way of coming to terms with time, process, change" (Herman 2002: 23) but it operates within and across texts, as well as in the formation and production of apparently well-formed, tellable narratives which seem to stand alone.

There are real questions to be asked, it seems to me, and work to be done, on understanding the differences between what intertextuality recognises as narratives or parts of narratives embedded within other genres (mostly written) and what sociolinguistic work identifies as, for example, a narrative constructed in and through the interactive process of another genre such as conversation, legal cross-examination or patient counselling. Are these the same thing or are they not? And what would be the implications of theorising the second in relation to the first or vice versa? This it seems to me is where we must return to questions that concern all the contributors to this book. Should we be recognising different genres of narrative, and what would the consequences of that be in theoretical terms? In the last section of this chapter I will begin to outline an answer to these questions.

Micro-analysis and genre

There is an extensive literature on the structure and function of narrative in a wide range of contexts from the oral mythologies of so-called primitive cultures to the literary narratives of Western democracies with, as we have seen above, a good deal of theoretical deconstruction of those differences. This deconstruction is one of the reasons why it is now difficult to maintain the binary distinctions between, for example, recount/construction, fact/fiction, and narrative/non-narrative among others. Narrative has become in poststructuralist contexts a ubiquitous term to cover what is seen to be a ubiquitous social practice but one that is rarely subjected to formal micro-analysis.

On the other hand, the critical vocabulary of narratology which deals with micro-analysis has been co-opted for the analysis of all kinds of spoken and written narratives, visual, film and media texts (Metz 1982; Heath 1981; Hartley 1982; Silverstone 1985) as well as for the sociolinguistic and ethnomethodological analyses included here and discussed above. It is worth commenting that the work in the latter fields pays on the whole less attention (except implicitly) to the questions of readership which emerged from narrative theory than is the case in work on media and film for example. The focus is much more on interactivity, and indeed in much of the work on collaborative conversational and interview construction of narratives, the distinction between reader and narrator is largely erased as it was in a very different political context in Barthes' (1975) work on authorship and readership.

Narratology is a complex field of study and that part of it which has been adopted into sociolinguistics comes largely by way of Labov and Waletzky (1967). It is worth rehearsing briefly some of the major elements which the theory identifies as central to the structure and function of narratives. In later forms of narrative analysis (e.g. Barthes 1979), usually applied to written, literary narratives, distinctions are made between what is being told – the actual chronological sequence of the events being narrated – called *histoire* – and the plot structure constructed by the teller – the order (temporality) of events as told – which is called *discours* (the Russian formalists identified the same distinction in their use of the terms *fabula* and *sjuzhet*). The act of story telling itself is distinguished from that which is told. In relation to what I have argued above, it is almost certainly the first of these – the act of story-telling – 'Listen, I will now tell you a story' – which constitutes narrative as a speech act. The principle parts of a narrative (as that which is told) are identified as *setting* (or orientation), *complication* (something that sets off the narrative train of events), *climax* (events come to a head, e.g. the hero and villain join in direct combat), *denouement* (resolution, e.g. the hero wins), and *coda* (or closing act, bringing the narrative to an end, *and they all lived happily ever after*) (Toolan 1988). *Focalisation* (the spatio-temporal perspective or orientation from which the story is told or seen) is important in some theories. *Character* was already important in Propp's early analysis (see above) but was less important in Labov and Waletzky's work (1967) and seems not to figure largely (except perhaps as 'identity') in the chapters of this book.

In most literary accounts of narrative structure, narratives embedded within narratives are recognised, since characters are very important in such narratives and they tend to tell one another stories within the main narrative frame (Mclean 1988). Thus although the reader/viewer is sometimes called the *narratee*, there may also be a *narratee* within the narrative (e.g. Miranda listening to her father's story at the beginning of *The Tempest*). It is often difficult to distinguish such a narratee from the *implied reader*, who, as Eco (1994) has argued, is implicit in every text: "Every text, after all (as I have already written), is a lazy machine asking the reader to do some of its work" (1994:3) ... "In a narrative text, the reader is forced to make choices all the time" (1994:6). The implied reader is a model reader, a "sort of ideal type whom the text not only foresees as a collaborator but also tries to create" (1994:9). The empirical, actual reader, is different and does not necessarily follow the text's or the narrative's instructions. An early example of the role of the reader at work in dialogue with a text, making (intertextual) sense of it in relation to all the other texts with which they are familiar, is offered by Barthes in his more poststructuralist account of reading in *S/Z* (1975), a study of Balzac's short story *Sarrasine*. Many of these understandings of the way narrative works at a micro-level, even if derived from studies of literary narratives, might be useful to those working on narrative as everyday social practice, but like the theories of readership mentioned above are not often referenced in sociolinguistic work.

Micro-analysis and theory

It is somewhere among these divergent positions that the micro levels of analysis and the macro or meta-level of narrative as social theory need to come together. Montgomery's work on the intelligibility of television news argues that this is a genre which is not narrative, or at least not only narrative. Part of his argument is about the relationship between the micro-levels of narrative analysis (the data) and the available theories of narrative. Thus he suggests that sociolinguistic work tends to focus too much on events and not enough on character and that if character were taken into account, actions or events would be seen to be coherent because protagonists have goal-based agendas. He questions whether this is always the case in television news and suggests that in this context intelligibility is sometimes provided by an alternative to narrative, the interaction between words and images. This, he suggests, is achieved through deixis and cueing sentences, which result in viewers inferring that the image is a representation of what the words say, and that there is overlapping or reciprocal reference between the visual and verbal tracks. The emphasis is on the factuality, the 'now-ness' (the eyewitness report), on showing, rather than telling, although reporters, in talking to one another, may act as if 'they were doing narrative'. This focus on micro-analysis is important but it does beg a number of questions. What do audiences actually do with this material? Is it not possible to construct multi-modal narratives involving both verbal and visual tracks? And in relation to genre, can we not have narrative eyewitness or factual reports? As Herman points out, Genette realised that "whereas the link between narration and perspective-taking may be organic and indissoluble, it is also complex, with seeing and speaking standing in a heteromorphic rather than an isomorphic relation to one another" (2002:301).

From my own recent research on the representation of asylum seekers and refugees in television news I recognise the validity of the effects Montgomery describes, but I would interpret these differently. It seems to me that the deixis and cueing which identify the visual and verbal tracks for a viewer could equally well be seen as *focalisation* processes. It is by seeing the visual track that viewers know how to frame the verbal track. It provides the perspective or orientation from which the 'story' seems to be being told and at the same time it tells a story which may sometimes clash with or override the factuality and now-ness of the verbal track. When this happens, the visual story may be the only story readers take away with them.

Thus the fact that a single image of large numbers of unidentified men, seen through a wire fence, running towards a tunnel entrance, accompanies a large percentage of the news stories about asylum analysed in a three month period in 2002–2003, seems to contribute in a significant way to the fact that viewers (in focus groups) believe that the story of asylum is about 'hordes' of men 'invading' Britain (Buchanan, Grillo-Simpson, & Threadgold 2003; MORI Poll 2003). The men in the image become the protagonists whose goal-based agendas have coherence for viewers. What is more, it is the cumulative 'everydayness' of this image and the narrative it always connotes, whatever else the news actually shows, tells or reports, and its iconicity (this is an image of how it is: we can see it) which converts this 'story' into myth, into common-sense understandings of asylum. So yes, there are very specific ways in which narrative is constructed in television news and they are generically different to, for instance, the collaborative conversational tellings of children's gendered play. Both have socio-cultural implications in the sense that they are both individual instances of social practice and practices which help to construct the social and the cultural. But neither is either kind of practice politically neutral. This is why a focus on the micro levels of data and analysis needs always to be framed and contextualised by the bigger picture of the logic of narrative as creative and constructive of social worlds and selves. Silverstone (1985) has been particularly acute in showing how relevant the structuralist analysis of narrative remains to the analysis of storying in a mass-mediated society but also how necessary the continued understanding of the link between narrative and myth – and the deconstruction of the apparent 'naturalness' of both – actually is as a way of framing that micro level of analysis.

Genre and narrative

The above example also illustrates at a number of levels the sheer difficulty of defining the differences between narrative and genre, and of dealing with the micro-levels of analysis in both cases. Perhaps it is that television news is the genre and that narratives of various kinds (images, reporters' talk, interviewee's stories) are embedded within it, while others are intertextually connoted. In genre theory, it has been recognised for some time that genres have obligatory and optional elements (Swales 1990). Is this also the case with narratives? It was almost the case with the accounts given by Propp and Levi-Strauss of fairy-tales and myth respectively, but narratology tends to present alternative accounts of narrative rather than a case for optional and obligatory elements of the same narrative phenomenon (Toolan 1988). And we know that narrative has been seen, among other things, as 'not a genre' because it seems to be an element of every genre (Swales 1990) and also as "a discourse genre and cognitive style that relies fundamentally on perspective taking" (Herman 2001:301). Should we also be asking which genres rely on narrative to function effectively?

In what follows I will briefly relate these questions and the issues raised in this chapter to some aspects of the way narrative has functioned in my own experience in the course of a series of related research projects on asylum and refugee issues in the UK. In the initial project, which involved setting up a media working group to monitor the Welsh media's representation of these issues, with a very specific agenda to change the way asylum stories were being written in the press, the rewriting of stories was part of a politics which mixed advocacy with research and knowledge production. It did involve micro-analysis and interventions designed to change both the genre (from sensational news report to human interest story or documentary or feature for example), the narrative (from a story of invading hordes using up scarce resources to a story of well integrated and educated people contributing to society) and the elements of story-telling (the perspective from which the story was told, the sources used, the attributes of characters, the goals of characters). The interventions were accomplished through interaction: meeting journalists, becoming an important resource for them in relation to the asylum issue, managing the media (Speers 2001; Buchanan, Grillo-Simpson, & Threadgold 2003). Clearly we were dealing with genres of news but using narrative to attempt to change these, and thus assuming that all news genres involve narrative. But narrative was also used here as theory, as practice, as politics and as strategy (Threadgold 2004).

The second project, funded by the Department for International Development (DFID), involved work in school classrooms in Swansea and Newport (Jewell 2004). It started as a creative writing/media literacy project. Attitudes to asylum needed to be changed. This required education and information which we would provide, and we would take asylum seekers into classrooms to help to change attitudes. Again, interaction, and interactions with difference, were key to the role of narrative in this project. We collaborated with three black African men, two of whom were refugees who had had their asylum claims recognised and been given leave to remain, and one of whom was still an asylum seeker. They came with us into classrooms where we first established what students knew of asylum and then used media texts to deconstruct current dominant representations and substitute alternative factual narratives. The children with whom we were working were aged from 12–14 and their initial attitudes and beliefs about asylum could have come directly from the pages of the tabloid press, and yet they had no difficulty deconstructing newspaper and television news about asylum. They knew how to 'do' their media literacy but significantly, it had not changed their beliefs. Offering alternative facts and figures and some stories might have made some impact but what really changed things were the embodied interactions in classrooms between white children from the South Wales Valleys, white academics, and black men from Sierra Leone, Malawi and Cameroon who could tell their stories of asylum seeking in the first person, as embodied realities. Bodies, and black bodies in particular, *mattered* in these classrooms. The children were encouraged to imagine, reposition themselves, as asylum seekers, to write stories and poems about what this would be like. Here, clearly we were using narrative as theory, as resource, and as a tool for the rewriting of belief and the repositioning of bodies.

The results of this work were clearest in the context of performance. One class decided to perform two plays about asylum seekers. In this case, the rewriting of selves and the storying was done within a performance framework. The genre was performance, a collaborative activity in the course of which many stories are embedded and characters move towards the resolution of the narrative problem which caused the plays to be written in the first place. The problem of asylum seeking had been introduced into the classroom by our research activity and our narrative politics. The plays were based in terms of 'story' on materials we had circulated in class and on one asylum seeker's 'live' narratives of what it had been like to be an asylum seeker and to have to use the Home Office voucher system for daily survival. The plays were structured around two binaries – the asylum seekers and the others – and within the 'others', those who were for and those who were against asylum. Both plays also delivered a moral message to their target audience. We should treat asylum seekers well because they are here through no fault of their own and deserve our sympathy. Both plays involved conversion stories where those who had been 'against' learned to understand why they should be 'for'.

I have argued elsewhere that rehearsal and performance enable us to see in microcosm some of what goes on in everyday life (but much more slowly and less visibly) in the processes involved in social change, and I have argued that performance actually enables us to see the struggles with the body which are involved in the taking on of new stories and positions (Threadgold 1997). In the case of these two performances what was fascinating in both rehearsal and performance was the "repeated stylization of the body ... which congeals over time ... to produce the appearance of a natural sort of being" (Butler 1990:33). These really very young children were already totally comfortable with the performance of the tabloid narrative of asylum and its dominant anti-asylum perspective. Those performing this role in the plays required relatively little rehearsal or coaching. And yet its very citation in this new context (iteration) must have begun to frame the performances and their meanings differently. Those performing the pro-asylum and 'converted to pro-asylum' roles required a great deal. They forgot their lines, they got their proxemics wrong, they forgot how to look and walk and stand on the stage in relation to the 'others' with whom they now had to identify. Those playing asylum seekers had equal difficulties in learning to perform bodies and words that 'do not matter'. It was on these roles that the bulk of rehearsal time was spent thus demonstrating the embodied nature of narrative roles (characters) and trajectories and the performative difficulties of changing them. But, if any changes in attitude were accomplished, it was through these struggles with the body and through embodied interactions as well as through telling stories differently. Telling stories differently in this case involved learning to live the self differently, the beginnings of changes to the habitus and very complex kinds of new embodied understandings. Arguably, it is only through such very local and specific shifts in understanding that larger social structures ever alter. This is why these very local exercises matter and why they inevitably work to increase our understanding of the relationship between micro and macro levels of social structure.

But there is a narrativity of a very different kind involved in measuring social attitudes. In the last two years in the UK context, it has been increasingly argued that the issue of immigration and asylum is among those of most concern to the general populace, and this claim is backed up by the statistical analysis of the results of large scale public opinion surveys, the last of these in November 2003 was commissioned by Migration Watch, a purportedly independent think tank (http://www.mori.com/polls/2003/immigration.shtml). These surveys appear to show that there is widespread support for tougher measures on both asylum and immigration and that, for example, 71% of people believe that asylum seekers who have arrived here from a safe country (one to which they could return without risk) in Europe should be sent back. Now the genre we are involved in here is 'public opinion survey' and yet, when we explore the questions being posed to participants we discover that they contain an embedded narrative. It is impossible to answer these questions without being 'interpellated' by them into a narrative that seems to derive itself from the tabloid reporting of asylum. One is positioned to answer questions about levels of government control of asylum, about the numbers of immigrants in the UK, about the numbers of asylum seekers who come to the UK each year, about whether they come because Britain is a 'soft touch', about whether immigration should be stopped. The narrative of large numbers of people coming to make demands on scarce resources and of the government losing control of the situation, a narrative which all major studies of media representation of asylum over the past five years show to be constant, in fact also informs these survey questions. To respond to the survey is to be implicated in the citation of that narrative. A different set of questions might produce evidence of a rather different set of public opinions. It matters therefore to be on the lookout for embedded or intertextually connoted narratives in analysing genres of social activity and to question the way in which they may be being used to support myths and hegemonic modes of interaction (the rejection of asylum seekers). In this case, these surveys are performative speech acts which function to accomplish what they articulate – to quite literally 'make' immigration the most important issue facing Britain.

To return to the questions I raised at the beginning of this last section then, I think we have to acknowledge that there are no easy answers, no easy ways of categorising or defining the many ways in which narrative operates. The chapters in this book tell a similar story. In almost every place we look it will be a slightly different thing. Perhaps this is what Derrida really meant by the differences between citation (repetition) and iteration (the constant possibility of difference and change). But what we do know, if we put together the kinds of detailed work that is done in the chapters of this book with the dense and difficult theories that have tried to understand the force of narrative as itself a way of theorising and embodying the social, is that narrative *matters*, and that the *matter* of narrative must continue to be the focus of research and theory if

Bauman, R. (1996). Transformations of the word in the production of Mexican festival drama. In M. Silverstein & G. Urban (Eds.), *Social interaction, social context and language: Essays in honor of Susan Ervin-Tripp* (pp. 301–27). Mahwah, NJ: Lawrence Erlbaum.

Bauman, R. & Briggs, C. (1990). Poetics and performance as critical perspectives on language and social life. *Annual Review of Anthropology, 19,* 59–88.

Bell, A. (1994). Telling stories. In D. Graddol & O. Boyd-Barrett (Eds.), *Media texts: Authors and readers* (pp. 119–136). Clevedon: Open University/Multilingual Matters.

Bennett, C. (1999). 'A sick business'. *The Guardian,* 18th November 1999.

Bennett, W. L. & Feldman, M. S. (1981). *Reconstructing reality in the courtroom.* New Brusnwick, NJ: Rutgers University Press.

Berger, P. & Luckman, T. (1966). *The social construction of reality.* Garden City, NY: Doubleday.

Berman, R. & Slobin, D. (Eds.). (1994). *Relating events in narrative: A crosslinguistic developmental study.* Hillsdale, NJ: Lawrence Erlbaum.

Biber, D., Johansson, S., Leech, G., Conrad, S., & Finegan, E. (1999). *Longman grammar of spoken and written English.* Harlow: Pearson Education.

Billig, M., Condor, S., Edwards, D., Gane, M., Middleton, D., & Radley, A. (1988). *Ideological dilemmas: A social psychology of everyday thinking.* London: Sage.

Blum-Kulka, S. (1993). 'You gotta know how to tell a story': Telling, tales, and tellers in American and Israeli narrative events at dinner. *Language in Society, 22,* 361–402.

Blum-Kulka, S. (1997). *Dinner talk: Cultural patterns of sociability and socialization in family discourse.* Mahwah, NJ: Lawrence Erlbaum.

Blum-Kulka, S. (2005a). Rethinking genre: Discourse genres as a social interactional phenomenon. In K. Fitch & R. Sanders (Eds.), *Handbook of language and social interaction* (pp. 275–301). Mahwah, NJ: Lawrence Erlbaum.

Blum-Kulka, S. (2005b). 'I will tell you the whole true story now': Sequencing the past, present and future in children's conversational narratives. In D. Ravid & H. Bat-Zeev Shyldkrot (Eds.), *Perspectives on language and language development: Essays in honor of Ruth Berman* (pp. 275–288). Dodrecht: Kluwer.

Blum-Kulka, S., Huck-Taglicht, D., & Avni, H. (2004). The social and discursive spectrum of peer talk. *Discourse Studies,* 6(3), 307–329.

Blum-Kulka, S. & Snow, C. (1992). Developing autonomy for tellers, tales and telling in family narrative-events. *Journal of Narrative and Life History, 2,* 187–217.

Boggs, S. (1985). *Speaking, relating, and learning: A study of Hawaiian children at home and at school.* Norwood, NJ: Ablex.

Bordwell, D. (1985). *Narration in the fiction film.* London: Methuen.

Bordwell, D. & Thompson, K. (1979). *Film art: An introduction.* Reading, MA: Addison-Wesley.

Borneman, J. (1992). *Belonging in the two Berlins. Kin, state, nation.* Cambridge: Cambridge University Press.

Bourdieu, P. (1990). *The logic of practice.* Cambridge: Polity Press.

Bourdieu, P. (1992). *Language and symbolic power.* Cambridge: Polity Press.

Briggs, C. (Ed.). (1996). *Disorderly discourse: Narrative, conflict and inequality.* Oxford: Oxford University Press

Brockmeier, J. & Carbaugh, D. (Eds.). (2001). *Narrative and identity: Studies in autobiography, self and culture.* Amsterdam: John Benjamins.

Bromley, R. (2000). *Narratives for a new belonging: Diasporic cultural fictions.* Edinburgh: Edinburgh University Press.

Brooks, P. & Gewirtz, P. (1996). *Law's stories: Narrative and rhetoric in the law.* New Haven: Yale University Press.

Bruner, J. (1986). *Actual minds, possible worlds.* Cambridge, MA: Harvard University Press.

Bruner, J. (1987). Life as narrative. *Social Research, 54*(1), 11–32.

Bruner, J. (1990). *Acts of meaning.* Cambridge, MA: Harvard University Press.

Bruner, J. (1991). The narrative construction of reality. *Critical Inquiry, 18,* 1–21.

Bruner, J. (2001). Self-making and world-making. In J. Brockmeier & D. Carbaugh (Eds.), *Narrative and identity: Studies in autobiography, self and culture* (pp. 25–28). Amsterdam: John Benjamins.

Buchanan, S., Grillo-Simpson, B., & Threadgold, T. (2003). *What's the story? Results from research into media coverage of refugees and asylum seekers in the UK.* London: Article 19.

Butler, J. (1990). *Gender trouble: Feminism and the subversion of identity.* London: Routledge.

Butler, J. (1993). *Bodies that matter: On the discursive limits of "Sex".* London: Routledge.

Caldas-Coulthard, C. (1997). *News as social practice: A study in critical discourse analysis.* Florianopolis: Universidade de Santa Caterina, Advanced Research in English Series.

Cameron, D. (1997). Performing gender identity: Young men's talk and the construction of heterosexual masculinity. In S. Johnson & U. H. Meinhof (Eds.), *Language and masculinity* (pp. 47–64). Oxford: Blackwell.

Cameron, D. (1998). Introduction: Why is language a feminist issue? In *The feminist critique of language: A reader* (pp. 1–21). New York: Routledge.

Chafe, W. (1980). The deployment of consciousness in the production of narrative. In W. Chafe (Ed.), *The pear stories: Cognitive, cultural and linguistic aspects of narrative production* (pp. 9–50). Norwood, NJ: Ablex.

Chafe, W. (1982). Integration and involvement in speaking, writing and oral literature. In D. Tannen (Ed.), *Spoken and written language: Exploring orality and literacy* (pp. 35–53). Norwood, NJ: Ablex.

Chafe, W. (1994). *Discourse, consciousness and time: The flow and displacement of conscious experience in speaking and writing.* Chicago: University of Chicago Press.

Chafe, W. (1997). Polyphonic topic development. In T. Givón (Ed.), *Conversation: Cognitive, communicative and social perspectives* (pp. 41–54). Amsterdam: John Benjamins.

Chafe, W. (1998). Things we can learn from repeated tellings of the same experience. *Narrative Inquiry, 8,* 269–285.

Chapple, A. & Ziebland, S. (2002). Prostate cancer: Embodied experience and perceptions of masculinity. *Sociology of Health and Illness, 24,* 820–841.

Chapple, A., Ziebland, S., Shepperd, S., Miller, R., Herxheimer, A., & McPherson, A. (2002). Patients' views of prostate specific antigen testing (PSA): A qualitative study. *British Medical Journal, 325,* 737–739.

Cheshire, J. (2000). The telling or the tale? Narratives and gender in adolescent friendship networks. *Journal of Sociolinguistics, 4*(2), 234–262.

Georgakopoulou, A. & Goutsos, D. (2000b). Mapping the world of discourse: The narrative vs non-narrative distinction. *Semiotica, 13*(1, 2) 113–141.

Gerhardt, S. (2004). *Why love matters: How affection shapes a baby's brain.* London: Brunner-Routledge.

Giles, H. & Coupland, N. (1991). *Language: Contexts and consequences.* Milton Keynes: Open University Press.

Goffman, E. (1959). *The presentation of self in everyday life.* Garden City, NY: Anchor Books.

Goffman, E. (1961). *Encounters: Two studies in the sociology of interaction.* Indianapolis, IN: Bobbs Merrill.

Goffman, E. (1963). *Behavior in public places: Notes on the social organization of gatherings.* New York: The Free Press.

Goffman, E. (1974). *Frame analysis.* London: Penguin Books.

Goffman, E. (1981). *Forms of talk.* Oxford: Blackwell.

Golding P. & Elliott, P. (1979). *Making the news.* London: Longman.

Goodwin, C. (1986). Audience diversity, participation and interpretation. *Text, 6,* 283–316.

Goodwin, M. H. (1990). *He-said-she-said: Talk as social organization among black children.* Indianapolis, IN: Indiana University Press.

Graddol, D. & Boyd-Barrett, O. (Eds.). (1994). *Media texts: Authors and readers.* Clevedon: Open University/Multilingual Matters.

Graddol, D. (1994). The visual accomplishment of factuality. In D. Graddol & O. Boyd-Barrett (Eds.), *Media texts: Authors and readers* (pp. 136–160). Clevedon: Open University/Multilingual Matters.

Greimas, A. J. (1966). *Semantique structurale.* Paris: Larousse.

Greimas, A. J. (1970). *Du sens.* Paris: Seuil.

Hall, K., Bucholtz, M., & Birch, M. (Eds.). (1992). *Locating power. Proceedings of the second Berkeley women and language conference.* Berkeley, CA: Berkeley Women and Language Group, University of California.

Halliday, M. A. K. & Hasan, R. (1989). *Language, context and text: Aspects of language in a social-semiotic perspective.* Oxford: Oxford University Press.

Hamilton, H. (1998). Reported speech and survivor identity in on-line bone marrow transplantation narratives. *Journal of Sociolinguistics, 2,* 53–67.

Harré, R. (1998). *The singular self: An introduction to the psychology of personhood.* London: Sage.

Harris, P. (2000). *The work of the imagination.* Malden, MA: Blackwell.

Harris, S. (2001). Fragmented narratives and multiple tellers: Witness and defendant accounts in trials. *Discourse Studies, 3*(1), 53–74.

Hartley, J. (1982). *Understanding news.* London: Routledge.

Hartley, J. (1996). *Popular reality: Journalism, modernity popular culture.* London: Arnold.

Hay, J. (1994). Jocular abuse patterns in mixed-group interaction. *Wellington Working Papers in Linguistics, 6,* 26–55.

Hay, J. (1995). Gender and humour: Beyond a joke. Unpublished Master's thesis, Victoria University of Wellington, Wellington, New Zealand.

Heath, S. (1981). *Questions of cinema.* Bloomington, IN: Indiana Univeristy Press.

Heath, S. Brice (1982). What no bedtime story means: Narrative skills at home and at school. *Language in Society, 11,* 49–76.

Heath, S. Brice (1983). *Ways with words: Language, life and work in communities and classrooms.* Cambridge: Cambridge University Press.

Heath, S. Brice (1986). Taking a cross-cultural look at narratives. *Topics in Language Disorders, 7*(1), 84–94.

Hebdige, D. (1979). *Subculture: The meaning of style.* London: Methuen.

Heffer, C. (2002). 'If you were standing in Marks & Spencers': Narrativisation and comprehension in the English summing-up. In J. Cotterill (Ed.), *Language in the legal process* (pp. 228–245). London: Palgrave.

Henkin, R. (1991). ktanim 'im harbe avar: shimushim yixudiyim shel zman avar bilshon yeladim (Little with lots of past: Special uses of past tense in children's language). *Leshonenu, 55,* 333–362. [in Hebrew]

Herman, D. (2001). Spatial reference in narrative domains. *Text, 21*(4), 515–541.

Herman, D. (2002). *Story logic.* Lincoln, NE: University of Nebraska Press.

Herxheimer, A., McPherson, A., Miller, R., Shepperd, S., Yaphe, J., & Ziebland, S. (2000). Database of patients' experiences (DIPEx): A multi-media approach to sharing experiences and information. *Lancet, 355,* 1540–1543.

Hobbs, P. (2003). 'You must say it for him': Reformulating a witness' testimony on cross examination at trial. *Text, 23*(4), 477–511.

Hollway, W. (1989). *Subjectivity and method in psychology.* London: Sage.

Holmes, J. (1998a). Victoria University's Language in the Workplace Project: Goals, scope and methodology. *Te Reo, 41,* 178–181.

Holmes, J. (1998b). Narrative structure: some contrasts between Maori and Pakeha story-telling. *Multilingua, 17*(1), 25–57.

Holmes, J. (1998c). Why tell stories? Constrasting themes and identities in the narratives of Maori and Pakeha women and men. *Journal of Asian Pacific Communication, 8*(1), 1–29.

Holmes, J. (1998d). The question of sociolinguistic universals. In J. Coates (Ed.), *Language and gender: A Reader* (pp. 461–483). Oxford: Blackwell.

Holmes, J. (2000a). Victoria University of Wellington's language in the workplace project: An overview. *Language in the Workplace Occasional Papers, 1,* 20.

Holmes, J. (2000b). Doing collegiality and keeping control at work: Small talk in government departments. In J. Coupland (Ed.), *Small talk* (pp. 32–61). London: Longman.

Holmes, J. (2000c). Women at work: Analysing women's talk in New Zealand workplaces. *Australian Review of Applied Linguistics, 22*(2), 1–17.

Holmes, J. (In press). Sharing a laugh: Pragmatic aspects of humour and gender in the workplace. *Journal of Pragmatics.*

Holmes, J., Burns, L., Marra, M., Stubbe, M., & Vine, B. (2003). Women managing discourse in the workplace. *Women and Management Review, 18*(8), 414–424.

Holmes, J., Johnson, G., & Vine, B. (1998). *Guide to the Wellington corpus of spoken New Zealand English.* Wellington: School of Linguistics and Applied Language Studies, Victoria University of Wellington.

Holmes, J. & Marra, M. (2002a). Having a laugh at work: How humour contributes to workplace culture. *Journal of Pragmatics, 34,* 1683–1710.

Holmes, J. & Marra, M. (2002b). Humour as a discursive boundary marker in social interaction. In A. Duszak (Ed.), *Us and others: Social identities across languages, discourses and cultures* (pp. 377–400). Amsterdam: John Benjamins.

Holmes, J. & Meyerhoff, M. (1999). The community of practice: Theories and methodologies in language and gender research. *Language in Society, 28*, 173–183.

Holmes, J. & Stubbe, M. (Forthcoming). Managing conflict in the workplace. *Australian Journal of Communication, 30*(1).

Hymes, D. (1975). Breakthrough into performance. In D. Ben-Amos & K. S. Goldstein (Eds.) *Folklore: Performance and communication* (pp. 11–74). The Hague: Mouton.

Hymes, D. (1996). *Ethnography, linguistics, narrative inequality: Toward an understanding of voice.* London: Taylor and Francis.

Jackson, B. (1988). *Law, fact and narrative coherence.* Roby: Deborah Charles.

Jacquemet, M. (1996). *Credibility in ourt: Communicative practices in the Comorra trials.* Cambridge: Cambridge University Press.

James, A., Jenks, C., & Prout, A. (1998). *Theorizing childhood.* Cambridge: Polity Press.

Jamison, K. R. (1996). *An unquiet mind: A memoir of moods and madness.* London: Picador.

Jaworski, A., Coupland, N., & Galasinski, D. (Eds.). (2004). *Sociolinguistics and metalanguage.* The Hague: Mouton.

Jefferson, G. (1978). Sequential aspects of storytelling in conversation. In J. Schenkein (Ed.), *Studies in the organization of conversational interaction* (pp. 219–248). New York: Academic Press.

Jewell, J. (2004). A home for refugees: Writing Wales differently. *Cyfrwng: Media Wales Journal, 1.*

Johnson, F. & Aries, E. (1998). The talk of women friends. In J. Coates (Ed.), *Language and gender: A reader* (pp. 215–225). Oxford: Blackwell.

Johnson, F. (2000). *Speaking culturally: Language diversity in the United States.* Thousand Oaks, CA: Sage.

Johnstone, B. (1990). *Stories, community and place.* Bloomington, IN: Indiana University Press.

Johnstone, B. (1993). Community and contest: Midwestern men and women creating their worlds in conversational storytelling. In D. Tannen (Ed.), *Gender and conversational interaction* (pp. 62–80). Oxford: Oxford University Press.

Jukes, A. (1993). *Why men hate women.* London: Free Association Books.

Kamler, B., Maclean, R., Reid, J., & Simpson, R. (1994). *Shaping up nicely: The formation of schoolgirls and schoolboys in the first month of school. A report to the gender equity and curriculum reform project.* Canberra/Geelong, Victoria: Department of Education, Employment and Training.

Kehily, M. J. (1995). Self-narration, autobiography and identity construction. *Gender and Education, 7*(1), 20–31.

Kendall, S. (1993). Constructing competence: Gender and mitigation at a radio network. Paper presented at the annual meeting of the American Association for Applied Linguistics, Baltimore.

Kerby, A. (1991). *Narrative and the self.* Bloomington, IN: Indiana University Press.

King, N. (2000). *Memory, narrative, identity. Remembering the self.* Edinburgh: Edinburgh University Press.

Kirby, V. (1997). *Telling flesh: The substance of the corporeal.* London: Routledge.

Kirkman, M., Maher, J., & Torney Souter, K. (Eds.). (2002). The fertile imagination: Narratives of reproduction. *Meridian: The Latrobe University English Review, 18*(2).

Kress, G. & Threadgold, T. (1988). Toward a social theory of genre. *Southern Review, 21*(3), 215–243.

Kuhn, A. (1985). History of narrative codes. In P. Cook (Ed.), *The cinema book* (pp. 208–222). London: British Film Institute.

Kuhn, E. D. (1992). Playing down authority while getting things done: Women professors get help from the institution. In K. Hall, M. Bucholtz, & B. Moonwomon (Eds.), *Locating power. Proceedings of the second Berkeley women and language conference*, Vol. 1 (pp. 318–325). Berkeley, CA: Berkeley Women and Language Group, University of California.

Kulick, D. (2003). Review of Jennifer Coates, 2003, Men talk: Stories in the making of masculinities. *Journal of Sociolinguistics, 7*, 628–630.

Kyratzis, A. & Ervin-Tripp, S. (1999). The development of discourse markers in peer interaction. *Journal of Pragmatics, 31*, 1321–1338.

Kyratzis, A. & Guo, J. (1996). 'Separate Worlds' for girls and boys?: Views from U.S. and Chinese mixed-sex friendship groups. In D. I. Slobin, J. Gerhardt, A. Kyratzis, & J. Guo (Eds.), *Social interaction, social context and language: Essays in honor of Susan Ervin-Tripp* (pp. 555–578). Mahwah, NJ: Lawrence Erlbaum.

Labov, W. (1972). The transformation of experience in narrative syntax. In *Language in the inner city: Studies in the black English vernacular* (pp. 354–396). Philadelphia, PA: University of Pennsylvania Press.

Labov, W. & Fanshel, D. (1977). *Therapeutic discourse.* New York: Academic Press.

Labov, W. & Waletzky, J. (1967). Narrative analysis: Oral versions of personal experience. In J. Helm (Ed.), *Essays in the verbal and visual arts* (pp. 12–44). Seattle, WA: University of Washington Press.

Lakoff, R. (1997). The O. J. Simpson case as an exercise in narrative analysis. *Discourse Processes, 23*, 547–566.

Leaper, C. (1991). Influence and involvement: Age, gender, and partner effects. *Child Development, 62*, 797–811.

Leith, D. & Myerson, G. (1989). *The power of address: Explorations in rhetoric.* London: Routledge.

Leith, D. (1995). Tense variation as a performance feature in a Scottish folktale. *Language in Society, 24*, 53–77.

Leith, D. (1999). Living with a fairytale: 'The Green Man of Knowledge'. *Changing English, 6*(2), 169–186.

Leith, D. (2002). Growing up with westerns: Masculinity and The Man from Laramie. *Changing English, 9*(2), 133–145.

Levi-Strauss, C. (1958/1963). *Structural anthropology* (Trans. C. Jacobson & B. Grundfest Schoepf). New York: Basic Books.

Lewis, G. (2002). *Sunbathing in the rain: A cheerful book about depression.* London: Flamingo.

Linde, C. (1993). *Life stories: The creation of coherence.* New York: Oxford University Press.

Lyotard, J. F. (1979/1984). *The postmodern condition: A report on knowledge* (Trans. G. Bennington & B. Massumi). Manchester: Manchester University Press.

Maclean, M. (1988). *Narrative as performance: The Baudelairean experiment*. London, New York: Routledge.

Mandelbaum, J. (1987). Couples sharing stories. *Communication Quarterly, 35*(2), 144–170.

Martin, J. & Plum, G. (1997). Construing experience: Some story genres. *Journal of Narrative and Life History, 7*, 299–308.

Matoesian, G. (1999). Intertextuality, affect and ideology. *Text, 19*(1), 73–109.

Matoesian, G. (2001). *Law and the language of identity: Discourse in the William Kennedy Smith rape trial*. Oxford: Oxford University Press.

McCarthy, W. B. (Ed.). (1994). *Jack in two worlds: Contemporary North American tales and their tellers*. Chapel Hill, NC: University of North Carolina Press.

McCrum, R. (2002). Interview with Joanna Trolloppe. *Observer Review*, February 3rd 2002.

Meinhof, U. H. (1994). Double talk in news broadcasts. In D. Graddol & O. Boyd-Barrett (Eds.), *Media texts: Authors and readers* (pp. 212–223). Clevedon: Open University/ Multilingual Matters.

Meinhof, U. H. (1997). The most important event of my life. A comparison of male and female written narratives. In S. Johnson & U. H. Meinhof (Eds.), *Language and masculinity* (pp. 208–228). Oxford: Blackwell.

Meinhof, U. H. (2001). Discourse and identity. In C. Bettoni et al. (Eds.), *Atti del lo congresso di studi dell'Associazione Italiana di Linguistica Applicata* (pp. 29–45). Perugia: Guerra Edizioni.

Meinhof, U. H. (2004). Europe viewed from below: Agents, victims, and the threat of the other. In R. Herrmann, T. Risse, & M. Brewer (Eds.), *Transnational identities: Becoming european in the EU* (pp. 214–244). Lanham, MD: Rowman and Littlefield Publishers.

Meinhof, U. H. (Ed.). (2002). *Living (with) borders: Identity discourses on east-west borders in Europe* (Border Regions Studies 1). Aldershot: Ashgate.

Meinhof, U. H. (Ed.). (2003). Bordering European identities. *Journal of Ethnic and Migration Studies*, special issue.

Meinhof, U. H. & Galasinski, D. (2000). Photography, memory and the construction of identities on the former east-west German border. *Discourse Studies, 2*(3), 323–353.

Metz, C. (1982). *Psychoanalysis and cinema: The imaginary signifier*. London: Macmillan.

Meyerhoff, M. & Niedzielski, N. (1994). Resistance to creolization: An interpersonal and intergroup account. *Language and Communication, 14*(4), 313–330.

Miller, J. F. & Chapman, R. S. (1998). *Basic SALT program for Windows. Version 5.0*. Language Analysis Laboratory, Waisman Center, University of Wisconsin, Madison.

Milroy, L. (1987). *Observing and analysing natural language*. Oxford: Blackwell.

Mishler, E. G. (1986). *Research interviewing: Context and narrative*. Cambridge, MA: Harvard University Press.

MORI poll carried out for Migration Watch UK, 16–21 January 2003, British views on immigration.

Nicolopoulou, A., Scales, B., & Weintraub, J. (1994). Gender differences and symbolic imagination in the stories of four-year-olds. In A. H. Dyson & C. Genishi (Eds.), *The need for story: Cultural diversity in classroom and community* (pp. 102–123). Urbana, IL: National Council of Teachers of English.

Ninio, A. & Snow, C. (1996). *Pragmatic development*. Boulder, CO: Westview.

Norrick, N. R. (1997). Twice-told tales: Collaborative narration of familiar stories. *Language in Society, 26*, 199–220.

Norrick, N. R. (1998). Retelling again. *Narrative Inquiry, 8*, 373–378.

Norrick, N. R. (2000). *Conversational narrative*. Amsterdam: Benjamins.

Norrick, N. R. (2001). Discourse markers in oral narrative. *Journal of Pragmatics, 33*, 849–878.

Norrick, N. R. (2004). Humor, tellability and co-narration in conversation. *Text, 24*(1), 79–111.

Norrick, N. R. (2005). Interaction in the telling and retelling of interlaced stories: The co-construction of humorous narratives. In U. Quasthoff & T. Becker (Eds.), *Narrative Interaction* (pp. 263–283). Amsterdam: John Benjamins.

Ochs, E. & Capps, L. (2001). *Living narrative: Creating lives in everyday storytelling*. Cambridge, MA: Harvard University Press.

Ochs, E. & Taylor, C. (1992). Family narrative as political activity. *Discourse and Society, 3*(3), 301–340.

Pahl, R. (2000). *On friendship*. Cambridge: Polity Press.

Parker, A. & Sedgewick, E. K. (1995). *Performativity and performance*. London: Routledge.

Penman, R. (1987). Discourse in court: Cooperation, coercion and coherence. *Discourse Processes, 10*(3), 201–218.

Polanyi, L. (1979). So what's the point? *Semiotica, 25*(3/4), 207–241.

Polanyi, L. (1982). Literary complexity in everyday storytelling. In D. Tannen (Ed.), *Spoken and written language: Exploring orality and litercay* (pp. 155–170). Norwood, NJ: Ablex.

Polanyi, L. (1985). Conversational storytelling. In T. A. van Dijk (Ed.), *Handbook of discourse analysis 3: Discourse and dialogue* (pp. 183–201). London: Academic Press.

Polanyi, L. (1989). *Telling the American story: A structural and cultural analysis of conversational storytelling*. Cambridge, MA: The MIT Press

Polss, L. (1990). Starting the story: A cross-cultural analysis of conversational story entrance talk. Unpublished M.A. Thesis, Hebrew University, Jerusalem.

Propp, V. (1928/1968). *Morphology of the folktale* (Trans. L. A. Wagner). Austin, TX: University of Texas Press.

Quasthoff, U. M. (1980). Gemeinsames Erzählen als Form und Mittel im sozialen Konflikt oder Ein Ehepaar erzählt eine Geschichte. In K. Ehlich (Ed.), *Erzählen im Alltag* (pp. 109–141). Frankfurt/Main: Suhrkamp.

Rampton, B. (1995). *Crossing: Language and ethnicity among adolescents*. London: Longman.

Rampton, B. (2000). Speech community. *Working Papers in Urban Language and Literacies, 15*. Also available at http://www.kcl.ac.uk/depsta/education/ULL/wpull.html

Riessman, C. K. (1990). Strategic uses of narrative in the presentation of self and illness: A research note. *Social Science and Medicine, 30*, 1195–1200.

Riessman, C. K. (1993). *Narrative analysis*. Newbury Park, CA: Sage.

Robertshaw, P. (1998). *Summary justice*. London: Cassell.

Rosmovitz, L. & Ziebland, S. (2004). Expressions of loss of adulthood in the narratives of colorectal cancer patients. *Qualitative Health Research, 14*, 187–203.

Rymes, B. (1995). The construction of moral agency in the narratives of high-school drop-outs. *Discourse and Society, 6*(3), 495–516.

Sacks, H. (1995). *Lectures on Conversation Vols. 1 and 2* (G. Jefferson Ed.). Oxford: Blackwell.

Sacks, H., Schegloff, E., & Jefferson, G. (1974). A simplest systematics for the organisation of turn-taking in conversation. *Language, 50*, 696–735.

Sarangi, S. & Roberts, C. (1999). The dynamics of interactional and institutional orders in work-related settings. In S. Sarangi & C. Roberts (Eds.), *Talk, work and institutional order* (pp. 1–57). Berlin: Mouton de Gruyter.

Sarbin, T. (Ed.). (1986). *Narrative psychology: The storied nature of human conduct.* New York: Praeger.

Scannell, P. (1996). *Radio, television and modern life.* London: Blackwell.

Schechner, R. (1985). *Between theatre and anthropology.* Philadelphia, PA: University of Pennsylvania Press.

Schegloff, E. (1992). In another context. In A. Duranti & C. Goodwin (Eds.), *Rethinking context*: *Language as an interactive phenomenon* (pp. 191–227). Cambridge: Cambridge University Press.

Schiffrin, D. (1981). Tense variation in narrative. *Language, 57*(1), 45–62.

Schiffrin, D. (1990). The management of a cooperative self in argument: The role of opinions and stories. In A. Grimshaw (Ed.), *Conflict talk* (pp. 241–259). Cambridge: Cambridge University Press.

Schiffrin, D. (1996). Narrative as self-portrait: Sociolinguistic constructions of identity. *Language in Society, 25*, 167–203.

Schiffrin, D. (2002). Mother and friends in a holocaust life story. *Language in Society, 31*, 309–353.

Searle, J. R. (1995). *The construction of social reality.* London: Penguin.

Sheldon, A. (1990a). Pickle fights: Gendered talk in preschool disputes. Special issue, 'Language and Gender.' *Discourse Processes, 13*(1), 5–31.

Sheldon, A. (1990b). 'Kings are royaler than queens': Language and socialization. *Young Children, 45*(2), 4–9.

Sheldon, A. (1992a). Conflict talk: Sociolinguistic challenges to self-assertion and how young girls meet them. *Merrill-Palmer Quarterly, 38*(1), 95–117.

Sheldon, A. (1992b). Preschool girls' discourse competence: Managing conflict. In K. Hall, M. Bucholtz, & B. Moonwomon (Eds.), *Locating power: Proceedings of the second Berkeley Women and Language Conference*, Vol. 2 (pp. 528–539). Berkeley Linguistic Society, University of California-Berkeley.

Sheldon, A. (1996). You can be the baby brother but you aren't born yet: Preschool girls' negotiation for power and access in pretend play. *Research on Language and Social Interaction, 29*(1), 57–80. Hillsdale, NJ: Lawrence Erlbaum Associates.

Sheldon, A. (1997). Talking power: Girls, gender enculturation and discourse. In R. Wodak (Ed.), *Gender and discourse* (pp. 225–244). London: Sage.

Sheldon, A. (2003). When the boy-cop wears a skirt: Nonstandard expressions of masculinity in a U.S. preschool. Ms. Paper presented at the *Eighth International Pragmatics Conference*, Toronto.

Sheldon, A. (In press). Talk as text. In R. Horowitz (Ed.), *Talking texts: How speech and writing interact in school learning.* Mahwah, NJ: Lawrence Erlbaum.

Sheldon, A. & Johnson, D. (1998). Preschool negotiators: Gender differences in double-voice discourse as a conflict talk style in early childhood. In J. Cheshire & P. Trudgill (Eds.), *The sociolinguistics reader*, Vol. 2 (pp. 76–99). London: Edward Arnold.

Sheldon, A. & Rohleder, L. (1996). Sharing the same world, telling different stories: Gender differences in co-constructed pretend narratives. In D. I. Slobin, J. Gerhardt, A. Kyratzis, & J. Guo (Eds.), *Social interaction, social context and language: Essays in honor of Susan Ervin-Tripp* (pp. 613–632). Mahwah, NJ: Lawrence Erlbaum.

Sherwin, R. K. (1994). Law frames: Historical truth and narrative necessity in a criminal case. *Stanford Law Review, 47,* 39–83.

Shuman, A. (1986). *Story telling rights: The uses of oral and written texts by urban adolescents.* Cambridge: Cambridge University Press.

Silverstein, M. & Urban, G. (Eds.). (1996). *Natural histories of discourse.* Chicago: University of Chicago Press.

Slobin, D., Gerhardt, J., Kyratzis, A., & Guo, J. (Eds.). (1996). *Social interaction, social context and language: Essays in honor of Susan Ervin-Tripp.* Mahwah, NJ: Lawrence Erlbaum.

Silverstone, R. (1985). *Framing science: Making of a BBC documentary.* London: BFI Publishing.

Smith, F. L. (1993). The pulpit and women's place: Gender and framing of the 'exegetical' self in sermon performances. In D. Tannen (Ed.), *Framing in discourse* (pp. 147–175). New York: Oxford University Press.

Somers, M. R. & Gibson, G. D. (1994). Reclaiming the epistemological 'other': Narrative and the social construction of identity. In C. Calhoun (Ed.), *Social theory and the politics of identity* (pp. 37–99). Cambridge, MA: Blackwell.

Speers, T. (2001). Welcome or over reaction? Refugees and asylum seekers in the Welsh media. Wales Media Forum, Cardiff School of Journalism, Media and Cultural Studies, Cardiff University.

Stubbe, M. (1998). Researching language in the workplace: A participatory model. *Proceedings of the Australian Linguistics Society Conference.* Brisbane University of Queensland. http://www.cltr.uq.edu.au/als98/.

Stubbe, M. (2000a). 'Just do it ...!' Discourse strategies for 'getting the message across' in a factory production team." In J. Henderson (Ed.), *Proceedings of the 1999 Conference of the Australian Linguistic Society.* http://www.arts.uwa.edu.au/LingWWW/als99/proceedings.

Stubbe, M. (2000b). Talk that works: Evaluating communication in a factory production team. *New Zealand English Journal, 14,* 55–65.

Stubbe, M. (2001). From office to production line: Collecting data for the Wellington Language in the Workplace Project. *Language in the Workplace Occasional Papers, 2,* 1–23.

Stygall, G. (1994). *Trial language: Discourse processing and discursive formation.* Amsterdam: John Benjamins.

Swales, J. (1990). *Genre analysis.* Cambridge: Cambridge University Press.

Symposium. (1994). Lawyers as storytellers and storytellers as lawyers: An interdisciplinary symposium exploring the use of storytelling in the practice of law. *Vermont Law Review, 18,* 565–762.

Tajfel, H. (1974). Social identity and intergroup behaviour. *Social Science Information, 13*(2), 65–93.

Tajfel, H. (1981). *Human groups and social categories.* Cambridge: Cambridge University Press.

Tannen, D. (1978). The effect of expectations on conversation. *Discourse Processes, 1,* 203–209.

Tannen, D. (1989). *Talking voices: Repetition, dialogue, and imagery in conversational discourse.* Cambridge: Cambridge University press.

Tannen, D. (1994). Gender differences in conversational cohesion. In D. Tannen (Ed.), *Gender and discourse* (pp. 85–135). Oxford: Oxford University Press.

Tannen, D. (1999). The display of (gendered) identities in talk at work. In M. Bucholtz, A. C. Liang, & L. A. Sutton (Eds.), *Reinventing identities: The gendered self in discourse* (pp. 221–240). Oxford: Oxford University Press.

Tedlock, D. (1983). *The spoken word and the work of interpretation.* Philadelphia, PA: Pennsylvania University Press.

Thornborrow, J. (2001). 'Has this ever happened to you?': Talk show narratives as mediated performance. In A. Tolson (Ed.), *TV talk shows: Discourse, performance, spectacle* (pp. 117–137). Mahwah, NJ: Erlbaum.

Thornborrow, J. (2002). *Power talk: Language and institutional interaction.* London: Pearson Education.

Threadgold, T. (1997). *Feminist poetics: Poeisis, performance, histories.* London: Routledge.

Threadgold, T. (1997a). Regulative fictions: Translations and performing subversions. *Law/Text/ Culture, 3,* 210–231.

Threadgold, T. (1997b). Narrative and legal texts: Telling stories about women who kill. Invited paper presented at the UTS Ultimo Seminar Series, May 1996. *UTS Review: Cultural studies and New Writing, 3*(1), 56–73.

Threadgold, T. (2004). Epilogue: Writing cultural studies differently. Special issue, Writing refugee lives. *Social Analysis: The International Journal of Cultural and Social Practice, 48*(3).

Todorov, T. (1969). *Grammaire du Decameron.* The Hague: Mouton.

Tolson, A. (1996). *Mediations.* London: Arnold.

Toolan, M. (1988/2001 2nd ed.). *Narrative: A critical linguistic introduction.* London: Routledge.

Troutt, D. (1999). Screws, koon and routine aberrations: The use of fictional narratives in federal police brutality prosecutions. *New York University Law Review, 74,* 18–122.

Tuchman, G. (1978). *Making news: A study in the construction of reality.* London: The Free Press.

Turner, V. (1987). *The anthropology of performance.* New York: PAJ Publications.

Urban, G. (1996). Entextualization, replication and power. In M. Silverstein & G. Urban (Eds.), *Natural histories of discourse* (pp. 21–44). Chicago: University of Chicago Press.

Van Dijk, T. A. (1988a). *News as discourse.* Hillsdale, NJ: Lawrence Erlbaum.

Van Dijk, T. A. (1988b). *News analysis.* Hillsdale, NJ: Lawrence Erlbaum.

Vine, B. (2001). Workplace language and power: Directives, requests and advice. Unpublished PhD thesis, Victoria University of Wellington, Wellington, New Zealand.

Watson, K. A. (1975). Transferable communicative routines: Strategies and group identity in two speech events. *Language in Society, 4,* 53–72.

Wenger, E. (1998). *Communities of practice.* Cambridge: Cambridge University Press.

Widdicombe, S. & Wooffitt, R. (1995). *The language of youth subcultures: Social identity in action.* New York: Harvester Wheatsheaf.

Wilentz, G. (2000). *Healing narratives: Women writers curing cultural disease*. New Brunswick, NJ: Rutgers University Press.

Wilson, J. (1989). *On the boundaries of conversation*. Oxford: Pergamon Press.

Wooffitt, R. (1992). *Telling tales of the unexpected: The organisation of factual discourse*. Hemel Hempstead: Harvester Wheatsheaf.

Wolfson, N. (1979). The conversational historical present alternation. *Language, 55*, 168–182.

Wolfson, N. (1982). *CHP: The conversational historic present in American English narrative*. Dordrecht: Foris.

Index

In the series *Studies in Narrative* the following titles have been published thus far or are scheduled for publication:

CL

306.
440
14
SOC